INTERNATIONAL TRADE, MIGRATION, AND CAPITAL FLOWS:

A Quantitative Analysis of Spatial Economic Interaction

Donald B. Freeman
York University

THE UNIVERSITY OF CHICAGO
DEPARTMENT OF GEOGRAPHY
RESEARCH PAPER NO. 146

1973

H
31
.C514
#146
1973

Research Papers are available from:
The University of Chicago
Department of Geography
5828 S. University Avenue
Chicago, Illinois 60637
Price: $5.00 list; $4.00 series subscription

For My Wife

ACKNOWLEDGMENTS

I offer my sincere thanks to the many people who, by their generous assistance and advice, have contributed to the completion of this study.

To my adviser, Professor Brian Berry, I owe a special tribute of appreciation. His guidance, encouragement, and perceptive suggestions have been invaluable at every stage of this research.

I wish to thank Professor Chauncy Harris, who carefully read the manuscript of this study and made many helpful comments which have led to its improvement.

I am very grateful for the financial support provided by the University of Chicago Department of Geography and Center for Urban Studies, which gave me the opportunity for graduate study, and to the University of Queensland and the Australian-American Educational Foundation, who awarded generous travel grants.

I consider myself very fortunate to have been able to work in the stimulating environment created by the students and faculty of the Department of Geography at the University of Chicago. To my colleagues who shared that experience, and to the members of a young and vigorous geography department here at York University, Toronto, I extend my appreciation of their interest and encouragement.

The massive task of programming and running the computer analyses in this study was ably undertaken by Rainer Zenner, programmer for the Geography Department at York University. The cartographic material was skillfully and expeditiously prepared by Mrs. Anna Parker, of the York cartographic staff.

Donald B. Freeman
York University
September 1, 1971

v

TABLE OF CONTENTS

Introduction
The Pattern of International Flows
Significance of International Economic Interaction
Selected Characteristics of National Economies
Illustration of Empirical Flow-Attribute Relationships
Resumé

Interdependence of Economic Attributes and Flows
Theoretical Relationships between Commodity and Factor Flows
Relations between Individual Flows and Attributes of National
        Economies
Spatial Models of Trade
Spatial Models of International Migration
Capital Flow Models with a Spatial Component
Bilateralism in International Transactions
Integrative Flow Study: Empirical Approaches

Structural Characteristics of Empirical Flow Models
Alternate Frameworks for Analysis of Flows
The Field Theoretical Model of Interaction
Operational Basis for Field Theory: The Technique of
        Canonical Correlation
Conclusion

LIST OF TABLES

LIST OF ILLUSTRATIONS

INTRODUCTION

This is an inductive study of international economic flows. It seeks to attain three interrelated objectives:

(1) identification and explanation of broad spatial and structural relationships in flows of economically-significant phenomena in the mid-1960's. Two levels of analysis are involved: the aggregate scale of economic behavior, focusing on general patterns of interaction among nations, and the level of detailed country-to-country flows, where far more complex patterns are involved;

(2) development of models to replicate observed patterns of interrelationship among flow phenomena, both at the aggregate scale, and at the level of country-to-country movement. Specific attention is paid to questions of substitution relations among flows, and the economic conditions, including deterrent effects of distance, which may impinge on the volume, nature, and direction of these flows;

(3) empirical testing of relevant theoretical concepts concerning commodity and production-factor flows. This is achieved by fitting the models to observed data, and leads to reevaluation of some aspects of trade and factor-flow theory. Concomitantly, the study attempts to illuminate areas within this broad field which may yield dividends to future studies of a more intensive and more detailed nature.

The economic flows considered in this study are commodity trade, human migration, capital movement, and information in the form of mail and telegraph messages. The inductive analytical stance we have adopted envisages that a framework stressing mutual interconnections among flows and national economic attributes is most appropriate for understanding observed patterns of economic interaction.

The problems of identification, description, and analysis of these flow phenomena are posed in Chapter I. Comparative description of flow maps is the initial tool for illustrating salient features and suggesting tentative interrelationships of spatial flow patterns. A preliminary explanatory context is also provided in the first chapter, through the medium of maps displaying hypothetically relevant patterns of national economic characteristics.

Tentative relationships emerging from the problem formulation in the first chapter are subjected to more detailed scrutiny in Chapter II. Here, the literature of Geography, Economics, and Political Science is drawn upon for

1

conceptual frameworks which appear useful in constructing models to replicate observed flow relationships. These deductive frameworks are classified accord-ing to the specific facets of economic interaction to which they apply.

Economic theories of international trade are examined in Chapter II from the point of view of the understanding they provide for questions of productive factor mobility, substitution relationships among flows, and the role of the spatial component in producing an orderly pattern of interaction. The Classical and Neoclassical trade theories, which assume immobility of productive factors, are discussed critically, and the usefulness in the present context of the "Modern" concepts of relative factor proportions and factor price equalization are evaluated.

Theories and ideas relating to international human migration and capital flow are then discussed. Particular attention is paid to the theoretical signifi-cance accorded to the effects of distance on these factor (and commodity) flows. Deductive models of trade-productive factor substitution are examined as a pre-lude to consideration of the need for empirical reinforcing of existing flow the-ories.

Characteristics of relevant empirical models are discussed in Chapter III. Linear-algebraic constructs are highlighted as being particularly suited to the type of problems posed in this study. The features of a Field-theoretic model, and the technique of canonical correlation, which renders it operational, are explained.

Application of this form of empirical model to general or aggregate-level patterns of interaction forms the content of Chapters IV to VII. In these chap-ters, the objectives of identification of major patterns of world economic flows, and the broad structural relationships among them, are achieved through objec-tive manipulation of multivariate data.

The basic steps of selection of variables and assembly of sample obser-vations are dealt with in Chapter IV. These steps follow the guidelines laid down in the previous chapters regarding theoretical considerations in structuring appropriate flow models.

A detailed definition of patterns in aggregate flows and economic charac-teristics of countries is then provided in Chapters V and VI. This identification of basic patterns, employing principal axis factor analysis and spatial grouping methods, plays an important role as a prelude to the mathematical delineation of broad flow-attribute relationships.

These aggregate relationships are described in detail in Chapter VII. The analysis of results emerging from the aggregate flow model provides a broad perspective on the interrelations among general forms of economic interaction and the kinds of economic attributes of nations which affect these relationships.

These results comprise, in their own right, an important part of the contribution which this study makes to the understanding of economic flows. They also provide a means of preliminary evaluation of input variables and model structure for the study of relationships among country-to-country flows, introduced in Chapters VIII and IX.

Chapter VIII deals with the selection of variables and sample observations for the model of country-to-country flows. Some problems in model construction, occasioned by the size of data matrices and the incidence of missing data, are also debated here.

Chapter IX complements the analysis of aggregate relationships given in Chapter VII by interpreting facets of interrelationships at the detailed scale of country-to-country interaction. It thus comprises the final step in attainment of the first two objectives enumerated as forming the focus of this study.

Contributions toward achievement of the third objective, the reevaluation of elements of economic flow theory in the light of empirical evidence from the study, are also made in these chapters dealing with the results of multivariate models. Chapter X draws together these threads of discussion emerging from the earlier chapters, focusing them on aspects of preexisting flow theory. It examines in particular the implications of empirical evidence for current notions concerning substitution among flows, and the role of distance in producing orderly patterns of interaction. By way of a conclusion to the study, Chapter X provides an evaluation of the efficacy of the models employed, reviews their shortcomings, and suggests avenues for future investigation into this general area of research.

The contributions of this study to current understanding of international economic interaction may thus be summarized as follows:

(1) it illustrates the application of a model format which stresses mutual interrelationships among flows and the economic environments in which they take place. This format is seen as a way of avoiding the pitfalls associated with pre-supposition of unidirectional causal linkages, common in previous flow models;

(2) it demonstrates that empirical analysis may be made to yield useful information concerning basic patterns of relationship in the realm of economic interaction. This may aid the development of theoretical constructs based on more realistic assumptions and capable of dealing with more complex facets of real-world flows;

(3) more specifically, it provides a generalized picture of some of the environmental conditions under which particular combinations or "mixes" of economic flows will take place, considering both the very broad aspects of inflow and outflow, and the very detailed scale of flows between pairs of countries.

CHAPTER I

INTERNATIONAL ECONOMIC INTERACTION:

PATTERN AND CONTEXT

Introduction

The contemporary international economy comprises a host of nation states, embodying a wide variety of economic, cultural, and political characteristics. These nations range from the very large and powerful, to tiny political entities more accurately described as city-states than as nations; from realms whose venerable histories span many centuries, to newly independent states whose names still carry an unfamiliar ring; from countries whose economies are highly industrialized, to those where traditional methods of subsistence agriculture or pastoralism still predominate. This diverse group of politically-independent entities is bound together by an interaction network of awesome complexity. Even a cursory examination of the complex flows among nations will, however, betray the pervading influence of economic motivation in many transactions comprising this network. Closer observation of the configuration of flows reveals, despite their acknowledged complexity, some dominant patterns and regularities which may confidently be considered amenable to profitable analysis.

The analysis of economic flows might logically begin with a preliminary display of general patterns in magnitude, composition, consistency, and spatial grouping of the flow phenomena. This would provide a background for subsequent inquiry into the ramifications of flows, in terms of their relationship with other features of the contemporary global economy. Of particular relevance would be the relation of specific types of international flow with alternate forms of interaction and with internal structures of an economic or political nature.

Thus, it would be appropriate at this juncture to display in summary form, and with a minimum of interpretive comment, the basic patterns of flow that comprise a major part of the contemporary international economy, to permit closer appraisal of their general dimensions and significance.

This chapter will therefore provide a brief sketch, in the form of a seri

4

of choropleth maps, of the broad outlines of commodity imports and exports, net inflow and outflow of investment capital, movement of long-term national migrants, and information flows in the form of mail and telegraph messages. Following this, a delineation of selected economic characteristics of nations will be provided by way of a context for the descriptive treatment of flows. As a consequence of this juxtaposition of flows and selected attributes, illustration of tentative patterns of relationship will be facilitated, and, concomitantly, problems of analysis should be more clearly discernible.

It should be noted here that, even in the simple displaying of factual data on commercial interaction and attributes, an element of subjectivity is unavoidable. The choice of suitable indices for measuring flows, and the selection of criteria for classifying or grouping countries on their scores or rating with respect to these indices, involve subjective judgement. A discussion of the general patterns of flow shown in Figures 1 to 5, and of attributes in Figures 6 to 9, would thus be incomplete without an explanation of the nature and peculiarities of the data employed, and the reasons for their selection.

The Pattern of International Flows

Aggregate Imports and Exports

Aggregate annual imports and exports of all commodities, in terms of their mean value in U.S. dollars for the three year period 1963-1965, [1] are shown in Figures 1 and 2. Data for these maps are taken from the Yearbook of International Trade Statistics for 1963, 1964, and 1965, published by the United Nations Department of Economic and Social Affairs. The aggregate data collected from the Country Tables of the Yearbook give fairly reliable measures of imports and exports of 139 countries, [2] comprising about 98 per cent of the aggregate trade of nations making data available in the period under examination. In volumetric terms, this total world trade amounted to over 153 billion U.S. dollars per year.

---

[1] A three year period was chosen for this study since this would be sufficiently long to suppress inordinate random variation yet not so long that secular trend influences would become appreciable. Cyclical aberrations are assumed to be minimal since in the 1963-1965 period, the international economy had recovered a state of "normalcy" following the somewhat depressed conditions of the previous few years.

[2] Statistics for each nation refer to transactions originating in or destined for the customs area of each country, which usually (although not invariably) is coextensive with the sovereign territory of that country.

6

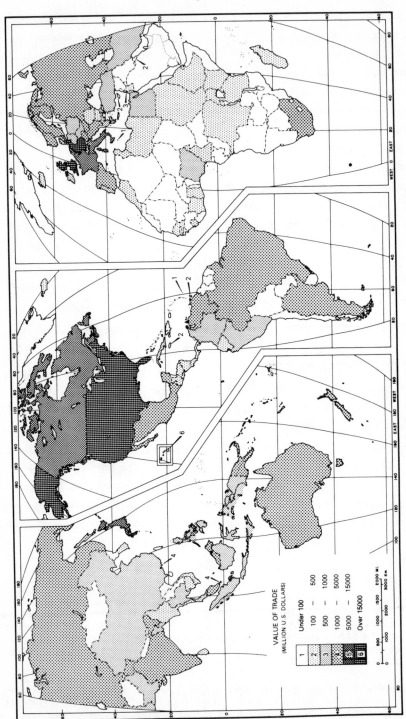

Figure 1.--Aggregate Annual Commodity Imports, 1963-1965

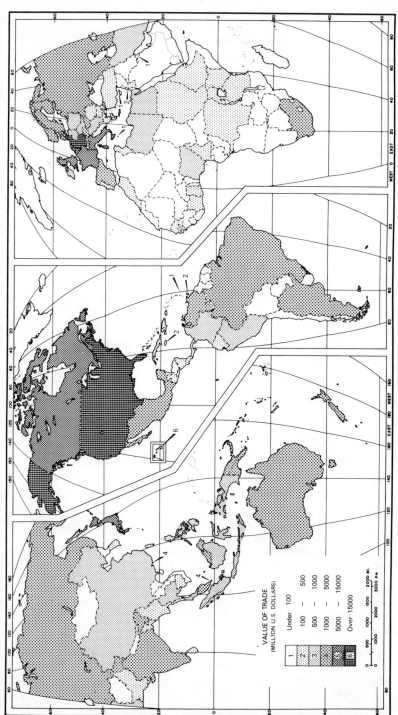

VALUE OF TRADE
(MILLION U.S. DOLLARS)

1	Under	100
2	100	–	500
3	500	–	1000
4	1000	–	5000
5	5000	–	15000
6	Over	15000

Figure 2. -- Aggregate Annual Commodity Exports, 1963-1965

Value of trade for each country is registered in units of national currency
however, and to achieve a standard scale it was found necessary to convert all
figures to U.S. dollars, using the mean of the quoted official exchange rates for
the period 1963-1965. [1]

Value of commodity imports and exports was chosen over volume in tons
(also listed in the Yearbook). The former clearly provides a more sensitive
barometer of economic impact of trade on national economies, where this is the
characteristic of trade flows which is of primary interest in the present context.

The patterns of import and export displayed in Figures 1 and 2 show
understandable similarity, but are by no means identical, as a later analysis of
the balance of trade for this period will show in more detail.

A number of countries are notable for the insignificance of their individual contributions to the world trade pattern, particularly some of the land-locked
states of Africa and Latin America. Yet other nations show a marked deficiency
in data on volume and composition of trade, and these have been identified in a
separate category. The most conspicuous group here comprises some of the
centrally planned economies within the Sino-Soviet spheres of influence. [2] The
lack of availability of adequate and reliable data on the economic behavior of
these nations has been a chronic cause of incompleteness and deficiency in general models of economic development and interaction in the past. Although some
information on economic behavior of centrally-coordinated economies has been
available for use in the maps that follow, subsequent inclusion of many communist nations in the main analysis has been ruled out by general paucity of data.
The detailed reasons for exclusion of specific countries will be dealt with in a
later chapter. [3]

---

[1] These were obtained from the Country Tables of the International Finan
cial Statistics published annually by the International Monetary Fund.

[2] A number of centrally-planned economies maintain official exchange
rates with other currency systems, converting at the rate of 0.90 new roubles
the U.S. dollar. This rate is employed by Albania, Bulgaria, Czechoslovakia,
East Germany, Hungary, Poland, Romania, and the U.S.S.R. in compiling trade
statistics. These nations are therefore included in the trade maps, but the basis
for the values shown must be borne in mind in making comparisons with non-
communist countries.

[3] Estimated data on certain economic attributes of command economies
exist in diverse sources, and have been used in several previous studies, although many agree that such data are not generally reliable. See Norton S. Gins
burg, ed., Atlas of Economic Development (Chicago: University of Chicago
Press, 1960), p. 102.

Countries contributing at least $100 million (U.S.) worth of exports to the world trade pattern, or accepting over $100 million worth of imports, predominate in the contemporary period. Within this group, the nations of Africa, Central America, and what was once Indochina rank lowest in total imports and exports, while the United States and West Germany are consistently highest. Britain, through an adverse balance of payments in this period, ranks somewhat lower, as do the rest of the Common Market countries, Canada, U.S.S.R., and Japan. In the middle categories are found most of the remaining "western" nations, several eastern European countries, India and adjacent south Asian countries, as well as much of Latin America. Small trade-oriented nations, such as the city-states of Singapore and Hong Kong, are also included in the intermediate categories.

The simple monetary value of trade, expressed in terms of United States dollar equivalence, provides no more than a crude estimation of the significance of elements in the pattern of commodity flow. Since official exchange rates have been employed in converting local currencies to U.S. dollars, the fact of vast disparities in the purchasing power of local currencies in local markets has been ignored. So, too, have the disparities between official exchange rates and somewhat more realistic conversion rates of an unofficial nature.

Likewise, no estimation of the relationship between total imports and exports and the populations or the overall level of productivity of various nations has been given in these maps. These aspects of trade will, however, be considered in detail in a later section.

Aggregate Movements of Labor

The contemporary pattern of international movement of labor is indexed by Figures 3 and 4. These show respectively the Total Long-term Immigration and Total Long-term Emigration for a number of countries making suitable data available, covering the three year period 1963-1965. Data for these maps are drawn from numerous sources, predominantly from appropriate tables of country-to-country movements published in national statistical yearbooks or abstracts. United Nations data on migration, as published in Table 27 of the Demographic Yearbook for 1966, give total movement of people into or out of a country, subdividing these into major categories of long-term movements and short-term, seasonal, vacational, or business movements among countries. However, the statistics on long-term migration compiled by the United Nations were found to be unsatisfactory for this particular study The primary reasons are their failure

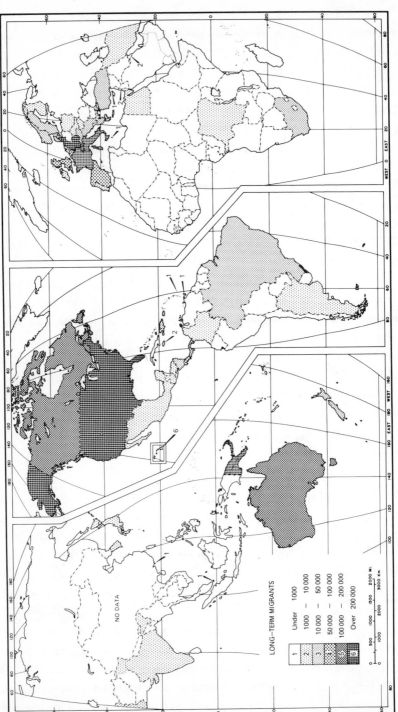

LONG-TERM MIGRANTS

1	Under 1000
2	1000 – 10 000
3	10 000 – 50 000
4	50 000 – 100 000
5	100 000 – 200 000
6	Over 200 000

NO DATA

Figure 3.--Total Long-Term Immigration: Mean Annual Flow for Period 1963-1965

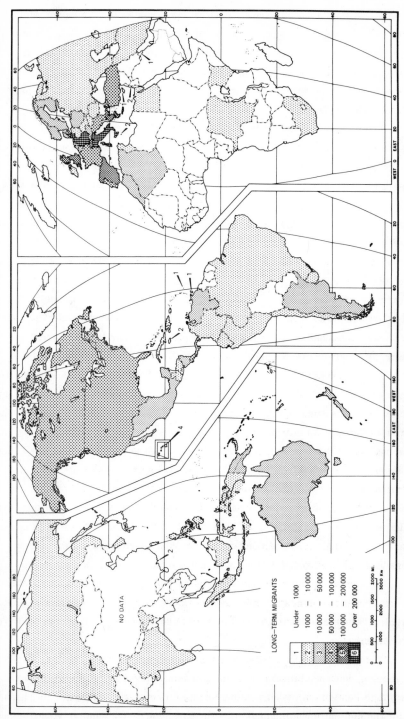

Figure 4. --Total Long-Term Emigration: Mean Annual Flow for Period 1963-1965

to distinguish individual country-to-country movements, their frequent omission
of emigration volumes (even for nations such as Canada and the United States),
and the fact that various subgroups are amalgamated for quite a number of countries. For these reasons, reliance has been placed on compiled aggregates of
country-to-country flows of long-term migrants, as recorded in various national
statistical abstracts.

The pattern of Immigration shown in Figure 3 highlights the position of
the New World (North and South America and Oceania) as a dominant destination
area for migrating labor. However, it also points to considerable movement
among European nations (particularly members of the European Common Market

The United States and West Germany, as major immigrant receptors,
dominate this pattern. Also highlighted are Canada and Australia (who have com
mitted themselves to massive immigration programs in post war years), France
Switzerland, and Italy. The high position of Italy in this pattern is partly the
result of a circular migratory movement of Italians to other common-market
countries (particularly West Germany) and Switzerland, usually of one to severa
years duration. This has meant the inclusion in Italian statistics of return move
ments under the heading of "long-term" migration, rather than as purely short-
term or seasonal forms of movement.

Britain, Spain, Belgium-Luxembourg, and Costa Rica are somewhat
lower on the list, but still appear to be major receptor countries (the statistics
supplied by Costa Rica appear, however, to be subject to question, possibly hig
lighting a disparity in interpretation of the long-term category of migration).
Other nations of the New World, particularly Brazil and Venezuela, New Zealan
and Republic of South Africa reveal continued and appreciable acceptance of
migrants, while the pattern of movement within the nations of Europe also involves significant influxes into Scandinavia, Austria, Greece, and Turkey. Wit
the latter two countries, the situation is undoubtedly similar to that outlined for
Italy, with cyclical return of laborers, from West Germany and Switzerland pre
dominantly, bolstering the statistics on long-term immigration.

Countries with only modest influxes of long-term migrants, or with negl
gible or unreported numbers, embrace the whole of continental Asia and Africa
(excluding Republic of South Africa) as well as south-east Asia and parts of
Latin America.

The pattern of Emigration bears considerable similarity to the immigration pattern, but reveals some notable differences besides. Once again, a pattern of high labor mobility of medium duration (one to several years) is respons
ble for the high outflows displayed for European countries such as West German

and Italy. The latter country, however, also clearly displays a strong component of emigration to New World nations in which return after a stay of only one or a few years is not a significant part of the pattern. Emigration streams from Turkey, Greece, Yugoslavia, and the Iberian peninsula focus on West Germany, Switzerland, France, and Scandinavia, while Britain provides a substantial stream of outmigration to Canada, the United States, Australia, New Zealand, and South Africa.

A notable part of the emigration pattern is the relatively large movement of long-term emigrés from the prosperous areas of the New World. This is a phenomenon that appears to have increased in the past few decades. It represents probably a "return to the cultural hearth" of ethnic groups making up the new countries, as well as the phenomena of increased mobility and changed attitude toward vacational travel that have become evident among younger age groups in Australia, New Zealand, Canada, South Africa, and the United States. In recent years, politically-motivated emigration from a number of western countries has become a significant part of the total pattern, as it has been for centuries from "older" areas of the world.

An aspect of this pattern worthy of note is the quite restricted flow of emigrants from the Soviet Union, a nation which, in terms of external population migration, acts essentially as a closed system. However, somewhat larger numbers do leave the U.S.S.R. than enter, mainly Jewish groups moving to Israel, or relatives of expatriates rejoining their families now living beyond the borders of the Soviet Union. Emigration from other communist nations of eastern Europe is, however, quite significantly greater, particularly from Yugoslavia, Czechoslovakia, and Poland. Most of this migration is directed toward nations of western Europe and North America, rather than to other countries within the communist bloc.

Recorded emigration from the larger, more populous nations of Asia is insignificant by comparison with the major streams emanating from western Europe. Japan, for example, actually records lower emigration volumes than immigration. India, the Philippines, and Indonesia likewise experience relatively small amounts of outmigration, as do Pakistan, Taiwan, Malaysia, and South Korea, and these movements are balanced to some extent by immigrant streams of about equivalent volume.

Aggregate Capital Inflow and Outflow

The global pattern of net capital imports and exports is summarized in Figure 5. The data on which this map is based represent the aggregation of several different forms of capital transaction, comprising bilateral grants, bilateral loans, and transactions involving multilateral financing agencies such as the International Monetary Fund (I. M. F.) and the International Bank for Reconstruction and Development (I. B. R. D.). Data are taken from the Yearbook of International Financial Statistics for 1963, 1964, and 1965, published by the I. M. F. , and are in U. S. dollars.

As the map shows, there is a marked division in this aggregate pattern between the group of countries commonly thought of as industrialized or "developed" and the remainder of the international community, which collectively are generally regarded as being "underdeveloped" in various degrees.

Thus, traditional capital-exporting nations such as the United States, Britain, France, and West Germany, the free-market countries of greatest industrial development and the largest generators of investment capital, dominate the pattern of capital outflow. These nations contributed annual volumes of investment exceeding $500 million each during the period under examination. Within the $100 to $500 million range lie such countries as the Soviet Union, Japan, Italy, Belgium, Canada, and Australia, which have more recently become significant contributors to the world supply of available investment capital

The countries mentioned above together form the base on which international loan and development institutions must rely for stability and security in the contemporary period. They have, indeed, become the key elements in the various multilateral programs for expansion of less developed nations (which will be discussed in detail in a later chapter).

Smaller values for capital export in Figure 5 may represent bona fide investments by small but capital-rich nations, as in the instance of Kuwait and Saudi Arabia, investment by a colonial administration in its oversea territories, as in the case of Portugal, or repatriation of capital from earlier loans maturing in this period, as appears to be the situation in Yugoslavia.

Investment inflow patterns for the same period are dominated by the more populous countries of the "third world," notably India and Pakistan (each receiving over $500 million per annum) and Brazil. An appreciable number of other nations received net sums in excess of $100 million per annum, including Bolivia and Chile in the Latin American realm, Algeria, Niger, United Arab Republic, and Republic of Congo in continental Africa, and Israel, South Vietnam

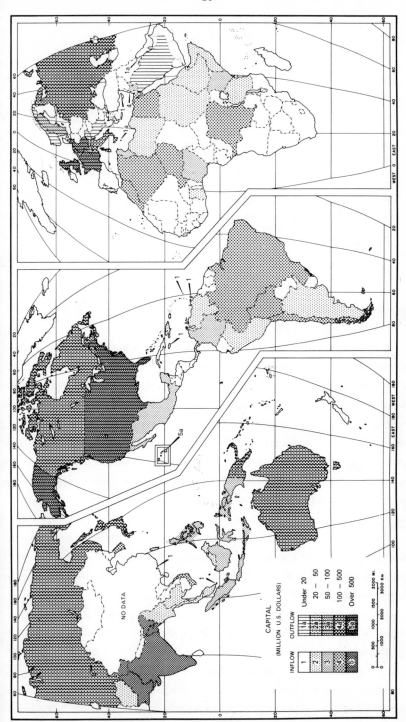

Figure 5.--Total Capital Flows: Net Inflow and Outflow for Period 1963-1965

and South Korea in Asia. Smaller net inflow ($50-100 million) was registered by such nations as Mexico and Colombia, Indonesia, the Philippines, Nigeria, Kenya, Tunisia, and Jordan. Relatively minor amounts (under $50 million) were received by the majority of the remaining "third world" countries.

With regard to the significance of this pattern of aggregate capital inflow a number of cautionary points must be borne in mind.

(1) The effectiveness of the investment received by a country will be largely a function of population number, structure, existing degree of industrialization, terms of the loan or grant, and many other factors. Hence the unqualified net capital flow cannot be considered simply as an index of rate or level of development.

(2) Certain elements of this pattern cannot be explained in purely economic terms. Some capital flows have political and strategic implications, as exemplified by the investment receipts of South Vietnam, United Arab Republic, and Israel in this period.

(3) Since values shown are net flows, obviously the full volumes of investment moving among countries are obscured to some extent.

Aggregate Information Flow: Mail and Telegraph Messages by Country of Origin

A further dimension of the degree of interaction among nations, in addition to the more tangible forms of movement (labor, capital, commodities), is the dissemination of information by the various communications media, of which mails and telegraph form a significant subset. Figure 6 displays the pattern of external information flow in the form of volume of mail and telegraph messages recorded by country of provenance. The data are derived from the United Nations Statistical Yearbook for 1963, 1964, and 1965. A larger than usual number of countries, however, do not collect data on external mail and telegraph flows, hence the map presents a pattern in which some significant gaps unfortunately appear.

Once again, the United States, Britain, and West Germany dominate this pattern, all contributing annual mail and telegraph outflows of more than 500 million messages. To this group also must be added the state of Brazil, although once again the data for this country seem questionable.

Somewhat lower on the scale of external mail and telegraph traffic (100-500 million items) are such countries as India, Australia, Mexico, and a number of west European nations, notably France and Italy. Smaller volumes (50-100 million) are recorded for Pakistan, Japan, Argentina, Venezuela, and several less populous European nations such as Portugal, Ireland, and Sweden. Of all the nations of Africa, only the Republic of South Africa falls within this inter-

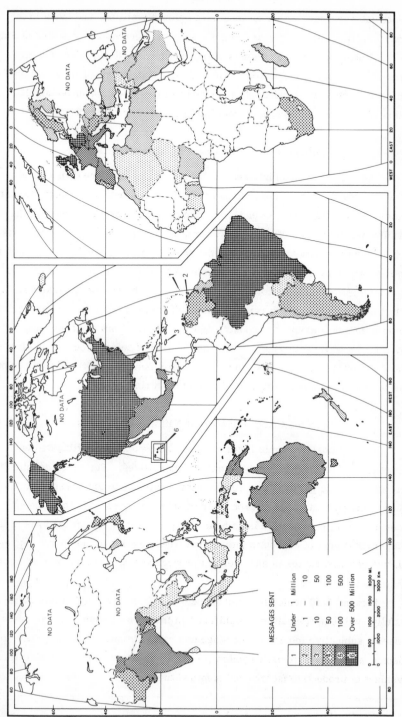

Figure 6. --Aggregate Information Flow: Mail and Telegraph Messages by Country of Origin. Annual Mean: 1963-1965

mediate category; most other nations have below 50 million, and many in fact below 10 million items per year. Significantly, the entropôt city-states of Singapore and Hong Kong record volumes of international mail and telegraph far in excess of the quantities expected in view of their population. This would tend to indicate possible causal links between oversea flows of commodities and the sending of commercial messages relating to commodity transactions.

Significance of International Economic Interaction

The set of six maps introduced above provides no more than a brief and rather impressionistic glimpse of the scale of the major types of international economic flows. However, even this cursory sketch provides a sense of the multidimensional nature of economic interaction. It points clearly to the existence of sustained flows of labor and investment capital at considerable volumes quantities which by any scale of measurement must be considered significant. The consideration of these flows would thus seem to be essential to the development of existing ideas which relate volumes of trade to other factors associated with economic development of countries of the world. This point may appear even more pertinent following a close examination of selected economic characteristics of interacting nations, and a tentative linking of aspects of flows to patterns in this set of commercial attributes of countries.

Selected Characteristics of National Economies

International economic flows are set in a context of multifaceted economic "personalities" of the community of nations themselves. The sheer complexity of global economic patterns is a considerable challenge to the researcher who wishes to capture an image of even their broadest outlines.[1] In the present instance, where the objective is an heuristic portrayal of salient features in the global environment of economic interaction, the selection of only a few representative characteristics is an uncertain procedure and, perhaps, our attempt is not a little temerarious.

Figures 7-10 depict selected aspects of national economies from which, hopefully, will emerge patterns significant in the present study. These maps represent subjective indices of the stage and rate of economic development, and of demographic characteristics which could play an important role in affecting movement of productive factors and commodities.

---

[1]See Ginsburg, op. cit., p. 1.

er Capita Gross National Product

Total Gross National Product, per capita Gross National Product, and
imilar measures have frequently been used as an index of the prosperity, pro-
uctivity, level of income, and level of development of countries, often as a
ole index, but more lately as one of a group of indices.[1]

Figure 7 presents the pattern of Per Capita Gross National Product for
ie period 1963-1965 inclusive. Data shown on this map are in U.S. dollars per
erson, per year, once again ignoring the differences in local purchasing power
nd exchange rates, which could alter the status of marginal countries in the
ategories shown here.

The highly-industrialized United States, and oil-rich Kuwait, emerge as
aving highest per capita productivity. Somewhat lower on the scale employed
or this map, with per capita incomes between $2,000 and $3,000 (U.S.) are
:anada, Sweden, and Switzerland. These countries stand somewhat ahead of
1ost remaining nations of northwest Europe and Australasia, which record
icomes equivalent to between $1,000 and $2,000 (U.S.) per annum. The latter
ountries can also quite clearly be considered "well-developed."

Some nations of western Europe, however, fall below this group of the
1oderately wealthy. Norway and Portugal, indeed, have per-capita annual
icomes of below 500 U.S. dollars (as does Yugoslavia). Spain, Ireland, and
ireece are, in per-capita terms, somewhat more prosperous, but still with
verage productivity values of under $1,000.

Intermediate levels of per-capita productivity or income embrace such
apidly industrializing nations as Japan, and also such raw-material-wealthy
ountries as Venezuela and Libya (which have vast oil deposits), Chile, and the
:epublic of South Africa (possessing plentiful mineral supplies). Somewhat
)wer per-capita national product ($100-500 U.S.) is observable in most of the
Ioslem world, Latin America, and several more developed southeast Asian
ations (Malaysia, Thailand, Taiwan, and the Philippines).

For much of the rest of the world, the picture is one of stark poverty and
xtremely low per-capita productivity, entrained in a vicious circle which en-
)lds between a third and two thirds of the world's population.

---

[1]The advantages and disadvantages of Gross National Product as a mea-
ure of economic development are debated more fully in Chapter III.

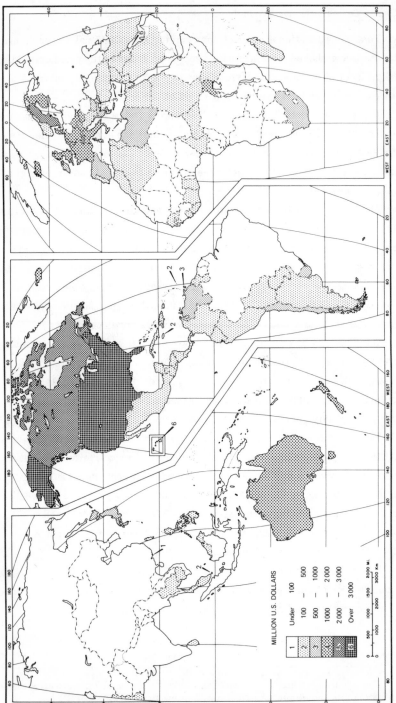

Figure 7.--Gross National Product per Capita: Mean Annual Value (U.S. Dollars) for Period 1963-1965

opulation Density

Population Density clearly has a deeply significant impact on economic haracteristics of nations and on their patterns of economic interaction. Five ategories of density, in units of number of persons per square kilometer of and surface in each country, are given in Figure 8. These data represent an verage for the period 1963-1965.

Figure 8 conveys only a very generalized impression of the global pattern of population distribution. It is clearly not sufficiently detailed for any lose analysis. The pattern could perhaps be loosely considered an index of opulation "pressure" on existing and future resources of various nations,[1] a actor which might exert considerable bearing on the economic outlook and behaior of many countries. Two great poles of high-density population emerge from ais map, these being western Europe and the islands and peninsulas of south nd east Asia, which comprise nations having densities generally exceeding 100 and in some cases 1000) persons per square kilometer.

The few countries (Malta, Singapore, Hong Kong, and Barbados) with opulation densities in excess of 1000/sq. km. are very small, and their combined populations are but a minute fraction of the total for the world regions in hich they are located.

Nations in intermediate categories are found on the periphery of the high ensity poles, but also in secondary concentrations such as equatorial Africa, orth and central America (including the Caribbean), and central Asia. The empty" areas of the world, i.e., those assemblages of countries with under) persons per sq. km. in Figure 8, embrace quite extensive areas of central nd Saharan Africa, South America, Canada, and Australasia.

ercent Increase in Population

Categories of positive and negative rate of population change, in terms of stimated Average Percentage Increase in Population for the period 1963-1965, re depicted in Figure 9. Included in this increase are migration and natural ncrease.

Rate of population increase has been found to be associated empirically ith several important economic dimensions of countries. An obvious associa-

---

[1]Exceptions to this generalization can, of course, be found. Pressure on xisting resources in thinly populated arid or cold areas (Arctic Canada, central ustralia, the Sahara) may be extremely high.

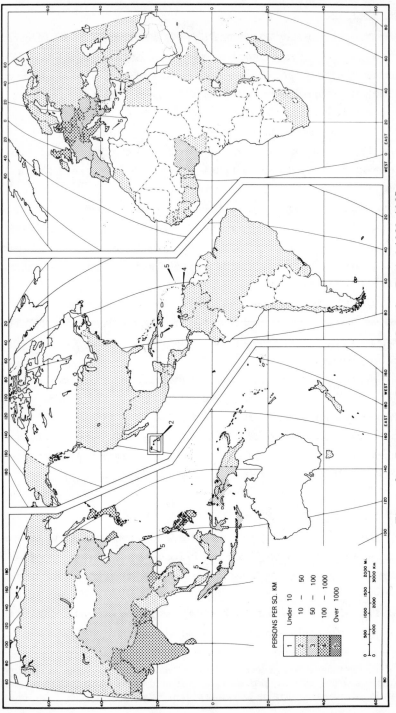

Figure 8.--Population Density: Mean for Period 1963-1965

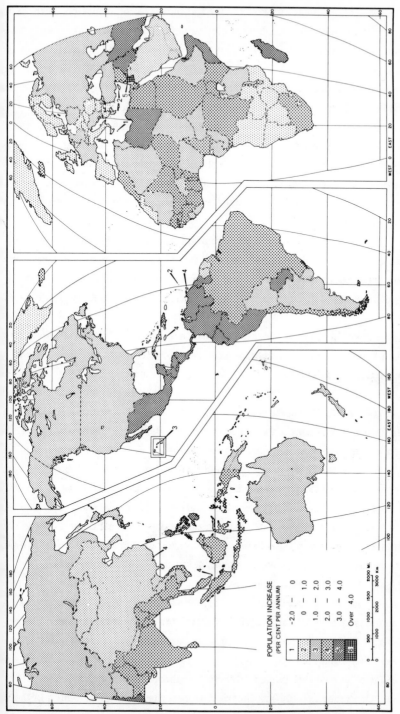

Figure 9.--Average Annual Percent Increase in Population for Period 1963-1965

tion is between increase in productivity and increase in population, measuring graphically the headway which a country is making in the struggle toward high economic prosperity. Casualties in this struggle are commonly found among nations at the lower end of the development scale, where traditional mores and lack of effective family planning programs have meant sustained and rapid rate of population increase without a commensurate increase in productivity.

In Figure 9, the nations of central and south America emerge as the most notable large enclave of very high population increase during the period under review. A combination of the relatively depressed economic status of these countries, low industrial-urban development, and traditional Catholic culture has produced an average annual growth rate exceeding 3 per cent for most of these nations.

Another large area of high population increase is the Moslem world, where countries like Jordan and Kuwait have increases of over 4 per cent per annum, and others (Libya, Iran, and Iraq) in excess of 3 per cent. Other outliers of very high increase exist in Malagasy, Somalia, Gambia, and the Philippines.

Somewhat lower increases (but still dangerously high in terms of pressure on rate of resource development) extend over much of the continents of Asia, Africa, and South America. Scarcely any countries of Africa for which data were available recorded increases below 1.0 per cent per annum during the period 1963-1965, and most exceeded 2.0 per cent. Countries in Asia and Latin America with large populations, such as India, Pakistan, Indonesia, and Brazil maintained increases which considerably exceeded 2.0 per cent per annum.

Some of the more prosperous countries of the new world displayed annual increases which also approached 2 per cent. The total populations of Australia, New Zealand, and Canada are perhaps small enough to have their growth significantly influenced by the sizeable immigrant intake which all three recorded during this specific period. All three are quite well developed in the sense of per capita income level, and have relatively low rates of natural increase.

In the "old" world, Common Market countries such as France, West Germany, and the Netherlands achieved greater than 1.0 per cent increases as did the Soviet Union, Poland, and Yugoslavia in the communist bloc. The remainder of Europe displayed, for the most part, somewhat lower rates of increase. Two countries, East Germany and Malta, actually recorded net loss in population during this period (clearly ascribable to out-migration in both cases). One other notably low increase is recorded for Japan, which is the o..

.rge nation in Asia having a rate of increase below 2.0 per cent. This low rate
. undoubtedly due in large measure to the effects of a vigorous birth control
.ogram and a rapid rise in industrial-urban development in the latter part of
.e post-war period.

rbanization

Since a strong empirical association exists between the maturity of a
.tion's urban-industrial structure and its rate and level of economic growth, an
.dex of urbanization was considered as potentially useful. Figure 10 portrays,
.r the period 1963-1964, the pattern of Percentage of Total Population in Metro-
.litan Cities, i.e., in cities having 500 thousand or more population. For the
.w nations in which no city of such a size existed, the population of the largest
.ty was used.

The strongly urban countries of the world, that is, countries having more
.an 50 per cent of their total population living in large metropolises are Austra-
.a, the United States, and Britain, to which must be added the small city states
. Singapore, Hong Kong, Malta, and Kuwait. Somewhat lower (40-50 per cent)
.t still highly urbanized are West Germany, Uruguay, Japan, and Barbados,
.llowed by Canada, the Low Countries, Israel, Panama, and the South Ameri-
.an nations of Argentina, Chile, and Venezuela.

Intermediate concentrations of metropolitan population are recorded for
.e rest of Europe (except for Norway and several eastern European nations
.hich have less than 10 per cent metropolitan population), New Zealand, South
.frica, and scattered countries in Latin America, the Middle East, and Asia.

For the rest of the world, urbanization is a relatively poorly developed
.henomenon, if we judge by percentage of population in metropolitan cities. The
.oviet Union, for example, ranks with such nations as Turkey, Brazil, Libya,
.nd South Vietnam as having only between 10 and 20 per cent of its population in
.rge cities. For the bulk of the countries in Africa and Asia, however, the
.ercentage is even lower, in most cases being less than 10 per cent.

Illustration of Empirical Flow-
Attribute Relationships

Having presented a summary sketch of major economic flow types and
.elected indices of national economic characteristics, it will now be necessary
. demonstrate evidence of the kinds of relationships between them hypothesized
. the introductory chapter. The questions to be asked in comparing the sets of

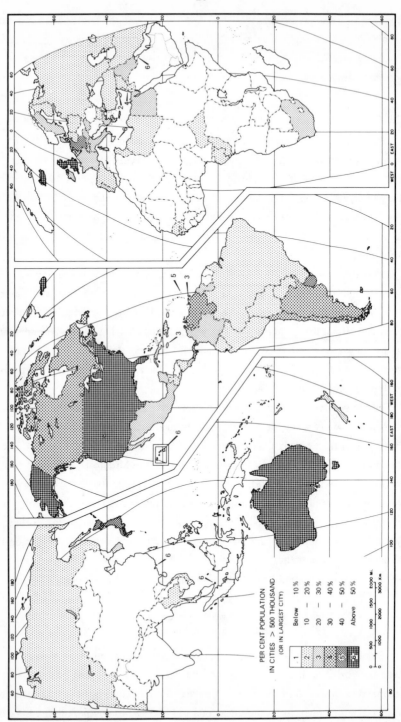

Figure 10.--Percent of Total Population in Metropolitan Cities: 1963-1964

maps described above, then, must focus on tentative empirical illustration of:

(1) correspondence in spatial and compositional patterns of economic flows, which may evince the effect of complementarity or substitutability of flow types;

(2) correspondence between flows and aspects of their economic context with emphasis on patterning in various potential stimuli to movement, and on evidence of an ordering effect produced by relative spatial positioning of nations with particular economic characteristics.

However, since it is difficult at this early stage (and at the broad scale we are using) to segregate neatly these two sets of relationships, we shall deal with them, for the time being, in the same general discussion. We shall also avoid exhaustive comparison between all possible combinations of flows and attributes, since the objective here is to illustrate, rather than inventory, observable relationships.

In some ways, and at an admittedly superficial level, general correspondences can be found in all the flow and attribute maps we have presented. This impression is imparted by the fairly consistent performance of a few distinctive clusters of countries across the spectrum of economic variables considered. Thus, the North Atlantic Community appears to maintain its relatively high position on the scales of all maps indexing level of interaction and development status, while African nations, with few exceptions, rank lowest. Closer observation, however, reveals a far more complex pattern of covariation. Relationships between specific sets of variables are brought out, and various subregions of the international community are shown to behave in quite different, and sometimes contrasting, ways with respect to the indices presented in the maps.

It is generally true that nations with greatest productivity appear also to have the greatest volume of trade. Thus, the United States and Canada, the two largest trading partners, have the highest Gross National Product per capita in straight dollar terms. This relationship tends to hold fairly strongly in lower categories as well. The contribution of trade to per capita income is well illustrated for the fortunate nations with large oil or mineral reserves, or which play the part of granaries for the surrounding less well-endowed nations. Specifically, Gross National Product per-capita of Venezuela, Kuwait, or Libya could not be explained without reference to external trade.

High Gross National Product per capita is also demonstrably related to total capital outflow, as revealed by the behavior of the United States, Canada, West Germany, and other prosperous nations. The converse, however, does not hold for all cases. The largest inflows of investment capital are funneled into the largest of the underdeveloped nations (India, Pakistan, Indonesia, Brazil), but for smaller third-world countries, the slightly better developed (United Ara Republic, Israel, Kenya, Chile, South Vietnam) seem to draw more investment capital than those with minimal per-capita income figures. High per-capita Gross National Product countries also tend to be significant destinations for long-term immigrants, as comparison of Figures 7 and 3 reveals. Once again, the United States, Canada, West Germany, Sweden, and Australia display rough corresponding positions on the scales of Immigration and Gross National Produ

Significantly, high rates of outmigration occur from moderately prosper ous countries on the periphery of the better developed new and old world nations or from these nations themselves. The first of these components suggests that relative closeness, and ability of migrants to pay for transportation, are possibly significant. The second component suggests a "backwash" effect of massive immigration programs in the newer and more rapidly developing countries.

Examination of the pattern of outmigration also reveals elements which are associated with demographic factors of origin countries. Very high density areas (but with at least moderate levels of per-capita income), show fairly high volumes of outmigration (e. g., Italy, Malta, Yugoslavia, Turkey, and British West Indies). The relationship of outmigration and absolute decline of population in Malta and East Germany has already been noted.

Population density of destination countries, as well as Gross National Product per-capita, appears significant in explaining patterns of immigration, specifically the larger flows to the United States, Canada, Australia, and New Zealand. However, in some cases (Israel, Switzerland, and West Germany) density of population in the destination country is already high. An explanatory factor here may be the level and rate of increase in productivity of the destination country relative to increases in its population. The differential in margina rate of productivity between origin and destination countries, and hence in their wage scales, may thus be prevented from converging and will consequently sustain the flow of labor.

Further correspondence may be observed between patterns of trade, migration, and capital flows, and the phenomenon of Urbanization as portrayed in Figure 10. The nations with highest percentage of population in large cities seem, at first glance, also to be magnets for large streams of migrants (indica ing, undoubtedly, a close relationship between urbanization and economic devel opment). These urbanized nations also appear to have somewhat lower rates of population increase, indicating a lower pressure on available resources and on accumulated capital available for international investment. They are also the largest suppliers of investment capital.

The urbanized centers of the world, then, may be hypothesized as forming "growth poles" whose relative prosperity is set in a circular pattern, [1] and
which act as the foci of interaction, in fact as the major stimuli of regional patterns of commodity and factor movements. They also reveal themselves as generators of information flow, as comparison of Figure 6 and Figure 10 will show.
Their importance as centers of trade is clearly indicated, in a comparison of
the maps of imports and exports with that of percent metropolitan population (Figures 1, 2, and 10).

To the extent that volumes of world trade are composed of the products of
highly-industrialized economies, the maps of trade and urbanization do show considerable correspondence. The discrepancies in these maps may be ascribed to
exports of raw materials by less urbanized nations with abundant natural resources, and to imports of food, and the ingredients of incipient industrial development, by those nations enjoying receipt of development capital from world
lending agencies.

Resumé

Many more patterns of correlation could be pointed out in the set of maps
of economic attributes and interactions. However, the specific patterns briefly
touched upon above serve to draw attention to the essential interdependence of
economic flows and the international economic environment in which these take
place. Some of the more important of these relationships may be reiterated here,
since they will form the focus of subsequent theoretical and empirical analysis:

(1) flows of Commodities, Labor, Capital, and Information exhibit patterns
    of general correspondence for important areas of the world, and of rela-
    tionship to certain broad economic characteristics (e.g., Per-capita
    Gross National Product);

(2) the apparent strengths of association among these flow patterns differ sub-
    stantially as more economic characteristics are considered and closer
    scrutiny is given to less prominent assemblages of countries. Demo-
    graphic factors (population density and rate of increase) and indices of
    economic development (% Metropolitan Population, Gross National Prod-
    uct per-capita) are revealed as having somewhat different (though con-

---

[1]This idea is discussed by Gunnar Myrdal, who used it to explain increasing disparity in rates of growth of "have" and "have not" countries. It has also
been described by Albert Hirschman and speculated on by numerous others as a
basis for programmed stimulation of development in less-prosperous countries.
For a review of this notion see Charles W. Hultman, Factor Migration: Trade
Theory and Growth Centers (Program on the Role of Growth Centers in Regional
Economic Development, Research Paper No. 29; Lexington: University of Kentucky, 1970).

nected) effects on patterns of Immigration and Emigration, Capital Inflo
and Outflow, and Commodity Imports and Exports;

(3) if a country's ability to export capital is taken as an index of the richnes
of its domestic capital supply, then patterns of capital endowment and
international migration show strong similarity. Both of these patterns
show interrelationship with the degree of urbanization as measured by
Percent Metropolitan Population, and with the level of per-capita productivity;

(4) the flow of information, represented by Mail and Telegraph Messages
Sent, appears to have stronger similarity with the configuration of trade
and perhaps with facets of the migration patterns, than with movement o
capital. Movement of information appears likewise to be associated wit
the urbanization and demographic measures listed, and suggests that it
may prove to be a useful index of total commercial/social interaction
among nations.

The drawing of comparisons between aspects of the flow and attribute pa
terns presented in this chapter has served to amplify the problems which comprise the focus of this study. The highly subjective and qualitative nature of the
procedure we have employed, and the tentative character of the associations
identified in this procedure, are freely acknowledged. However, the available
tools of analysis for attacking complex problems such as this are far more
powerful and, with careful use, far more accurate. In the chapters which follo
we shall endeavor to use these tools to examine the systems of interrelationshij
which bind the countries comprising the global economy.

The result of this more rigorous analysis should be a set of inductively-
based generalizations concerning economic flows and their mutual effects on
groups of nations, both at the general or aggregated level, and also at the disaggregate scale of country-to-country interaction. Yet even more may be
learned by paying close attention to cases which do not fit neatly into general pa
terns, and by attempting to account for their failure to conform. However, it
would be appropriate to initiate this closer analysis by reviewing the fund of co
cepts which have emerged to explain the mechanisms of economic interaction
and their effects on national economic characteristics. This review will form
the focus of the following chapter.

CHAPTER II

INTERNATIONAL TRADE, MIGRATION, AND

INVESTMENT: CONTRIBUTIONS TOWARD

AN INTEGRATIVE SPATIAL THEORY

Interdependence of Economic
Attributes and Flows

The group of nations which comprise the international economy, together with their economic attributes and the relationships which bind them, could be thought of as a vast system whose elements (objects, attributes, and interactions) are in a continual state of flux and a universal condition of interdependence. An important implication of this perspective on the international economic system is that any analysis of international trade, or migration of labor, or movement of capital would give only a partial or incomplete picture without explicit consideration of possible mutual interdependence of these forms of interaction. The theoretical consideration of flow interrelationships, in other words, is seen to be as much a part of the development of an adequate model of economic interaction as the linking of individual flows with internal attributes of nations making up the interaction system.

In the present instance, achieving the objective of understanding international economic interaction involves the joint investigation of two sets of theoretically-occurring relationships:

(1) complementarity or substitutability among different types of economic flows;

(2) causal connections among attributes of national economies and individual or mixed flows, whether these connections are unidirectional (asymmetrical) or circular and cumulative (symmetrical).

For convenience we have grouped the myriad every-day interactions of an economic nature into two categories: flows of commodities, and flows of those factors of production (labor and capital) which can be considered more or less mobile.[1] The primary objective of the study, then, becomes the tracing of theo-

---

[1]Land, the third major factor of production, is considered immobile in the

retical relationships between commodity and factor movements, after which, guided by the resultant deductive framework, we can employ inductive methods to gain further understanding of real world patterns.

Theoretical Relationships between Commodity and Factor Flows

Basic Conditions for Trade and Factor Movement

What are the major factors governing the structure, direction and consistency of factor and commodity movements? Numerous economic, political, and cultural influences, of varying shades of significance, could be suggested intuitively in answer to this question. Cultural traditions, for example, may affect the volume and value of certain commodities entering into trade or may explain the absence of some otherwise common items in the trade baskets of certain countries. The level of technology and the prevailing development ideology may also be expected to play a part in deciding how much capital or labor and what kinds of goods will be imported or exported by a nation. However, for the present it will be assumed that all such influences may be expressed by a purely economic index, this being the differential in prices of commodities and factors at points of origin (supply) and destination (demand).

Is there, in fact, a relationship between prices for commodities and prices of the factors needed to produce these commodities? It could be answered that the demand for factors is a derived demand, stemming from the final demand for commodities, and that a differential in demand for factors in two countries (and consequently in their relative prices) reflects a similar demand (and price) differential for commodities produced from them.

Such a differential, on the assumption of parity of currency exchange rates and free mobility of factors and commodities, could clearly result in either a flow of commodities or a movement of factors from the low-price to the high-price market.

In other words, trade and factor flows, under certain conditions, could constitute alternate and freely interchangeable responses to essentially the same set of stimuli.

---

present context, despite occasional instances of the transfer of sovereignty over land from one country to another: such transfers do not normally enter into international economic transactions. Ancillary factors such as entrepreneurial ability and technology, which are themselves mobile, are not considered as separate entities in this study.

This statement is, admittedly, overly simplistic, as it ignores many important factors in the real world which tend to complicate the relationship between factor and trade flows. In particular, it does not take account of the supply and demand situations in a multi-commodity, many-market system such as the world economy. Here one must grapple with (among other things) questions of factor endowments and production functions on the supply side, and commodity substitutability and taste changes on the demand side.

Nor does this simple relationship take cognizance of impediments to movement of commodities, labor, and capital that may hypothetically occur. When the existence of such frictions is acknowledged, quite different relationships among types of flow can arise.

Alternative Modifications of the Basic Flow Model

The introduction of such modifications to the simple model of interaction stated above may produce three results:

(1) maintenance of the substitution relationship between trade and factor movement, with a clear dominance of one form to the virtual exclusion of the other;

(2) substitution among flow types, but without complete dominance of either form;

(3) complementary (rather than substitutionary) relationship among flow types.

The modifications needed to produce the first of these three results are either prohibitive tariffs or complete factor immobility at an international level together with a comparative advantage in production of at least two commodities in two potential trading partners. The result may still be called a general model of economic interaction since all possible kinds of movement are formally considered although a number are summarily dismissed by rigid assumptions.

Models Assuming Factor Immobility

Factor immobility is, in essence, the situation envisaged by the classical trade theorists Ricardo and Torrens, whose independent discovery of the principle of comparative advantage[1] set the stage for development of trade theory in

---

[1] The notion of comparative advantage can probably be explained most simply by means of a brief illustration. Let us suppose that two nations, A and B, have identical outlays of $100 million which can be invested either in the production of steel or wheat. With its outlay, A can produce either 6 million tons of steel, or 2 million tons of wheat, whereas B, with the same outlay, can produce

classical and neoclassical economics.[1]

In the classical trade model, comparative advantage in production was envisaged as arising out of price or cost differentials caused by disparities in labor productivity in the two countries. This notion, which is the essence of the Labor Theory of Value, overlooked the role of richness of resource endowment and the ancillary role of capital in raising productivity, and for these and other reasons was subsequently discredited. However, the essential notion of comparative advantage, which is not necessarily dependent on the labor theory of value for its operability, was rescued by neoclassical scholars,[2] who removed the offending and unnecessary labor theory and restored the concept of comparative cost to the respectable position it has since occupied as a cornerstone of economic trade theory.

However, in the eyes of the neoclassicists, economic interaction among nations was still composed exclusively of commodity trade (the assumption of factor immobility remained) and their basic model still comprised only the two country-two commodity case. Moreover, their explanation of trade still relied on the assumption that fixed factor costs and identical tastes and demands ex-

---

only 2 million tons of steel or 1 million tons of wheat (perhaps due to inefficiency or lack of social overhead capital).

For each ton of steel A wishes to produce, it must forego 1/3 ton of wheat. However, for each ton of steel B wishes to produce, it must do without 1/2 ton of wheat.

Now if A concentrates on steel and can sell its excess at the rate of 1 ton of steel for more than 1/3 ton of wheat, it would be in its best interest to import all of its wheat needs.

Similarly if B can buy 1 ton of steel for less than 1/2 ton of wheat, it will obviously want to import steel and concentrate on domestic wheat production.

Thus, a basis of trade exists between A and B, A exporting steel and importing wheat from B even though in absolute terms A can produce more of both commodities than B for the same outlay.

[1]Excellent reviews of the classical trade theory are given in John S. Chipman, "A Survey of the Theory of International Trade: Part 1, The Classical Theory," Econometrica, Vol. XXXIII (1965); and in: Jagdish Bhagwati, "The Pure Theory of International Trade: A Survey," Economic Journal, LXXIV (1964), 4-26.

[2]Embellishments of the classical theory, which have come to be known as neoclassical concepts, were made in the early part of this century by Alfred Marshall and Francis Edgeworth in the form of a general (but aspatial) equilibrium model. This was later expanded by such economists as James Meade and Wassily Leontief who refined the analytical tools of community indifference curves (for demand analysis) and production possibility curve (for depicting supply patterns). For a succinct account of the development of neoclassical concepts see Jagdish Bhagwati, ed., International Trade (Middlesex, England: Penguin Books, 1969), pp. 10-12.

sted in both trading partners, as required by the comparative cost formulation.

The conditions under which commodity movement will completely replace factor movement have more recently been rigorously demonstrated by Samuelson,[1] who shows that, in the two-country, two-factor, two-commodity case, commodity and factor price equalization will be mutually determined if:

(1) production functions are linear-homogeneous (i. e., if the factor combinations determine absolute and relative marginal productivity),

(2) if specialization of production is ruled out by the nature of resource endowment and

(3) if the amount of one factor required by one commodity is consistently greater, at all price levels, than that required by the second commodity.

Theoretical Application of Prohibitive Tariff Assumption

The alternate modification of the simple model, i. e., the imposition of prohibitive tariffs on all commodity imports would, of course, induce complete autarky (self-sufficiency). Such a condition would run counter to the assumption of economic motivation in international transactions (since it is at variance with the demonstrated economic advantages of specialization and at least partial commodity trade as revealed by the comparative advantage model). Not surprisingly, then, consideration of prohibitive tariff structures in economic theory has featured highly specific application rather than incorporation in any general structure. Its main uses have been as an analytical device, as for example in the study of commodity-factor substitution relationships,[2] and in specific aspects of the theory of protection of domestic industry.[3]

Any attempt to introduce more realistic assumptions into the basic interaction equation clearly entails rejection of both the above limitations of the simple model of economic interaction postulated earlier, and thus acceptance of the second and third possibilities (i. e., partial substitutability or complementarity of factor and trade flows).

---

[1]Paul A. Samuelson, "Prices of Factors and Goods in General Equilibrium," Review of Economic Studies, XXI (1953-1954), 1-21.

[2]Robert A. Mundell, International Economics (New York: Macmillan, 1968), pp. 85-90.

[3]The theoretical efficacy of prohibitive tariffs in raising real wages of those industries relying on relatively scarce productive factors is reviewed in P. Samuelson and W. Stolper, "Protection and Real Wages," Review of Economic Studies, IX (1941), 58-73.

Theories Based on Partial
Trade-Factor Substitution

For the second modification (i. e., existence of limited substitution conditions among commodities and factors) we must remove the assumption that
commodities are infinitely mobile and factors completely immobile at the inter
national level. That is, we accept the existence at all scales of analysis of so
non-prohibitive impediments or frictions to movement of both goods and factor
of production. Obviously, if we retain the assumption that supply and demand
conditions in trading partners are such that the communities are indifferent as
to which form of movement takes place, the volumetric composition of mixed
commodity-and-factor flows will be regulated simply by the severity of the impediments acting on each type of flow.

In other words, an increase in trade impediments between the two coun
tries would stimulate movement of factors, and an increase in frictions to mov
ment of labor and/or capital would stimulate trade.

Robert A. Mundell[1] demonstrates the existence and modus operandi of
this relationship in a rigorously developed model involving two countries, two
commodities, and two productive factors, one of which (capital) is considered
mobile. Mundell's study proceeds deductively, developing the case in which
total substitutability of commodities for factors takes place, where one commo
ity is taken to be labor-intensive and the second capital-intensive. A modifica
tion is then introduced to permit capital mobility, resulting in an upset of relative marginal products on the two factors in the two countries. With the assistance of a small and temporary tariff imposition, this adjustment removes the
economic advantage of commodity trade.

The conclusions of Mundell's study reinforce the notion that commodity
flows and factor movements are, in a limited sense, substitutable. We are
shown that the key to an understanding of the volume of each kind of flow entering into the aggregate pattern of movement between pairs of interacting countri
may be found in the nature of frictions to individual flow types.

If we remove the assumptions of fixed and identical demand conditions
and fixed (but not necessarily homologous) factor combinations in both potentia
trading partners, the range of possible relationships between flows of factors
and commodities becomes suddenly very large. One would intuitively expect
that, in the absence of these assumptions, all or most real-world situations

---

[1]Robert A. Mundell, "International Trade and Factor Mobility," Americ
Economic Review, XLVII (June, 1957), 321-35.

nvolving mixed flows could now be theoretically embraced. But the rigorous
)asis of the comparative cost model has also been removed in the process, so
ve are faced with the problem of setting up new hypotheses to explain observed
)atterns.

This problem was faced by the Swedish economist Eli Heckscher and his
)upil Bertil Ohlin--authors of a novel and provocative conceptual scheme which
las since been termed the Modern Theory of Trade.[1] The ideas of these two
:esearchers were developed essentially as an alternative to the classical com-
)arative-cost formulation, attempting to avoid the pitfalls surrounding the un-
•ealistic classical assumptions concerning the bases of comparative cost and the
stimuli to trade.

'actor Proportions and Trade Predominance

The well known Heckscher-Ohlin theorem, around which the Modern The-
•ry of Trade revolves, may be stated succinctly as follows:

> International (or interregional) trade results from differences in relative
> factor endowments from country to country; exports of a particular nation
> will thus comprise those commodities in whose production a predominant
> quantity of the relatively abundant factor is employed, and its imports will
> include commodities having predominant amounts of factors scarce in that
> country.[2]

\s a corollary to this proposition, Ohlin states that unhindered commodity trade
among countries tends to equalize prices of productive factors, thus acting as a
substitute for international factor movements.[3]

The basic Heckscher-Ohlin model, however, retains the static character
)f previous comparative advantage formulations and is based on quite stringent
assumptions. For example, the following conditions for trade are assumed to

---

[1]The work of these scholars was stimulated by John Williams' earlier
ttack on the implications of the assumption in existing theory concerning abso-
ute internal factor-mobility and complete international factor immobility. See
. Williams, "The Theory of International Trade Reconsidered," Economic
ournal, XXXIX, No. 154 (June, 1929), 195-209.

[2]Bertil Ohlin, Interregional and International Trade (Cambridge, Mass.:
arvard University Press, 1933), p. 34.

[3]In its original, stronger form (attributable to Heckscher), this proposi-
ion was known as the "factor price equalization theorem." Samuelson and
erner have demonstrated that, under the original assumptions of the Heckscher-
)hlin model, the stronger case applies. See P. A. Samuelson, "International
'rade and the Equalization of Factor Prices," Economic Journal, LVIII (1948),
63-84.

be exogenously fixed or determined:[1]

(1) the supply of productive factors

(2) the technical knowledge which, with the relative factor prices, governs the combination of factors

(3) the character and structure of tastes or demand

(4) the conditions of ownership with regard to factors (i. e., the distribution of income and purchasing power).

Thus, in the basic Ohlin model, the condition of factor immobility is retained at the international level, production functions are assumed identical in all countries for production of a particular commodity, and each production function is taken as subject to constant returns to scale.

Ohlin is by no means unaware of the lack of realism of these rigid assumptions. He uses them initially to build the simple framework of his trade model since they are indispensable to the construction of the mutual-interdependence theory of factor and commodity pricing on which the rest of his theory of trade relies. However, he proceeds in due course to examine the theoretical state of his system when certain of these assumptions are relaxed.

When the assumption of interregional immobility of factors is relaxed, the element which conditions trade and factor movements, according to Ohlin, the relative severity of obstacles to the movement of each. This follows from the fact that price, wage, or interest rate differences in the mutually-interdependent international system could be virtually neutralized by either factor or commodity flows.

In considering the nature of obstacles to commodity movement, Ohlin dwells at considerable length on the behavior of transfer costs, noting the importance here of understanding concepts of industrial and agricultural location theory. He also deals with problems of tariff barriers, import restrictions, and disparities in the general administrative and commercial systems of different countries. In treating the subject of obstacles to factor movement, Ohlin notes that these comprise not so much economic deterrents as psychological aversion on the part of the laborer and entrepreneur against change or uncertainty.[2] He goes further, however, and states that the setting up of an impediment to flows of one type of factor would generally result in a restriction of flows of other factors, leading to an important converse of this statement, namely, that the demand for labor and capital is most commonly a joint demand.[3]

---

[1] Ohlin, op. cit., p. 305.

[2] Ibid., p. 115.

[3] Ibid., p. 224.

Ohlin, however, does not seem to accept in his model that movements of commodities and movement of factors can be theoretically of equal significance. On at least one occasion he asserts that trade renders unnecessary the movement of factors in whole or in part, and that factor flows may simply be called forth when trade is unable to produce full price equalization among countries, and then only if the factor price differences are sufficient to overcome the barriers to movement of labor and capital. He seems, in other words, to revert to the assumption of relative immobility of productive factors despite lengthy discussion of variations of this postulate and their hypothetical effects.

Ohlin does, however, acknowledge the criticism of the French economist Byé concerning his basic assumption of lower relative mobility of productive factors. He answers this criticism by saying that:

> One can agree with Byé that very little explicit and formalized analysis is available regarding the effect on international trade of various degrees of international mobility of the factors of production, but such an analysis would hardly overthrow the main body of existing doctrine. In the short run, labor supply is almost fixed. In the long run it varies under the influence of changes in the demand for labor in each country, and it is not difficult to pay due attention to the possibility of migration.[1]

In other words, although Ohlin sets up a framework (factor price equalization) which clearly makes room for the possibility of mixed-flow responses, and gives this framework a logical basis (international disparities in relative factor endowments), he virtually dismisses the possibility of developing a general interaction theory by failing to postulate formally the conditions which would govern the relationships among the flows themselves. Instead, he relies on an untested, empirically based assumption that, by some unstated measure, factor movements are of lower significance and hence unworthy of explicit incorporation in his general trade theory.

Complementary Factor and Commodity Movement

The third modification to the general interaction model outlined earlier in this chapter envisions the movement of commodities, labor, and capital as a joint response to a set of stimuli rather than as alternative or substitute responses. This appears to be a highly specific case within the general set of commodity-factor flow relationships, and perhaps for this reason has received little treatment in existing trade or factor movement theory.

---

[1] Ibid., pp. 312-13.

There is, of course, no difficulty in conceptualizing the relationships among the factor flows themselves. As has already been pointed out, Ohlin considers labor and capital to be subject to joint demand and hence to combine in complementary flows to receptor nations. The reason, as is verified by numerous empirical studies, stems from the participation of these two factors, in various proportions, in almost all productive activities. In some cases, e. g., the transference of a migrant's savings to the country of destination, or the remittance of money by expatriate laborers to their relatives in the country of origin, the flows of labor and capital are very closely tied indeed.

The conditions under which commodities might move in unison with productive factors are, however, less clear. It is theoretically possible that economic interaction between an older, labor and capital-rich country and a new country rich in resources but poor in labor and capital will comprise mainly flows of factors initially. If, as a result, the productive factor disparities between the two nations are narrowed sufficiently, being accompanied by a rise in aggregate incomes in both, the volume of trade between the two nations may be stimulated.[1] But the determination of the exact conditions under which such complementary trade-factor flow relationships would be established cannot be determined deductively: further investigation of these relationships must be based on empirical analysis.

Relations between Individual Flows and
Attributes of National Economies

As a generalization, it would be legitimate to assert that the question of any kind of substitutionary or complementary relationships among flows themselves has been ignored or overlooked in most models dealing with specific, solitary forms of interaction. Despite this shortcoming, many such models of individual flow types have been very important and useful aids to an understanding of the factors generating flow phenomena.

In the present context, however, we will examine only those constructs which illustrate a movement toward the inclusion of concepts of space or distance among the factors giving rise to individual forms of interaction. These comprise the essential stepping stones toward a general, integrative spatial model of flow.

In dealing with such constructs, a number of appropriate methods of

---

[1]Ibid., p. 118. Carl Iversen, Aspects of the Theory of International Capital Movements (New York: Augustus Kelley, 1967), pp. 182-83.

model classification exist and could be used. A method of approach which suggests itself as particularly useful would be to treat separately the various models dealing with explanation of trade flows, migration, and capital movements, and within these divisions to emphasize those frameworks which have some form of spatial or distance component. Generally, the latter are more empirically based, although this is not exclusively the case.

Spatial Models of Trade

Although Bertil Ohlin was indeed aware of the frictional effects of distance or space as well as of the potential mobility of productive factors, and gives these questions some consideration in his theoretical treatment of trade, his conclusions, and the formalized expression of his model, in effect exclude them from a position of significance. It must be pointed out that, in this connection, Ohlin's assertion concerning the low relative mobility of productive factors in comparison with commodities is an inductive rather than deductive question, and Ohlin's work could perhaps be faulted for its failure to supply such empirical verification for this crucial plank in his theory. Ohlin likewise falls short of a truly spatial theory by failing to take formal and precise account of location and distance factors. In the words of August Lösch:

> Ohlin's solution is not so radical, partly because he did not really break away from the theory of trade between countries (the "regions" he constructs are essentially no more than truncated countries), and partly because he did not penetrate deeply enough into location theory. Ohlin gives the impression of not having completely overcome the prevailing theory's characteristic failure to think in terms of space. [1]

Lösch proposes, as an alternative, a dynamic theory of trade which stresses the spatial aspects of price shifts, defining the configuration of such shifts as wave-like ripples in international commodity-price surfaces which may or may not be modified by political boundaries. However, Lösch does not provide a rigorous mathematical statement of his theory, and to date his trade model has not been accorded any significant empirical testing which would verify its operability.

Gravity Models in Trade Studies

A promising alternative line of development to the predominantly deductive, geometric analyses considered above has been the construction of spatial

---

[1] August Lösch, "Eine neue Theorie des internationalen Handels," Weltwirtschaftliches Archiv (September, 1939). E. Henderson, translator, "A New Theory of International Trade," International Economic Papers, VI (1959), 50-65.

trade models in an econometric form, begun independently by economists in Finland and Holland. In essence, the earlier models of the Finnish researcher K. Poyhonen and P. Pulliainen, and of the Dutch economist J. Tinbergen are expansions of the familiar gravity model,[1] expressing dyadic (pair-wise) interaction among trading partners as a function of theoretically relevant "mass" characteristics of the partners themselves and of a retarding effect related to their physical distance apart.

Within the discipline of Geography the gravity model has been used for a number of years in models replicating flow phenomena.[2] Models relating spec

---

[1]In its most general form, the gravity model is usually written:

$$X_{ij} = k \frac{P_i (W_i) P_j (W_j)}{W_d d_{ij}^n}$$

where P_i, P_j are mass factors,

d_{ij} is distance between points i, j,

W is a weighting factor,

and k is a scalar constant.

The Poyhonen-Pulliainen model is expressed by:

$$X_{ij} = k \frac{C_i C_j P_i^a P_j^b}{d_{ij}^n}$$

whereas the Tinbergen formula is:

$$X_{ij} = k \frac{P_i^a P_j^b}{d_{ij}^n}$$

P_i, P_j are Gross National Product of origin and destination countries, d_{ij} the distance between their main economic centers, exponents a, b and d are elasticities of trade with respect to Gross National Project and distance. k is a proportionality constant, while C_i and C_j in the Finnish model are indices expressing "openness to trade," such as resource endowment, tariff levels, etc.

In a review of these models, the Belgian economist Waelbroek has suggested that the factor of prices in origin and destination countries, and the elasticity of substitution attendant upon relative price differences, be added to the gravity model. See Jean Waelbroek, "The Growth Propelled Exports Model of International Trade: Empirical Basis and Dynamic Stability" (unpublished Research Paper, Université Libre de Bruxelles and Massachusetts Institute of Technology, 1966), pp. 5-16.

[2]Gunnar Olsson, Distance and Human Interaction: A Review and Bibliogphy (Review and Bibliography Series No. 2; Philadelphia: Regional Science Research Institute, 1965).

ically to commodity movement were developed by Robert H. T. Smith and Peter Gould[1] (who effectively made operable the concepts of complementarity and transferability first put forward by Edward Ullman),[2] and tested using simple gravity-type formulations. The most elegant of such models, however, has been propounded by Brian J. L. Berry, developing and refining the work of one of Tinbergen's pupils, Hans Linnemann. Since this particular line of approach has strongly influenced the development of the model to be tested in the present study, it merits closer attention here.

The Linnemann study addresses the problem of explaining "why the size of international trade flows differs so much between different pairs of countries."[3] Linnemann submits that the lack of congruity of production and domestic demand provides the ultimate reason for commodity trade, that such incongruity engenders in each country a condition of "potential supply" and "potential demand" for commodities offered on the world market, but that, because of trade impediments, e.g., transport costs and tariffs, no country will be able to realize its full potentialities as far as trade with foreign countries is concerned.

The notions of potential supply and potential demand employed by Linnemann are in no way synonymous with the concept of Potential as employed by

---

[1]Robert H. T. Smith and Peter R. Gould, "Method in Commodity Flow Studies," Australian Geographer, VIII (1961), 73-77.

[2]The notions of complementarity and transferability were considered by Ullman to be basic to the understanding of any form of economic flow. In introducing the notion of complementarity, Ullman states:

In order for two areas to interact, there must be a demand in one and a supply in the other. Thus an automobile industry in one area would use tires produced in another but not buggy whips produced in still another. Specific complementarity is required before interchange takes place.

This concept is modified by an adaptation of the Intervening Opportunity notion:

Complementarity, however, generates interchange only if no intervening source of supply is available.

Transferability is a factor which Ullman equates with the friction of distance operating against physical movement:

A final factor required in an interaction system is transferability or distance, measured in real terms of transfer and time costs.

See Edward L. Ullman, "The Role of Transportation and the Bases for Interaction," in Man's Role in Changing the Face of the Earth, ed. W. L. Thomas, Jr. (Chicago: University of Chicago Press, 1956), pp. 862-80.

[3]Hans Linnemann, An Econometric Study of International Trade Flows (Amsterdam: North Holland Publishing Co., 1965), p. 4.

Stewart, Warntz[1] and others in accounting for population movements, or by Harris, Ray and others in measuring the locational pull of the market.[2] While the latter are a derivative of the gravity formula and imply a field of interaction probabilities around a given point,[3] the Linnemann concept is derived purely from a consideration of characteristics relating to each point that could be considered part of the "mass" factors, e.g., size of a country's national or domestic product, size of population, and (of secondary importance) level of per-capita income.[4]

It is interesting, however, that Linnemann rejects both the comparative-cost and relative-factor-proportions concepts as a viable explanatory framework for trade study. He asserts that comparative advantage is neither static nor exogenous to the trade model, as classical theory implies, since it changes with technological innovation, and the concomitant change in factor proportions may be stimulated quite markedly by trade.[5]

In mathematical form, the trade flow model devised by Linnemann is expressed by:

$$X_{ij} = \beta 0 \; \frac{(E_i^{\partial})^{\beta 1} \; (M_j^{\partial})^{\beta 2}}{(R_{ij})^{\beta 3}}$$

where E^{∂} is potential supply,

            M^{∂} represents potential demand,

            R_{ij} is an index of resistance.

These are then recast in a multiple regression model, featuring the variables actually collected from international statistical sources and intended as indices of the more abstract concepts in the above model.

---

[1] John Q. Stewart, "Empirical Mathematical Rules Governing the Distribution and Equilibrium of Population," Geographical Review, XXXVII (1947), 473-75. And also: William Warntz, Toward a Geography of Price: A Study in Geo-Econometrics (Philadelphia: Regional Science Research Institute, 1959).

[2] Chauncy D. Harris, "The Market as a Factor in the Localization of Industry in the U.S.," Annals of the Association of American Geographers, XLIV (1954), 315-48. And also: D. Michael Ray, Market Potential and Economic Shadow (Research Series No. 101; Chicago: University of Chicago, Department of Geography, 1965).

[3] The general formula for population potential (P_i) of any point is given by

$$P_i = k \sum \frac{W_j}{d_{ij}^n}$$

[4] Linnemann, op. cit., pp. 10-21.   [5] Ibid., p. 21.

Further attention will be given to the _form_ of the Linnemann trade model in a later chapter dealing expressly with technical aspects of model development rather than the conceptual aspects which are the main concern of the present section. It should be noted, however, that this model was refined by Berry[1] in his study of commodity flow in India to include concepts of potential supply and demand more attuned to the present state of geographic understanding of these concepts, and that this model was accorded regional testing in India by Reed.[2]

Where immobility of productive factors is assumed, the Berry-Reed model forms the most general and theoretically comprehensive construct yet devised to explain volume of dyadic (i. e., pair-wise) trade, since it takes into account the probability of interaction among the dyads themselves, as well as the probability of interaction by a member of a dyad with the field of outside potential trade partners. This model will also be examined in greater detail in the section dealing with development of model structures.

Spatial Models of International Migration

The development of migration theory, in contrast to international trade and investment flow theories, showed an early emphasis on spatial frameworks for analysis. The pioneering nineteenth century treatises by Henry Carey and Ernest G. Ravenstein[3] gave explicit attention to the ordering effect of distance on patterns of human migration. Indeed, Ravenstein's "laws of migration" could be described as a prototype of the familiar gravity model, numerous variations of which have been employed in more recent migration analyses. A brief survey of the relevant concepts and models devised to replicate and explain international migration patterns will bring this fact clearly to light.

Many studies of migration of human populations make a clear distinction between _refugee_ movements, caused by catastrophic political or social upheaval (and, occasionally, natural disaster) from the more orderly migrations of people in response to predominantly economic stimuli, this latter form of movement

---

[1] Brian J. L. Berry, Essays on Commodity Flows and the Spatial Structure of the Indian Economy (Research Series No. 111; Chicago: University of Chicago, Department of Geography, 1966).

[2] Wallace E. Reed, Areal Interaction in India (Research Series No. 110; Chicago: University of Chicago, Department of Geography, 1967).

[3] Henry C. Carey, Principles of Social Science (Philadelphia: J. Lippincott, 1858). E. G. Ravenstein, "The Laws of Migration," Journal of the Royal Statistical Society, XLVIII (1885), 167-235.

being termed <u>national migration.</u> The theories of migration referred to in this section deal, quite obviously, with the latter form of movement only.

Studies of population movements at the international level form a distinc field of investigation within the broader realm of migration analysis. This is a consequence of the capacity of nation states to apply legislative restrictions and controls to immigration (and in some cases emigration), conditions which do no generally apply at the interregional level. Other important distinctions, of course, attend the difference in scale of international as opposed to intranationa migration. Therefore, although in some respects international migration reveals considerable similarity in pattern, causes, and consequences to internal regional population movements, the present examination of concepts which have evolved from migration studies will emphasize development of frameworks of migration at a global scale. What follows, then, is a focused discussion of rele vant concepts, rather than a comprehensive treatment of general migration theory. An up-to-date and penetrating review of the field of migration study is available in Paul J. Schwind's analysis of Regional Migration in the United State

Frameworks for analysis of international migratory movements general permit relevant concepts to be divided into:

(1) those relating to stimulus conditions, i.e., factors which generate move ment,

and

(2) concepts relating to frictional effects acting against movement.

Stimulus to migration is commonly postulated as being predominantly economic but demographic stimuli are often linked with the push-pull mechanism generat ing population movements. As Spengler explains,

> Migration between countries takes place because the migrant expects trans ference of himself (and possibly his family) to the country of destination to augment the index of welfare (usually an economically dominated index) by which he guides his conduct. [2]

The "push" factors associated with augmentation of this welfare index are, according to Spengler,

(1) the rates of absolute and relative natural increase in country of origin,

(2) changes in occupational structure (e.g., movement of surplus agricultural labor to cities),

---

[1] Paul J. Schwind, Migration and Regional Development in the United Stat (Research Paper No. 133; Chicago: University of Chicago, Department of Geog raphy, 1971).

[2] Joseph J. Spengler, "Effects Produced in Receiving Countries by Pre-1939 Immigration," in Economics of International Migration, ed. Brinley Thom (London: Macmillan, 1958), p. 37.

(3) the progress of urban-industrial growth,

(4) relative demand for different categories of labor,

and

(5) transportation costs relative to income.

'Pull" factors conditioning the movement of migrant labor to receiving countries are:

(1) domestic natural increase in recipient country,

(2) rate of expansion of settlement in (and accessibility of) suitable cultivable land,

(3) urban-industrial development,

and

(4) availability of capital. [1]

These general stimulus conditions have been augmented, developed and ested in numerous empirical studies of migration. The influence of economic cycles in the destination country on fluctuations of migrant streams is shown by Olsson[2] for the case of outmigration from Sweden to the United States. Olsson likewise discovers a relationship between severe unemployment in the origin country and the behavior of emigrant flows, but this relationship is not borne out by studies in the United States, particularly those by Philip Nelson, [3] which also reveal low correlation between intensity of migration and income levels.

Both Nelson and Esse Lovgren[4] stress the importance of non-economic stimuli to migration, particularly the effect of expatriate relatives and friends of potential migrants, both as a source of information about the job possibilities n receptor countries and as a magnet for fresh streams of migrants.

Effects of Distance on Migration

In this regard, these studies, and various others, also stress the ordering effect of distance on migration. Physical distance is recognized in this context as behaving in the manner of a surrogate for two important underlying effects:

---

[1] Ibid., pp. 43-51.

[2] Gunnar Olsson, Distance and Human Interaction: A Review and Bibliography (Review and Bibliography Series, No. 2; Philadelphia: Regional Science Research Institute, 1965), p. 23.

[3] Philip Nelson, "Migration, Real Income, and Information," Journal of Regional Science, I, No. 2 (1959), 43-74.

[4] Esse Lovgren, "The Geographic Mobility of Labor," Geografiska Annaler, XXXVIII (1956), 344-95.

(1) the cost of transport for migrating families and their personal belonging which bears a close relationship to distance,

(2) the availability of information on job opportunities, living conditions, an other facts concerning prospective destination countries, which likewise exhibit a "falling off" with distance of such countries from the home cou try of the potential migrant.

Replication of migration patterns has been achieved in both deterministi and probabilistic[1] frameworks, and both have yielded extremely useful results. For the present purpose, however, where aggregate rather than individual migratory behavior is the subject of interest, and where broad international relationships are being investigated involving resultant flows of labor and their economic, demographic, and physical stimuli or deterrents, the models which adopt a deterministic cast are perhaps more relevant.[2]

Gravity Models in Migration Studies

The previously mentioned gravity or Pareto models are probably the most common of the deterministic models, giving an explicit relationship of the migratory movement with physical distance.[3]

The simply gravity formula

$$X_{ij} = k \frac{P_i P_j}{d_{ij}^n} \quad \text{where } n = 1 \text{ or } 2$$

was developed and employed in studies by Reilly, Zipf, Stewart, and others[4] to demonstrate the inverse relationship ("distance decay") of migratory volume with distance. The operation of distance as a surrogate for probability of migrants encountering intervening opportunities for settlement was explored by Stouffer,[5] and from his work arose the concept of population potential, employe

[1]See for example the study by Torsten Hägerstrand in Migration in Swede A Symposium (Lund Studies in Geography, Series B, No. 13, 1957). And also: Richard Morrill, Migration and the Spread and Growth of Urban Settlement (Lu Studies in Geography, Series B, No. 26, 1965).

[2]Walter Isard, Methods of Regional Analysis (New York: Wiley, 1960), Chapter 3, "Migration Estimation."

[3]Recently Berry and Schwind have suggested that the regularity predicted by gravity models may in fact be a measure of aggregate random effects. See B. J. L. Berry and P. J. Schwind, "Information and Entropy in Migrant Flows Geographical Analysis, I, No. 1 (1969), 5-14.

[4]Morrill, op. cit., p. 38.

[5]S. A. Stouffer, "Intervening Opportunities: A Theory Relating Mobility and Distance," American Sociological Review, V (1940), 845-67.

in a number of subsequent migration studies. Ajo,[1] for example, demonstrates a relationship in the level of migration among areas with accessibility, or "income potential," of the origin point to the total field of economic opportunity comprising all possible destination points.

Brief mention must also be made of a variety of deterministic migration model that employs an input-output structure. Lovgren,[2] for instance, analyzes flows among regions using a system in which relative volumes of movement among areas are expressed as constant coefficients in an input-output matrix. This structure will not be employed in the present study, however.

Capital Flow Models with a Spatial Component

The subject of spatial movement of investment capital has been given scant attention by economic geographers. Its treatment has, indeed, been almost entirely relegated to the abstract realm of monetary theory in economics, and the question of any ordering effect of distance upon the volume and direction of capital flows has been largely ignored. Very few studies exist, therefore, to provide background concepts of a kind relevant to the present study.

The reasons for this state of affairs are probably to be found in the extremely complex nature of capital transactions, and in the fact that the mechanisms governing the participation of flows of investment funds in the international economy are, at best, only partially understood. Moreover, the recent increase in participation by national governments and multilateral agencies in the process of capital investment or economic aid has added the dimension of non-economic (i.e., strategic or political) aspects to the problem.

When used in connection with the two other broad groups of productive factors (land and labor), "Capital" is generally taken to imply the "material means of production produced by man,"[3] i.e., goods not for immediate consumption but earmarked for involvement in increasing the production of other goods and services. However, this definition presents problems in dealing with concepts of _mobility_ of capital, since a flow of investment capital between two counries does not necessarily imply a physical movement of capital goods between

---

[1]R. Ajo, Contributions to Social Physics (Lund Studies in Geography, Series B, No. 11, 1953).

[2]E. Lovgren, Mutual Relations between Migration Fields (Lund Studies in Geography, Series B, No. 13, 1957).

[3]Carl Iversen, Aspects of the Theory of International Capital Movement New York: A. M. Kelley, 1935), p. 20.

the same two nations. [1] Something other than physical goods is involved, and this "something, " whose price is expressed in interest rates, could be defined as a claim or title to other productive factors (land, labor, technological or entrepreneurial inputs) for a set period. In the words of Carl Iversen,

> The original agents of production - labor and land, the 'goods of highest order' - may be used either directly to produce immediate satisfactions or in an indirect roundabout way to produce capital goods that will bring great satisfaction at a later date. The new elementary productive service, a supply of which is required in order to obtain this greater future satisfaction, is waiting . . . [i. e.,] . . . what takes place when capital moves from country to country is exactly that part of the supply of waiting or capital disposal in one country is put at the disposal of people in another. [2]

Iversen did not produce a formally-stated model of international capital movements, and wrote at a time prior to the rise of large-scale government and multilateral lending. However, his detailed and penetrating analysis of the nature, causes and consequences of private capital transactions provides a wealth of a priori notions which may be useful in the present context.

Basic Conditions Affecting Investment Flows

Although cautioning the reader concerning the mutual interdependence of capital transactions and other economic phenomena, Iversen draws "functional relationships" between capital flows and certain other factors which may for convenience be considered "primary" or causal.

A differential in interest rates in two countries, large enough to outweigh the cost of transfer of capital (occasioned by obstacles to its movement), is the main primary or explanatory condition of those enumerated by Iversen. [3] However, the ultimate cause of such transfers may be found in " . . . any change in the primary elements - the 'basic data' - of the interrelated price systems of

---

[1] Frequently, complex triangular or polygonal interactions take place as loans from one country to another are eventually liquidated by exports of capital and/or consumer goods involving numerous other countries.

[2] Given this definition of investment capital, certain qualitative differences within this concept must be dealt with; e. g.:
(1) "Short term" and "long term" capital; here the difference is mainly in the intention of the investor, not so much in the form of the investment: short-term loans, for example, are largely speculative.
(2) "Real" and "equalizing" movements, i. e., those flows from capital-rich to capital-poor countries designed to take lasting advantage of highest interest rates in the latter (real) and those movements of capital which effect compensate for other economic disturbances and so maintain equilibrium in balance of payments (equalizing).

[3] Iversen, op. cit., p. 94.

he trading countries." Thus, changes in consumer tastes and demands, in conditions of ownership of those factors of production governing income distribution,
n the supply of productive factors, and in technological aspects of production,
nay cause adjustment of interest margins and thus initiate capital movements.

There is also the possible involvement of a psychological rather than
purely economic motive, i.e., the inclination of the investor to spread his capi-
al over a great number of investments in order to minimize his risk. This
could lead to a situation in which capital will flow even among countries having
he same interest rates. In this regard, the investment policies of banks, insurance firms, and investment trusts are seen by Iversen to have appreciable impact on patterns of capital flow. [1]

Effects of Distance on Capital Flows

In examining the impediments to international capital movements, Iversen
reviews the way in which the strong classical assumption of complete capital
immobility arose in the thinking of Adam Smith, John Stuart Mill, David Ricardo,
and their disciples. He restates the obstacles to international capital movement
enumerated by John Cairnes, [2] (these being

(1) geographical distance,

(2) difference in political institutions,

and

(3) difference in language and social customs),

and notes the culmination of this stringent immobility assumption in the writings
of Alfred Marshall.

Iversen comments on the empirical fact (which conflicts with his notion of
risk-spreading as a stimulus to oversea investment) of a general reticence among
investors to commit capital in the international investment arena unless a thresh-
old difference in interest rates between domestic and foreign capital markets is
attained. He further suggests that the difference between domestic and foreign
interest rates necessary to call forth a flow of capital can be used as a measure
of the cost or friction attendant on international transfer of capital. [3]

---

[1] Ibid., p. 144.

[2] John Cairnes, Some Leading Principles of Political Economy Newly Expounded (New York: Harper and Brothers, 1874), p. 361.

[3] Iversen, op. cit., p. 107.

The actual underlying causes of friction, then, as seen by Iversen and others, [1] are not so much the monetary expense of shipping capital disposal fr⟨ one country to another, but are the less tangible outgrowth of psychological fa⟨ tors on the part of potential investors. The most notable of these factors is a⟩ aversion to uncertainty and risk inherent in lending abroad, a reticence often deepened by the fact of a "distance decay" effect in the amount of information available to investors on opportunities and regulations surrounding capital inv⟨ ment at increasingly greater distance from their own location.

Gravity Models in Capital Flow Studies

Of particular relevance to the present discussion is a second notable st in which Otis Duncan examines the financial role of the modern western metro⟩ lis. [2] Here the concern is self-consciously with movement of capital over spac The scale is interregional rather than international, and a stronger empirical base permits some fairly conclusive evidence to be drawn in favor of the hypot esis that loan and investment capital flows, like more tangible varieties of con merce, behave as functions of distance. Duncan's test involves the fitting of t⟩ varieties of gravity model to data on flows of funds between Federal Reserve Zones in the United States, and data on financial hinterland-serving functions ⟨ Standard Metropolitan Statistical Areas.

Bilateralism in International Transactions

Many of the flow models discussed above are based on a common assun tion that explanation of volumes of flow between two countries can be understoc purely in terms of conditions at, or differences between, the countries them- selves. This essentially bilateral view of interaction was encountered mostly an implicit assumption, or as a simplifying condition in the statement of a theo It does, however, become explicit in models based on the gravity formula whic involve specification of "mass" and distance variables for interacting dyads. Some discussion of the implications of this assumption may serve to illustrate problems which must be overcome in formulating our own inductive approach t⟨ international flow study.

The widely adopted view of international trade that finds expression in t comparative advantage formulation is one which stresses the dominance of bi-

---

[1] This idea is shared by Bertil Ohlin. See Ohlin, op. cit., p. 115.

[2] Otis D. Duncan et al., Metropolis and Region (Baltimore: Johns Hopki⟩ Press, 1960).

teral control mechanisms. The explanation for volumes of dyadic flow, in her words, is sought in the conditions of supply and demand in the two counies which render mutually profitable an exchange of commodities, in the proction of which the exporting country enjoys a comparative, if not absolute, roductivity advantage. In this view of trade, the influence of other potential ading partners on the magnitude of this specific interchange is ignored, and it assumed that achievement of equilibrium in trading patterns is the result of lateral accommodation and agreement among pairs of trading partners.

The realism of such assumptions is clearly open to question. Even in an xchange system based on barter arrangements and where productive factors re prohibited from moving, purely bilateral patterns would not necessarily ecome dominant. Multilateral commodity agreements, the development of ntrepôt functions in some nations, and the "dumping" or donating of commodies by some nations, would be likely to render flow patterns inexplicable in erms of the bilateral, comparative-advantage model hitherto favored by trade eorists.

In the contemporary world economy, the existence of a system of interational credit and the possibility of productive factor movements has made the attern of economic interactions even more complex. Payment for commodity nports can be made in the form of equilibrating movements of capital, or by the rovision of services such as the carriage of goods or passengers in nationallyvned fleets, and the bunkering of foreign vessels calling at a nation's ports. Iultilateralism in commercial transactions is, moreover, now institutionalized y the formation of supranational "clearing houses" for capital and technical aid. he roles of the International Monetary Fund and International Bank for Recontruction and Development have been partly to remove the undesirable effects hich resulted from a system in which bilateral agreements had proved to be neffective in maintaining stability.

Bilateralism in productive factor movement has not been emphasized as eavily in past explanatory models as was the case with regard to trade. As reviously noted, the existence of a joint demand for labor and capital is recogized as a common feature of the market for productive factors, but it seems lso generally recognized that quite disparate sources of supply of labor and apital may in reality contribute to the satisfying of this joint demand. A numer of models dealing with factor movement are equally guilty with trade models f adopting a purely bilateral view of the phenomenon they seek to explain. In nany of these, the bilateralism is also expressed in the structure of the model (the gravity formula, again, being a typical example) rather than as one of the stated assumptions on which the model is based.

Integrative Flow Study: Empirical Approaches

Our review of existing conceptual contributions to spatial analysis of flows suggests that the elements of an integrative flow theory exist, albeit in a disjointed, fragmented, and incomplete form. However, further progress toward inclusion of realistic conditions in deductive models (for example, consideration of multilateralism, continuous price surfaces, multiple currency exchange rates, and complex commodity/factor substitution relationships) wou involve momentous problems.

It is significant that some important attempts have been made at overcoming these and other problems through empirical rather than strictly theore cal avenues, employing inductive rather than deductive procedures. These attempts to incorporate complexities of the international economy in interactio models would be more appropriately discussed in the context of an examinatior of inductive flow models, particularly as these relate to the emergence of procedures to be employed in the present study. These topics will be dealt with i the following chapters.

CHAPTER III

EMPIRICAL ANALYSIS OF
INTERNATIONAL FLOWS

The models of transaction flows discussed in the previous chapter share
deductive, theoretical approach rather than an empirical one. Inductive rein-
orcement of this deductive approach remains deficient, however. There is a
rucial lack of rigorous and sharply focused empirical testing of the bases and
.ssumptions of transaction theory.

The reasons for this lag in empirical analysis are at least partially con-
.ected with the complexity of the phenomena themselves, and partly with the
earth of adequate statistical material with which to index or measure their
.ehavior. The mathematical techniques necessary for such analysis have been
.dopted only quite recently by social scientists in general and by economists and
eographers in particular. Their use has awaited the development of large
apacity digital computers, which have facilitated the application of multivariate
.rocedures.

Structural Characteristics of
Empirical Flow Models

Most flow models have been couched in a form which is intrinsically
.ilateral, and which does not lend itself readily to the sort of modification which
.ould permit consideration of multilateral effects. Initially, then, we shall be
.ealing in this chapter with bilateral models. Within these, however, a basic
.istinction can be made between models which express a symmetrical relation-
.hip (i. e., where two-way flows are considered) and those which express an
.symmetrical (one-way) relationship.

Symmetrical bilateralism is the underlying principle in all basic gravity
.odels, which are among the most common forms to be employed in the replica-
ion of spatial interaction patterns. A characteristic of the gravity model which
s relevant here is its consideration of dyadic interaction as if it existed in vacuo,
.gnoring the potential influence of "third parties" on the flow between a specific

pair of points. In addition, the $P_1 P_2/d$ model replicates, strictly speaking, th*
probability* of interaction between points. This probability value theoretically
applies to a summation of interaction in both directions between the points in
question, where this probability is proportional to relevant mass and distance
characteristics pertaining to these points. Thus, the distance value represent*
a friction against movement between points irrespective of direction. The values associated with the termini of flows subsume both "push" and "pull" effect*
each value acting as a "scalar" whose magnitudes, in combination, function as
estimates of the probability of interactions both originating and terminating in
that point. Put in other words, use of the basic gravity formula is theoretical*
most appropriate for replication of interaction turnover between pairs of point*
disregarding effects of the environment of these points. It is also appropriate
for analysis of situations in which the classical comparative advantage type of
bilateral, balanced trade is encountered.

For explanation of unidirectional flows, refinements of the gravity formula have been used. One such refinement is the making of a formal distincti*
between "push" and "pull" effects, so that appropriate magnitudes can be at-
tached to origins and destinations of particular unidirectional flows. The resu*
ing model is thus one characterized by asymmetrical bilateralism.

Models which follow this prescription (i.e., separating "push" and "pul*
effects) are not common, but some good examples do exist. For instance, in *
study which examined patterns of grain movement to New England from the res*
of the coterminous United States, Robert H. T. Smith distinguished population
the destination area as the relevant "pull" factor, while surplus grain producti*
in the origin states became the "push" factor which Smith employed to produce
yardstick of "expected" flow volume. [1]

While it would appear theoretically more valid to employ this discrimin*
tion between the magnitudes in a model applied to one-way flows, it is not alwa*
made in practice. The model developed by Linnemann, which we introduced in
the previous chapter in connection with theoretical development in trade study,
illustrates a model form in which this distinction is not, in fact, made. Although applied to exports and imports of partner countries, Linnemann's mode*
employs the same scalars in both cases, rather than specific "push" and "pull"
variables. A more detailed study of this and similar models will be useful in
the present context, helping to explain the operational characteristics of an
important form of flow model.

---

[1] Robert H. T. Smith, "Toward a Measure of Complementarity," *Econom*
Geography, XL (1964), 1-8.

Linear Models of Bilateral Interaction

Linnemann's model, which develops the earlier work of Tinbergen, is essentially an expanded gravity formulation based on an association of "potential" supply and demand variables and linear distance, which together provide a measure of "expected" dyadic interchange in the international economy. Simple reordering of scalar variables[1] has produced a "multivariate single-equation regression" model which, with sequential modification, becomes the essential form of flow model in various phases of Linnemann's study. The basic form of the Linnemann model was given above, but it may be restated in linear econometric form as:

$$X_{ij} = \partial_0 \, Y_i^{\partial 1} \cdot N_i^{-\partial 2} \, Y_j^{\partial 3} \, N_j^{-\partial 4} \, D_{ij}^{-\partial 5} \, P_{ij}^{\partial 6}$$

where Y = Gross National Product,

N = population size,

D = geographical distance between "centers of gravity" of economy of countries,

P = preferential trade factor.

In a subsequent refinement of the model, Linnemann added a variable (C_{ij}) to represent commodity composition of trade between two countries.

It will be noted that, in this equation, the model's independent variables are combined multiplicatively rather than additively as in the general econometric form, and are aimed at explanation of dyadic rather than aggregated flows. Linnemann's discussion of the reasons for this structure is rather perfunctory. He merely quotes a comment by Robert Ferber and P. J. Verdoorn[2] to the effect that " . . . interactions in economic life are often of geometric rather than arithmetic form." What Linnemann is tacitly acknowledging, by the use of such a form, is the catalytic effect which the presence of some variables may have on the behavior of others, and explicitly with respect to their relationship with the dependent variable. Thus, for example, since cost of transporta-

---

[1] Justification for the use of scalars is provided, in Linnemann's view, by the fact that variables such as Gross National Product and Population of origin and destination points incorporate both the element of demand for goods and the productive capacity which engenders a supply of merchantable commodities. A further (but unstated) practical consideration is, of course, the unavailability of more finely-detailed data needed to facilitate such a separation of individual stimulus effects.

[2] Robert Ferber and P. J. Verdoorn, Research Methods in Economics and Business (New York: Macmillan, 1962), pp. 85-86.

tion does not bear a linear relationship to distance traveled, consideration of these two variables in a trade model must be multiplicative.

The econometric form of Linnemann's model lends itself to empirical testing by least-squares multiple linear regression, [1] a common technique app. cable to situations of this sort. The model becomes linear in its logarithmica. transformed state, as shown:

$$\log X_{ij} = \log a_o + a_1 \log X_1 + a_2 \log X_2 \ldots + a_n \log X_n$$

Where the regression coefficients $a_0, a_1, a_2 \ldots$ then become the value which indicate the nature and significance of the explanatory role played by eac independent variable $X_1, X_2 \ldots X_n$.

The actual selection of explanatory indices must, of course, be derivec from our theoretical understanding of the factors relating to stimulus or hindrance to international trade.

A rather similar Pareto-type model was developed by Yeates[2] to expla

---

[1]For a full discussion of this technique and its application in Geography, see Leslie J. King, Statistical Analysis in Geography (Englewood Cliffs: Pren tice Hall, 1969), pp. 135-51.

[2]The form of Yeates' model is:

$$\frac{Y_{jI}t}{X_{Ij}t} = a + b_1(TN1_j t) + b_2(PC1_j t) + b_3(TCOSTS_{Ij}) + d_1(EEC_j)$$
$$+ d_2(EFTA_j) + d_3(SA_j) + d_4(DA_j) + d_5(COMM_j)$$

where Y_{jI} = imports by Italy from the jth country in either 1954 or 196: (in millions of United States dollars)

X_{Ij} = exports by Italy to the jth country in either 1954 or 1963 (ir millions of United States dollars)

$TN1_j$ = total national income of the jth country in either 1954 or 19 (in billions of United States dollars)

$PC1_j$ = per capita income of the jth country (TN1/population) in either 1954 or 1963 (in United States dollars)

$TCOSTS_{Ij}$ = transport costs between Italy and country j

EEC_j = country j in EEC in 1963? Yes = 1, No = 0

$EFTA_j$ = country j in EFTA in 1963? Yes = 1, No = 0

SA_j = country j in sterling area in 1963? Yes = 1, No = 0

DA_j = country j in dollar area in 1963? Yes = 1, No = 0

$COMM_j$ = country j have a Communist government in 1963? Yes = 1, No = 0

For further discussion of this model see Maurice H. Yeates, An Introduction t Quantitative Analysis in Economic Geography (New York: McGraw-Hill, 1968) pp. 129-41.

lyadic flows of exports and imports, at two time periods, emanating from or terminating in Italy. Yeates likewise employs common scalars to explain unidirectional flows. He makes considerable use in his model of "dummy" variables, i.e., nominal as opposed to ordinal or interval data scales, which record presence or absence in a country of certain conditions deemed to be relevant to dyadic trade volumes.

Interpretation of Parameters in Linear Models

A corollary of this approach, exemplified by the models of Linnemann and Yeates, is that the equations for imports and exports will have different parameters, assuming, of course, that we discount the unrealistic condition of bilateral balancing in trading patterns.[1] These parameters are, in familiar econometric fashion, interpreted by Linnemann as elasticities, "linked to the income elasticity of foreign supply and foreign demand, respectively . . ."[2] Linnemann does not seem to give any serious attention to the possibility that these parameter differences may result from variation in "random shocks." These are stochastic elements which would attend the application of an incomplete model (i.e., in this case a model incorporating gross proportionality variables rather than separate and more finely drawn "push" and "pull" effects). In his failure to accord importance to this possibility, Linnemann is, however, by no means alone. Perhaps the majority of deterministic models applied to commodity and factor flows have displayed the same strategy.

Models with a Multilateral Component

In view of the patently multilateral character of many economic interactions at the global level, it might be argued that this condition should be reflected in any model which attempts to replicate flows among nations. The need for consideration of the many-sided, complex nature of many interactions has, in fact, been recognized and put into effect in a number of more recent empirical models. The concepts which permit the incorporation of outside influences on dyadic flows are those based on the idea of intervening opportunity or interaction potential.[3]

---

[1] Linnemann himself makes initial use of this assumption of bilateral balancing in trade, but recognizes its rather unrealistic nature and later removes it as a basic premise, considering it subsequently as a special case of the more general unbalanced trade situation. See Linnemann, op. cit., pp. 48-49.

[2] Ibid., p. 54.   [3] See p. 44.

However, models using potential concepts for measurement of interaction have not been an unqualified success in practical terms, despite their superior theoretical qualities vis-a-vis gravity-based formulations. The drawback to potential models as explanatory empirical frameworks are noted by Reed,[1] who employed the concept of potential in examining flows of goods in a regional context in India.

The context of Reed's discussion is the testing of the econometric flow model proposed by Berry. Although Berry's model is similar to that developed by Linnemann, it is considerably improved in respect of the conceptual underpinnings of the variables selected, incorporating explicit measures of potential fields surrounding pairs of points. The basic form of the Berry-Reed model is

$$X_{ij} = a_o \, S_i^{a1} \cdot D_j^{a2} \cdot d_{ij}^{-a3} \cdot R_j^{a4} \cdot Q_i^{a5}$$

where S_i = supply at i,

D_j = demand at j,

d_{ij} = distance ij,

R_j = contribution of S_i to supply space potential at j,

Q_i = contribution of D_j to demand space potential at i.

The practical problems which Reed encountered in testing this model relate to the "multiple counting" of components in the set of independent variables, as a consequence of including several interaction-potential variables. For instance, Reed draws attention to an aspect of Stouffer's intervening opportunity concept, which envisages the level of interaction between points d miles apart as being proportional to total probability of interaction between each point in question and all outside points within a radius d. Logically, this probability (if points are uniformly distributed) should be closely proportional also to distance d. Thus the distance variable itself may be used as a surrogate for intervening opportunity measures with a fair degree of practical success.

Where potential rather than absolute values are employed as independent variables in a flow model (as in Reed's study), the cumulative effect of the distance variable used in the calculation of potential measures becomes problematical. Where the distance measure itself is used conjointly with various potential variables, yet higher intercorrelation among independent variables may result, in violation of the requirements of multiple regression procedures which form the operational basis for linear flow models.

---

[1] Reed, op. cit., pp. 181-94.

Relevant Implications of Model Structure

The preceding discussion has several important implications for the present study. First, the explicit recognition of multilateral influences on volumes of flow, whether aggregated or dyadic, has been highlighted as being theoretically desirable. Yet serious practical problems are seen to attend the use of Potential measures in models based on the explanatory power of independent variables. Purely bilateral (gravity) models have without doubt demonstrated practical usefulness, but if we are to give consideration to the theoretical basis for their operation, we should conclude that models using gross scalar variables ideally apply only to symmetrical interaction. Alternately, separate "push" and "pull" factors should be distinguished where asymmetrical flows are the subject of analysis.

Alternate Frameworks for Analysis of Flows

Berry's India study is significant for more than its introduction of potential measures in a linear flow model. It is perhaps of greater interest for its pursuance of a more satisfactory way of displaying empirical relationships between dyadic flows on the one hand and economic stimuli on the other, avoiding the limitation of the essentially bilateral gravity-based formulations. Berry envisions the set of interregional economic relationships as an example of a "Field" of interaction probabilities, where the concept of a Field involves the abstract notion of potential interaction among a set of regions as well as direct dyadic or bilateral interconnections. The usefulness of the Field concept lies in its amenability to expression in the form of a multivariate model in which aggregate or multilateral as well as dyadic interactions, and corresponding disparities in relevant characteristics, are seen as two sets of variates between which particular relationships may be identified. The formal statement of concepts underlying this approach has been given the name Field Theory, and the method by which these relationships can be unraveled is a linear algebraic procedure involving the multivariate techniques of principal axis factor analysis and canonical correlation.

The Field Theoretic Model of Interaction

Originally derived from the realm of physics, the "Field" concept was first used in the social sciences by Kurt Lewin[1] as a framework for studying the

---

[1] See Kurt Lewin, Field Theory in Social Science (New York: Harper Torchbooks, 1951).

complex interplay among various forms of social interaction, and social conditions which engender or might potentially engender interaction.

The theory was given a more explicit mathematical statement by Rummel who employed it as a framework for analysis of social and political interaction focusing on those of a discordant or violent nature. Rummel's work provides a clear geometric illustration of the basic concepts of a Field as well as a formal mathematical statement of such notions as "system," "state," and "boundaries" within a Field.

In Berry's work, the concept of a Field embraces the concepts of formal and functional regionalization, [2] where the places which form the elements of regions are organized in rows of two geographic matrices A and B. The columns of matrix A become relevant attributes of places, and A can then be labeled the Attribute Matrix, while the columns of B are occupied by kinds of interaction taking place between pairs of places, and B may be termed the Behavior Matrix. A tracing of formal and functional relationships within this spatial Field of attributes and interactions is then achieved by establishing basic structural dimensions and broad regional patterns. This is carried out by first using factor analytic and objective grouping techniques, and then "mapping" structural and behavioral spaces so formed into each other in an optimizing fashion by canonical correlation.

The immediate usefulness of this procedure in the present instance should now be quite clear. We can define the world economy as a Field, in which the various nations are the objects, their relevant economic characteristics are the attributes, and the flows of commodities, labor, capital, and information are the interactions of predominant interest. Our objective, in this Field Theory context, is to establish the nature, significance, and direction of mutually-reinforcing relationships (highlighted by our discussion of interaction theories) among the elements of our sets of attributes and interactions.

Essentially we are interested in the unraveling of dyadic interrelationships, where each country is conceived of as entering into a set of transactions with other individuals to the extent that certain conditions in those countries are disparate. However, before proceeding with such a complex analysis, it would appear useful to take an intermediate step by considering first a Field of aggregated rather than dyadic or disaggregated behavior.

---

[1] R. J. Rummel, "A Field Theory of Social Action with Application to Conflict within Nations," General Systems Yearbook, X (1965), 183-211.

[2] Berry, op. cit., pp. 189-90.

Four particular advantages arising out of such an intermediate phase can be listed.

(1) It will permit an overview of the general patterns of behavior and economic structure of the whole set of countries, providing us with a picture of the propensities of certain countries or groups of countries for certain types of interaction.

(2) An interpretation of these aggregate patterns may throw light on many specific aspects of detailed dyadic flow complexes, enabling us to better understand the intricacies of country-to-country flows and the factors associated with them.

(3) From a technical viewpoint, it may permit the identification of variables which perhaps do not contribute as much to an understanding of the economic relationships among nations as our a priori deliberations might indicate, enabling us to eliminate such variables or select more appropriate alternatives for the dyadic phase of study.

(4) Since the aggregate patterns are essentially much simpler than the dyadic, the intermediate phase may provide clearer illustration of the basic technical procedures involved.

Operational Basis for Field Theory: The
Technique of Canonical Correlation

The Field-theoretical formulation outlined above can be made operational in both aggregate and disaggregate cases by canonical correlation. In this technique, the objective is to find a quantitative and significant relationship between two sets of variates. The linear-algebraic method of achieving this objective was introduced by Harold Hotelling, who coined the term "canonical" correlation as an acknowledgement of the fixed relationship between sets of variates produced from original input variables. A full mathematical statement with appropriate proofs may be gleaned from works by Hotelling, Anderson, and Rao. [1]

Obviously, the method of division of the variables into the original two sets is exogenous to the canonical correlation algorithm, and to the extent that data may be partitioned subjectively (by discrimination among certain purportedly significant characteristics) this has important ramifications for the interpretation of the results of this process.

In the present instance, for example, subjective discrimination among the sample objects is on the basis of (a) "internal" versus "external" characteristics (aggregate level) and (b) dyadic differential in characteristics versus

---

[1] Harold Hotelling, "Relations between Two Sets of Variates," Biometrika, XXVIII (1936), 321-77. Theodore W. Anderson, An Introduction to Multivariate Statistical Analysis (New York: John Wiley, 1958). Calyampudi R. Rao, Advanced Statistical Methods in Biometric Research (New York: John Wiley, 1952).

dyadic interaction (disaggregated level), but this division is in keeping with the basic concepts of Field Theory. In other circumstances, more objective defini tion of sets might be achieved by such multivariate statistical methods as multi ple discriminant analysis.[1]

Previous empirical use of canonical correlation in Geography has been limited, but within very recent years it has become more common.[2] As we have seen, Berry uses it to discuss interaction in India. Gauthier[3] employs it to draw relationships between development of road networks in Brazil and re gional economic growth. Other studies using this technique are by Greer-Wootten on the social/demographic patterns of Montreal[4] and by Ray on spatial interrelationships of economic and cultural differences in Canada.[5]

Canonical correlation is in many ways similar to principal components or principal axis factor analysis, in that it involves the construction of linear functions which are made up of elements of the original variables. It is differe however, in that it involves the replacing of each of two sets of variates by a canonical variate comprising linear combinations of the variables in each set.

Thus, if we have p variables $X_1, X_2 \ldots X_p$ for a sample of n observa tions, and these variables are divided into two groups with joint variance:

$$X_1, X_2, \ldots X_p \text{ and } X_{p+1}, X_{p+2}, \ldots X_{p'}$$

our objective is to obtain a pair of linear functions (U_t and V_t) of these variable (which have been standardized or reduced to a form with zero-mean and unit variance) that have a maximum (canonical) correlation R. That is,

for $U_t = k_1 z_1 + k_2 z_2 + \ldots + k_p z_p$ (1)

and $V_t = k_{p+1} z_{p+1} + k_{p+2} z_{p+2} + \ldots + k_p z_p$ (2)

---

[1] See King, op. cit., pp. 204-12, for geographic applications of discrimi nant analysis.

[2] For a review of the usage of this technique in Geography see D. Michae Ray and Paul R. Lohnes, "Canonical Correlation in Geographical Analysis" (unpublished research paper, State University of New York at Buffalo, Novemb 1970).

[3] Howard L. Gauthier, "Transportation and the Growth of the Sao Paulo Economy," Journal of Regional Science, VIII, No. 1 (1968), 77-94.

[4] Forthcoming in the University of Toronto, Department of Geography Research Series.

[5] D. Michael Ray, "The Spatial Interrelationships of Economic and Cul tural Differences: A Canonical Ecology of Canada" (unpublished research pape University of Buffalo, 1970).

the value of R must be maximized, given that

$$\text{variance of } U_t = 1 = \sum_{i=1}^{\hat{p}} \sum_{j=1}^{\hat{p}} r_{ij} k_i k_j \qquad (3)$$

$$\text{variance of } V_t = 1 = \sum_{i=\hat{p}+1}^{p} \sum_{j=\hat{p}+1}^{p} r_{ij} k_i k_j \qquad (4)$$

$$\text{and} \qquad R = \sum_{i=1}^{\hat{p}} \sum_{j=\hat{p}+1}^{p} r_{ij} k_i k_j \qquad (5)$$

where this will be a maximum given the condition that $U_t, V_t = 1$.

While correlation of U_t and V_t is maximized, there must be zero correlation (orthogonality) of U_t and V_t with other canonical variates $U_1, V_1, U_2, V_2 \ldots$ $U_{t-1}, V_{t-1}.$[1]

The solution thus calls for the construction of a matrix $\sum$ comprising submatrix elements which are in fact the variance-convariance matrices of the variable sets $X_1, X_2 \ldots X_{\hat{p}} = [X]$, and $X_{\hat{p}+1} \ldots X_p = [Y]$

$$\text{i.e.,} \qquad \sum = \begin{pmatrix} \Sigma XX & \Sigma XY \\ \Sigma YX & \Sigma YY \end{pmatrix} \qquad (6)$$

From the equation for U and V we identify coefficients α and β such that

$$\begin{pmatrix} -\lambda\,\Sigma XX & \Sigma XY \\ \Sigma YX & -\lambda\,\Sigma YY \end{pmatrix} \cdot \begin{pmatrix} \alpha \\ \beta \end{pmatrix} = 0 \qquad (7)$$

Solution of the determinantal equation

$$\begin{vmatrix} -\lambda\Sigma XX & \Sigma XY \\ \Sigma YX & -\lambda\,\Sigma YY \end{vmatrix} = 0 \qquad (8)$$

yields a set of p eigenvalues which comprise the required R values for pairs of U and V, and which will be extracted in descending order of significance.[2]

A set of vectors called eigenvectors, corresponding to the (positive) eigenvalues, are also extracted from equation (7), these eigenvectors yielding the coefficients α and β which are part of the equations for U and V.

Thus, in a manner reminiscent of principal components analysis we produce a set of eigenvalues, and corresponding sets of variates arranged in eigenvectors, which are mathematically independent, and which are arranged in descending order of statistical significance. An illustration is provided by Table 5

---

[1] King, op. cit., p. 218.

[2] If the number ($\hat{p}$) of original variables in the set $X_1, \ldots X_{\hat{p}}$ is equivalent to the number ($p-\hat{p}$) in the set $X_{\hat{p}+1} \ldots X_p$, then the p eigenvalues will be given as positive numbers. However, if $\hat{p} < (p-\hat{p})$, there will be only $2\hat{p}$ positive eigenvalues and the remainder will be zero.

of Chapter VII, where there are ten eigenvectors or canonical variates, comprising loadings of the two sets of factor-variates, each with its corresponding eigenvalue (canonical correlation).

Conclusion

The technique of canonical analysis, then, provides the appropriate means of fitting a model couched in Field-theoretic form. It will be evident tha a model of this form is eminently suited to the replication of situations such as the particular one being considered in the present study. More explicitly, it w: be obvious that flows between partners (dyads) may be arranged in a matrix of INTERACTIONS, of N flow types by M dyads, for each of which a set of relevai economic influences may be identified and arrayed in a matrix of ATTRIBUTES of the partners involved in commerce. These attributes may be actual in the sense that they directly regulate the volume of dyadic movement in the case of specific pair of countries, or potential in that they indirectly influence the volume of movement by conditioning the environment (i.e., the total spectrum of relationships within the international economy) within which actual dyadic move ment must take place.

The form of the model employed in this study, therefore, is essentially reflection of the conceptual framework which is at the core of our attempt to understand patterns in the gamut of international economic interaction. We hav seen that any empirical approach--and indeed any theoretical approach with rea istic assumptions--to this problem must accept the possibility of complex inter actions among the various alternative forms of flow. It must acknowledge com plex relationships among the economic conditions (indexing deep-seated cultura political effects) which comprise stimuli to commerce. In particular, the mutually-reinforcing nature of relationships between flows and attributes of nation must be recognized.

The fourth chapter of this study will begin initial probing of the practica problems of modeling economic flows, by detailing the processes of selection c variables and sample observations, and of setting up an aggregate model of the international economic scene. This will, hopefully, provide insight and guidan in approaching the infinitely more complex area of dyadic flow among nations.

CHAPTER IV

AN AGGREGATE MODEL OF TRADE AND FACTOR
FLOWS: SOME PRELIMINARY CONSIDERATIONS

Even the most sophisticated models built to replicate the causal connections of pair-wise economic interactions are ultimately only as good as the
assumptions on which they are based and the data with which they are made operational. To stand the test of empirical verification, a model must rest on plausible assumptions. It must, in other words, have basic premises that are consistent, i.e., that are not mutually contradictory, and that accord with our best
knowledge of the processes that operate in the real world, i.e., that do not
unduly distort reality.[1] The data selected for empirical testing of a model
should, moreover, comprise valid and appropriate indexes of the theoretical
variables specified in the model.

The present chapter is designed as a means of appraising these considerations, a preliminary and heuristic step in the process of building a multivariate
dyadic model of economic flow interrelationships. It introduces a general survey
(continued in Chapters 5 and 6) of the global patterns of economic interaction, as
these are revealed by aggregate values for inflow and outflow of commodities,
migrants, and capital in the context of selected data pertaining to characteristics
of the economy of each nation.

It will also be necessary in this chapter to discuss the sample of countries
for which data have been amassed, and to discuss the bases for acceptance or
rejection of countries potentially eligible for inclusion in the aggregate-level
study.

Assembly of Data: The Need for Classification

Attempts to describe the welter of national characteristics relating to living
standards and commercial dealings with other nations make frequent use of some

---

[1]This is not to deny the importance of some more abstract models whose
assumptions are highly stringent but which nevertheless greatly increase our
understanding of specific facets of structure and process in real world systems.

form of taxonomic system to produce an orderly enumeration of attributes and interactions. Such a system is also necessary to facilitate the identification of patterns of economic behavior, and for the formulation of valid generalizations about these patterns. Commonly such taxonomic aids take the form of a scalin of attributes, so that a particular country will occupy a position on a continuum or in a hierarchy, with respect to a particular attribute or set of attributes. Perhaps the most frequently encountered system of scaling of national attribute utilizes the notion of economic development, in which countries are ordered according to their performance on indices which measure progress with respec to improvement in material living standards. What is tacitly understood in suc a system is that progress through this hierarchy or continuum is theoretically feasible for any country. Thus, the comparison of the "stage of development" a country with others on the scale becomes more than simply an intellectual exercise, having strong implications for economic policy at national and supra national levels.

The question of the kinds of national attributes which are most appropri ate as indices of economic development has been the subject of considerable pr vious research. Simple measures of gross or per capita monetary income or productivity are now generally regarded as being insufficient, by themselves, t convey an accurate picture of a nation's developmental progress. Consequently the inclusion of other aspects, often only obliquely related to productivity, is a common feature in studies dealing with economic growth.

Thus, the sectoral structure of economies has been considered most important by some researchers,[1] who see economic progress in terms of sectoral change away from heavy reliance on agricultural/extractive sectors towa a more balanced structure with secondary and tertiary activities giving the lea to economic expansion. Yet others[2] see technological change as a dominant cr terion for ordering nations in a hierarchy of economic growth. The truly multi variate nature of the phenomenon of economic development has been given ex plicit recognition in some recent studies. The Atlas of Economic Development

---

[1]H. A. Innis and W. T. Easterbrook, "Fundamental and Historical Elements," in Canada, ed. George Brown (United Nations Series; Berkeley and Lo Angeles: University of California Press, 1960), pp. 155-64. And also: Walt W Rostow, The Stages of Economic Growth: A Non-Communist Manifesto (Cambridge, 1961).

[2]Hans Carol, "Stages of Technology and Their Impact upon the Physical Environment: A Basic Problem in Cultural Geography," Canadian Geographer, VIII, No. 1 (1964), 1-7.

edited by Norton Ginsburg[1] displays maps of 48 variables which relate to such characteristics of countries as health and educational attainment of the population, degree of urbanization, level of power generation, and development and use of internal transportation networks. Adelman and Morris[2] have compiled a list of indicators of national growth status which encompasses political and social factors, such as stability of government, importance of indigenous middle class, and social cohesiveness, as well as predominantly economic attributes like size of the traditional agricultural sector. Where statistical data were lacking for some of these attributes, "dummy" variables, or qualitative assessments, were compiled on the basis of the best knowledge of expert consultants.

A similar, but even more detailed and comprehensive list of socially and politically-relevant variables was collected by Bruce Russett et al. for use in studies of the factors underlying certain observed behavior patterns among interacting nation-states. This list is published in the World Handbook of Political and Social Indicators. [3]

In both the Ginsburg and Adelman-Morris studies, and in a subsequent study by Russett, [4] ordering of the multitude of attributes was achieved by application of multivariate statistical techniques of factor and principal components analysis. The chapter by Berry[5] in Ginsburg's Atlas, for example, concluded in the identification of underlying dimensions of economic and related behavior of nations, giving a relatively objective method of classifying countries with regard to significant aspects of development.

The specific relevance of such taxonomic methods to the present analysis is quite clear: they constitute an efficient means of establishing basic structures in the gamut of national characteristics which our study identifies as being related to economic interaction, and on which the nations in the study sample may be classified. To a certain extent, also, the studies mentioned above provide

---

[1]Norton S. Ginsburg, ed., Atlas of Economic Development (Chicago: University of Chicago Press, 1961).

[2]Irma Adelman and Cynthia T. Morris, Society, Politics, and Economic Development: A Quantitative Approach (Baltimore: Johns Hopkins Press, 1967).

[3]Bruce Russett, et al., World Handbook of Political and Social Indicators (New Haven: Yale University Press, 1964).

[4]Bruce Russett, International Regions and the International System (Chicago: Rand McNally, 1967).

[5]Ginsburg, op. cit., pp. 110-19.

guidance in the selection of appropriate variables and constitute a basis for com
parison of some of the results of the present study. They point explicitly and
significantly to the relationships between certain facets of economic developmer
and the volume and character of economic interaction among nations. This latter theme will be developed in some detail in a subsequent section.

The Aggregate Model: Variables Selected

The actual selection of variables for the aggregate phase of this study
proved to be a difficult task. The difficulty arose mainly in the important but
uncertain step of choosing empirically-derived indices, which might act as vali
measures of the theoretically-generated concepts alluded to in the phase of deductive model-building described in Chapter II. It is obviously not always poss
ble, despite careful selection, to arrive at a set of satisfactory empirical variables which unequivocally represent quite abstract concepts.

It must be stressed, however, that guidance for the selection of variable
in this study was indeed drawn from a consideration of the measures which wou
most appropriately express basic and often intangible concepts. Since this process involved a complex sequence of subjective decisions as well as fairly obje
tive selection procedures, an elaboration of the data selection phase is warrant
here.

The actual data set accumulated for use in this aggregate stage of model
building is, in some significant aspects, rather different from the data to be
amassed for the testing of a truly dyadic model. The phenomena being examine
at this exploratory aggregate level are essentially the external economic dealings of a country with all other nations taken together (which, in the later dyadi
phase of analysis, are themselves considered as attributes of a country), and
those facets of the country that could be described as "internal" characteristics
Indeed, the objective of this aggregate analysis could be stated simply as a stud
of mutually-reinforcing aspects of the face a nation presents to the commercial
world and its own internal economic structure. The emphasis of this study is
the highlighting of trends which might themselves be used as guidance in the
development of a more detailed dyadic model.

In summary, variables selected as relevant to this aggregate phase of
enquiry have been chosen with the following requirements in mind:

(a) suitability with regard to the a priori conceptual framework discussed in
    the previous chapter; i.e., selection of appropriate indices to measure
    "stimuli" and "deterrent" forces;

(b) appropriateness for testing specific hypotheses which are part and parcel of the theoretical underpinnings of the study;

(c) ability to satisfy questions concerning data comparability and completeness, where these must be considered as important criteria for selection, having also a strong bearing on size and nature of the study sample;

(d) evidence concerning variables from previous studies must be used as guidance in the matter of likely success or failure of certain measures as predictor variables.

Aggregate Interaction Variables

Figures 1 to 6 in Chapter I summarized the general patterns of aggregate economic interaction among the nations of the contemporary world. Their introduction in the first chapter was considered to be an appropriate way of drawing attention to the reality of complex factor-commodity flows among nations and the need for an essentially integrative approach to the study of such economic interactions. However, for the larger purposes of this study, a somewhat expanded set of measures of the external relations of countries seems desirable. This should provide more detailed information on the many important facets of the trading characteristics of nations, their propensities for importing or exporting capital, their attractiveness or lack of attractiveness to potential migrants, and their involvement in the international flow of information.

Trade Variables

Thirty-three variables were selected to represent the behavior of nations with regard to commodity trade. This number included Total Exports by Value (U.S. dollars) and Total Imports (also in U.S. dollars) whose world patterns appear in Figures 1 and 2. Since these variables give only the sparest outline of the nature of trade emanating from or terminating in a particular nation, the addition of variables detailing the commodity composition of aggregate trade was deemed advisable. Data were thus assembled to show the primary categories of trade for each country following the convention of the Standard International Trade Classification.[1] A ten-fold categorization of commodities entering into world trade was thus available for both imports and exports of countries,

---

[1] The Standard International Trade Classification (S. I. T. C.) is a 4-digit numerical system for the standardized description of the myriad goods which enter into world trade. The code was first employed by the United Nations in 1950 (revised in 1960), to identify 625 subgroups of commodities, which form 177 groups, 56 divisions and 10 major sections. In the present study, the 10 major groupings only are employed (see Table 1).

adding useful detail to the simple picture provided by total trade figures. The source of these data was, as with the aggregate data, the Country Tables of the Yearbook of International Trade Statistics, 1963, 1964, and 1965, published by the Department of Economic and Social Affairs of the United Nations. Once aga the data are in the form of monetary value (units of local currency), this form being most significant in the present context as a measure of the importance of the trade flow to the economy of a nation. For the sake of international compar ability, conversion of these local currency values to U.S. dollar equivalence wa undertaken subsequent to collection of raw data, using official exchange rates quoted for this period (1963-1965) in the Yearbook of International Financial Sta tistics of the International Monetary Fund. Values used in this study, then, are the (arithmetic) mean annual flow value (U.S. dollars) for the period 1963-1965, categorized according to the S.I.T.C. code.

As was pointed out in Chapter I, both imports and exports are worthy of inclusion because in a large number of cases, these two do not balance at the end of any given period. Thus, for some countries, there may be a surplus of exports over imports, referred to as a "favorable" balance. For others, imports may be larger, in which case the nation is regarded as having an "unfavor able" balance. Equilibrating movements of capital (and other means) may be adopted to effect balance of payments in these circumstances. In any event, the size of this differential between exports and imports has significant repercussions for other economic attributes of a nation, and thus the variable Ratio of Imports to Exports was included in this study.

For the same basic reason, the balance in various categories of commod ity trade composition is included, enabling us to identify nations which are large food importers, net exporters of industrial products, raw materials and fuels, and so on. The thirty-three variables describing relevant aspects of aggregate commodity trade are summarized in Table 1.

Migration Variables

A group of five measures were selected to describe the international movement of labor. Two of these, Long-term Immigrants and Long-term Emigrants were briefly discussed in Chapter I and their spatial configurations are shown in Figures 3 and 4. The three additional variables included are Total Immigration, Total Emigration, and Migration Saldo.[1]

[1]This term is frequently used in migration literature to express the balance between total immigration and emigration for a given country, at the end o

TABLE 1

AGGREGATE INTERACTION MODEL:
TRADE VARIABLES

1	S. I. T. C. Exports: Food
2	Beverages
3	Raw Materials
4	Fuels
5	Vegetable Oils
6	Chemicals
7	Manufactures
8	Transport Equipment
9	Miscellaneous
10	Commodities and Transactions, Not Elsewhere Specified
11	Total Exports
12	S. I. T. C. Imports: Food
13	Beverages
14	Raw Materials
15	Fuels
16	Vegetable Oils
17	Chemicals
18	Manufactures
19	Transport Equipment
20	Miscellaneous
21	Commodities and Transactions, Not Elsewhere Specified
22	Total Imports
23	S. I. T. C. Trade Balance (positive or negative): Food
24	Beverages
25	Raw Materials
26	Fuels
27	Vegetable Oils
28	Chemicals
29	Manufactures
30	Transport Equipment
31	Miscellaneous
32	Commodities and Transactions, Not Elsewhere Specified
33	Total Trade Balance

The values for long-term immigration and emigration, as explained in Chapter I, are collated from data on dyadic movements published by individual destination countries. However, the statistics on Total Immigration and Total Emigration were drawn from Table 27 of the United Nations Demographic Yearbook for 1966, which gives only gross or aggregated volumes of movement for migration. Indeed, for a considerable number of countries, the Yearbook gives data in which the number of migrants specifically indicating the permanent or

a given period. It can, consequently, assume both positive and negative values for individual countries.

long-term nature of their change of residence is not identified. The total migration measures are thus somewhat coarser than the variables long-term immigrtion and emigration, measuring a noticeably broader aspect (short and long-ter movement) of migratory streams.

The questions of comparability and reliability are especially problemati cal in the case of migration statistics. An attempt was made to maintain the greatest possible level of comparability in international migration data by using only those tables which clearly indicated the long-term nature of migrants, and wherever possible using data for immigrants to the country compiling the statis tics rather than emigrants from that country. This was done in the (empiricall justified) belief that greater accuracy and reliability could be assumed in a nation's count of the migrants entering its borders with intent to make it their permanent or quasi-permanent home. As earlier pointed out, these data were found to be sufficiently detailed to permit the inclusion of long-term migration statistics in the dyadic phase of the study, from which country-by-country aggr gates of long-term immigration and emigration were compiled for use in the present exploratory phase. Sources of these data are listed in an appendix to this study.

The fifth migration variable, Migration Saldo, records simply the balance obtained by subtracting total emigration from total immigration for the three-year period and averaging to give net gain or loss of population due to arrivals or departures. While it undoubtedly incorporates the long-term migra tory effect it also includes a proportion of the short-term movements, the "unr turned" short-term residents of the country at the close of the period for which statistics have been gathered.

Thus, migration saldo measures a somewhat broader aspect of population movement than simply the number of people whose recorded intent is to change permanently their country of domicile, instead giving the de facto balance at the end of each year. The desirability of adding this extra dimension h been the main reason for inclusion of this variable in the group of migration statistics.

Details of the age, sex, and occupational structures of migratory strea although desirable in an analysis of this type, were not available in a sufficient comprehensive or reliable form, and thus have not been included.

Capital Flow Variables

Eight variables constitute the group of measures which attempt to describe the behavior of capital flows to and from the nations of the contemporary
world. The most general of these, Net Capital Flow, was introduced in Chapter I with the objective of acquainting the reader with the magnitude of flows of
this productive factor vis-a-vis the volume of commodity and labor movements
in the world economy. These data, obtained from the United Nations Statistical
Yearbook can be accepted as a measure of the total real flow of investment capital. This comprises capital which has been negotiated by a country from a single creditor under short or long term loan agreements (bilateral loans) or under
the guise of an official donation (bilateral grants). However, it also includes
capital negotiated from an international or supranational lending institution such
as the International Monetary Fund (I. M. F.) or the International Bank for Reconstruction and Development (I. B. R. D.).[1]

Additional information concerning the nature of international capital movement has been added in the form of data on Bilateral Grants, Bilateral Loans
and Multilateral Capital Receipts, derived also from the United Nations Statistical
Yearbook. Further elaboration of the patterns of negotiation by nations with
multilateral funding institutions is given in the variables I. M. F. Drawings,
I. M. F. Repurchases, I. B. R. D. Borrowers, and I. B. R. D. Lenders. These
data are drawn from the Yearbook of International Financial Statistics of the
I. M. F. All data on capital movement are given in U. S. dollars.

---

[1]The International Monetary Fund and the International Bank for Reconstruction and Development both had their origins in the problem of reestablishing
normal relations among trading countries after the Second World War. The
main function of the I. M. F. is essentially the "damping down" of balance of payments disequilibria by creating an atmosphere in which national currencies enjoy greater international confidence and exchange stability, and the obviating of
competitive devaluations such as those which plagued the trading scene during
the 1930's.

Few communist states are members of the I. M. F., and several non-
communist countries (such as Switzerland) have likewise declined to participate.
The numbers of countries subscribing to the I. M. F. have grown in the past few
years as newly independent third-world nations have seized on the opportunities
available to member countries. In 1965, 105 nations were members of the I. M. F.

The I. B. R. D. has the objective of encouraging domestic investment in
less-developed nations by acting in the capacity of guarantor, promoter, and
source of technical assistance to private investment ventures. Its membership
is restricted to countries who have subscribed to the I. M. F.

An excellent, detailed account of the scope and activities of these two
financial agencies is given in: M. A. G. van Meerhaeghe, International Economic
Institutions (New York: Wiley, 1966).

Information Flow Variables

Augmenting the pattern of Mail and Telegraph Messages Despatched from various nations, which was displayed in Figure 6 (Chapter I), are the variables Mail Received and Telegraph Messages Received. These provide a balanced and comprehensive picture of the flow of an important form of information to and from countries. In the present phase of the analysis the flows of mail and of telegraph messages despatched from various nations have been disaggregate and are treated as separate variables.

Aggregate Attribute Variables

As was the case with regard to interaction variables, the attribute variates introduced in Chapter I have, for the larger purposes of this study, been augmented by a number of other economic indices. The expanded group of variables selected to form the Matrix of Attributes of countries was once again chosen on the basis of the underlying conceptualization of the spatial interaction model outlined in Chapter II. Since economic flows are thought to be conditioned by certain combinations of economic/demographic stimuli and by the deterrent of distance (as expressed by the gravity analogy), the set of variables representing the relevant attributes[1] of countries can be conveniently grouped and discussed under the headings Stimulus Variables and Deterrent Variables.

Stimulus Variables

We have asserted earlier that, in theory, the composition of interaction among nations is dependent on essentially the same set of attributes of nations. However, our discussion of the operation of these types of interaction, and our heuristic survey in Chapter I, indicate that certain groups of attributes are likely to impinge more strongly on some of the main interaction forms than on others. We recognize, of course, that for each attribute an influence (albeit possibly quite minor and indirect) will be felt on all interaction forms, but such an influence will not apply uniformly in all cases. This line of thought has led to the division of relevant attributes, for present purposes, into:

(1) general stimuli (conceived of as possibly influencing all types of interaction fairly equally)

---

[1] I. e., those characteristics of nations which could be considered contributors to the factor and commodity price differentials which economic interaction theory recognizes as the immediate generator of movements of labor, capital, and trade goods.

(2) specific stimulus variables (relating predominantly to either migration or trade, capital movement or information flow).

General Stimulus Variables

In the category of general influences on the gamut of possible economic interactions could be placed a number of demographic, economic, and related variables which provide a comprehensive coverage of the state of a country's development. Of the demographic variables, Total Population, Population Density (briefly discussed in Chapter I), and Total Economically-active Population provide a broad index of the distribution of consumers and producers of commodities and capital and the founts of potential migration. To these are added nine variables which examine the details of occupation structure of the economically active population:

(1) population engaged in agriculture,

(2) workers in extractive industries (mining, quarrying, forestry, and fishing),

(3) manufacturing population,

(4) population engaged in building and Public Works,

(5) population in electrical, water and gas supply services,

(6) population engaged in commerce, banking, and insurance,

(7) transport and communication workers,

(8) service personnel,

(9) otherwise economically engaged population.

These are given in absolute numbers of workers in each category. They may be considered indexes of the propensity of nations (which obviously may differ considerably in the structure of economically-active population) to import or export various types and amounts of labor, commodities, or investment capital.

Into the same general category fall a number of variables measuring aspects of a nation's productivity or aggregate income. Foremost of these are the familiar measures of Gross National Product, Gross Domestic Product, National Income, [1] and Gross Fixed Capital Formation. These yardsticks of a

---

[1] Gross National Product is a monetary measure of the value of all goods and services produced in a country in a given year, arrived at by totalling all costs in all forms of production employing the country's own productive factors. National Income measures, at factor cost, the current earnings of a nation's factors of production, thus virtually representing Gross National Product minus indirect taxes and capital consumption allowances, etc. Gross Domestic Product normally refers to an index of industrial production, in monetary terms, giving in terms of the value added by industry a measure of volume of production at factor cost.

nation's output are given in absolute and per-capita form, where the latter (as illustrated in Chapter I) provides a sense of the effectiveness of productive output in raising the average income of the population.

Complementing these aggregate measures of productivity is a set of seven variables which show the Industrial Origin of the Total Domestic Product of a country. These variables detail, respectively, the proportion of Domestic Product contributed by:

(1) Agriculture,

(2) Secondary Industry,

(3) Manufacturing (singled out as a major subsector of (2)),

(4) Construction,

(5) Transport/Communication,

(6) Wholesale/Retail Trade Sector,

and

(7) other undifferentiated productive activities.

It should be pointed out that these variables also complement rather than duplicate the occupational structure data discussed earlier. Because of a number of complicating factors, e.g., degree of capital intensiveness in various productive sectors, application of diminishing returns to investment, and quality of physical resources, there is no theoretical or empirical reason why numbers of people employed in an economic sector should be closely paralleled by productivity of that sector. Indeed, in some sectors, notably agriculture, there even seems to be an inverse trend between the two: lower numbers of workers (but with greater capital inputs) commonly achieve higher productivity levels.

A further group of measures has been added to the list of general stimulus variables, a group which might be classed as surrogates for less tangible attributes of countries which nevertheless are relevant to the volume of interaction.

The first two of these, Metropolitan Population, and Metropolitan Population as Percent of Total Population (introduced in Chapter I), attempt to express qualities of a nation that might be described as its degree of urban-industrial development and its internal economic/political coherence or cohesiveness. The relationship between degree of urbanization and the rapid growth of industrialization is empirically evidenced in the maps displayed in the first chapter of this study. Some evidence also exists for the association of well-developed urban hierarchical structures and degree of economic development.[1] The third surrogate

---

[1] Alan Pred, The Spatial Dynamics of U.S. Urban Industrial Growth: 18

ate variable, <u>Total Surface Area</u> (or Size) of a nation, here roughly indexes
he probability of obtaining diversity in physical resources of a country and per-
aps quantity of certain classes of resources such as arable land, minerals and
ossil fuels. Used in this context, <u>Surface Area</u> is not universally accepted by
revious researchers. Linnemann, for example, dismisses it as of no theoret-
cal importance for the explanation of trade.[1] Ohlin accepts the validity of con-
idering <u>land-intensiveness</u> of nations as an explanatory variable, but likewise
ejects simple area as an index of resource endowment.[2] Van Meerhaege,
owever, asserts (with supporting empirical evidence) that surface area can
alidly be thought of as a rough measure of probable resource potential,[3] and
he present author shares this view.

pecific Stimulus Variables

Variables which seem to relate more specifically to the volume of trade
hat might be expected among nations, and also the capacity of nations for export
r import of capital, include a nation's <u>Gold Holdings</u>,[4] <u>Financial Reserves</u>, and
oreign Exchange Supplies. These data, at least for the period under review,
rovided a fair indicator of the international confidence which a nation's economy
ight command, i.e., of the ability of a country to pay its trading debts where
incurred an "unfavorable balance of payments."

Identification of the more prominent trading nations of the world is aided
y inclusion of the variables <u>Ratio of Imports to G.N.P.</u> and <u>Ratio of Exports to</u>
.N.P. The propensity of nations to attract foreign investment capital is mea-
ured in part by the variable <u>Discount Rate</u>. This provides an idea of the varia-
on among countries in the interest which accrues to investment in those counies, by measuring the rate at which the central bank makes loans to other
anks or institutions.

---

914 (Cambridge, Mass.: M.I.T. Press, 1966). Brian J. L. Berry, "City Size
istributions and Economic Development," <u>Economic Development and Cultural</u>
<u>hange</u>, IX (1961), 573-88.

[1]"The limited importance of natural resources in determining the extent of
country's participation in world trade is one of the reasons for disregarding the
nd area of a country as a trade explaining variable in our analysis." Linne-
ann, <u>op. cit.</u>, p. 23.

[2]Ohlin, <u>op. cit.</u>, pp. 24-27. [3]Van Meerhaeghe, <u>op. cit.</u>, pp. 15-17.

[4]The recent international deemphasizing of the Gold Standard has decreased
e importance of this element for some national economies, but this development
ok place after the period being studied in the present instance.

Variables which appear to focus more specifically on the stimulus to population migration comprise the Level of Unemployment, which is thought to act in a negative fashion on potential in-migration, Cost of Living, Wage Level, and Ratio of Wages to Living Cost, all indexing the prosperity of a country's employed population. The wage index and living cost index are both based on a primary datum of the mean wage per hour and living cost in the United States of America, which is taken as 100 in both variables. All other countries are then ordinally scaled according to this base figure for the United States.

Deterrent Variables

At this stage of the study, a single variable, distance, is seen as being the sole universal deterrent or friction acting on all forms of interaction. As stressed earlier, however, certain attributes of the nations themselves, while acting as stimuli for some forms of interaction or for some specific trading partners, may in fact operate as severe impediments to other forms of interaction.

At the aggregate level of analysis, it should be noted, the measurement of actual distance (whether in linear units or in cost or time equivalence) has no meaning. In analyzing relationships between external behavioral aspects of a nation and its internal attributes, we cannot use a relative concept such as simple distance, which implies a dyadic spatial relationship of an object at one point in a co-ordinate system with one or more other points.

It is possible, however, to develop from the friction of distance notion a monadic variable which might then be added to the group of characteristics of nations which are hypothesized to explain interaction. This "manufactured" variable will be based on the notion of Accessibility of a country to the main market/productive population clusters of the world, i.e., a country's location with respect to the global field of urban population potential.

The method of calculating for each nation a measure of its accessibility to this total field is briefly as follows:

(1) transform the latitude-longitude expression of a city's location into a new Cartesian coordinate system with a single reference point or origin;

(2) compute the weighted mean center of metropolitan population for each country with respect to this new origin;

(3) calculate the pair-wise angular distances between successive pairs of national "centers of gravity" of metropolitan population;

(4) derive from this table of distances the measure of a country's Accessibility to the world urban population field.

Thus, for every nation in the study sample, the values for population, latitude, and longitude were collected for urban centers which exceeded one-half million people[1] in the time period under study. These coordinates were then restated in a Euclidean system whose origin $(0, 0)$ is at the intersection of the Greenwich meridian (the y-coordinate), and a line (x-coordinate) which represents 90 degrees south latitude, i.e., the south pole. All points in this transformed system are thus positive. A point at the equator and the international date line would then have transformed coordinates of 90.0, 180.0; the city of Glasgow (55°54N, 4°25W) has the approximate transformed coordinates (145.625, 355.600). Thus every large urban center has been located in a Cartesian coordinate system where the x and y coordinates measure angular distance) such that, for any point i,

$$0 < x_i < 180,$$

$$0 < y_i < 360.$$

The locations of urban centers having populations greater than 500 thousand for each country are used to find the weighted mean center $(w_n)_I$ of the urban population of a nation by the formula:

$$w_n \, lat_I = \frac{\sum_{j}^{k} (P_j \, lat_j)}{\sum_{j}^{k} P_j}, \quad w_n \, long_I = \frac{\sum_{j}^{k} (P_j \, long_j)}{\sum_{j}^{k} P_j}$$

It follows that the shortest angular distance d between two points $i_{(x_1 y_1)}$ and $j_{(x_2 y_2)}$ may be found using simple Pythagorean geometry:

$$d_{ij} = ((x_1 - x_2)^2 + (y_1 - y_2)^2)^{1/2}$$

The accessibility value C is found for a nation i by the following formula reminiscent of the Population Potential measure:

$$C_i = \sum_{i=1}^{k} \frac{P_j}{d_{ij}}$$

where P_j is the metropolitan-urban population of nation j,

d_{ij} is the angular distance between weighted mean centers of urban population in i, j.

---

[1] Where no city of such size exists in a nation, the largest urban center is taken irrespective of its population.

The Study Sample: Nations Selected

In theory, any nation which asserts administrative control over a clear demarcated segment of the global economic space is eligible for inclusion as a observation in the data matrices for this study.[1] In the contemporary world, more than 150 nations would thus qualify. The number of countries actually selected, however, is considerably smaller, due to a set of circumstances related to the ability and willingness of nations to collect and disseminate the kin of data that would be suitable for use in this study.

In some instances, for example, countries still remain under colonial status, in most cases being denied a full measure of independence in the admin istration of their internal economic processes, not to mention their dealings with other nations. In other instances, nations may be too poorly developed in an administrative and economic sense to permit the carrying out of regular an reliable census procedures. The United Nations may, in some such cases, undertake the collection of data in these countries for its own purposes, or (as is more likely) estimates of various characteristics will be given by the nation government in lieu of painstakingly-gathered census material.

In the present study, where 50 interaction and 41 attribute variables ha been identified as potentially useful, consistent gaps appear in the data matric for some countries which come under the rubric of "underdeveloped."

Other nations, for various political or strategic reasons, do not make certain data available, and hence less reliable "estimates" may be the only me sures that come to hand for important economic characteristics of such countries. The centrally-planned economies are a significant group in this particu lar category.

Since, in the present study, the maintenance of the highest possible sta dard of data comparability and reliability is certainly desirable, this will have to be effected at the expense of complete universality of the study; i. e., the

---

[1] Here we make the assumption that independent nations, besides being classed as separate political units, may also be considered to have some mea sure of separate functioning and existence in an economic sense. I. e., we assume that a nation-state is a meaningful unit for collection of data relating levels of productivity and rates of increase in income, and associated factors affecting these variables. This assumption could, however, be criticized on the grounds that it ignores the question of spatial autocorrelation among the observations. I. e., it ignores the question of mutual influences among nation in the real world which would affect their individual behavior, and thus rende invalid any statistical inferences about their aggregate behavior (since this assumes individual observations are independent and autonomous). The problem of spatial autocorrelation remains a troublesome obstacle to valid statisti cal manipulation of geographic series.

ntire population of the community of nations cannot be used. However, the con-
lusions of this study will carry little weight if some semblance of universality
s not retained. Hence, a compromise must be struck in selecting the set of
bservations comprising our empirical base. Nations with some gaps in data
vill be retained, and estimates inserted for the missing values (these estimates
vill be means for the distribution of that variable over the sample of countries).
above a critical level of data omission, however (12 variables in both attribute
nd interaction matrices), nations will be rejected.

The resulting set of observations cannot be considered a random sample
f all nations, since the smaller, less developed, and centrally-planned econ-
mies have higher rates of exclusion from the study than do the better developed
r non-communist nations. It is admittedly unfortunate that this degree of up-
vard bias has been introduced into the study. It is believed that such bias will
e insufficient to invalidate the broad generalizations which should be possible
s a result of this phase of analysis.

The set of observations for the aggregate analysis, chosen in the manner
utlined above, comprised 108 nations. These are listed (alphabetically for
najor world regions) in Table 2.

It will be observed from Table 2 that fairly good coverage has been
chieved in most of the major regions of the world. Unfortunately, large gaps
o occur for southern Africa, as well as east Asia, where the exclusion of The
²eople's Republic of China must undoubtedly lead to a somewhat biased picture
f regional economic patterns.

The data assembled for the 108 nations in the observation set, however,
rovide a basis for construction of an aggregate model which may confidently be
xpected to have acceptable levels of accuracy and comprehensiveness.

The Aggregate Model: Summary
Restatement of Objectives

In this initial phase of analysis, the objective is to find answers to the
ollowing questions:

(1) what are the underlying patterns of variation for which the selected variables are indexes?

(2) what spatial patterns emerge from a consideration of similarities and
differences among nations with respect to aggregate economic behavior?

(3) what (if any) are the empirical interrelationships among such forms of
external commerce? Specifically, are there, at the aggregate level,
predictable substitution relations among a country's trade, migration,
and capital flow patterns? And what are the predictor variables?

TABLE 2

THE AGGREGATE STUDY: SAMPLE NATIONS

AFRICA				
Algeria	001	Dominican Republic	037	Malaysia	075
Cameroon	002	El Salvador	038	Pakistan	076
Central African		Guatemala	039	Philippines	077
Republic	003	Honduras	040	Singapore	078
Chad	004	Jamaica	041	Syria	079
Congo (Brazzaville)	005	Mexico	042	Thailand	080
Congo (Dem. Rep.)	006	Nicaragua	043	Turkey	081
Dahomey	007	Panama	044	South Vietnam	082
Ethiopia	008	Trinidad and			
Gabon	009	Tobago	045	EUROPE	
Gambia	010	U.S.A.	046	Austria	083
Ghana	011	Argentina	047	Belgium-	
Ivory Coast	012	Bolivia	048	Luxembourg	084
Kenya	013	Brazil	049	Bulgaria	085
Liberia	014	Chile	050	Czechoslovakia	086
Libya	015	Colombia	051	Denmark	087
Malagasy	016	Ecuador	052	Finland	088
Malawi	017	Guyana	053	France	089
Mali	018	Paraguay	054	West Germany	090
Mauritania	019	Peru	055	Greece	091
Morocco	020	Uruguay	056	Hungary	092
Niger	021	Venezuela	057	Iceland	093
Nigeria	022			Ireland	094
Senegal	023	ASIA		Italy	095
Sierra Leone	024	Afghanistan	058	Malta	096
Somalia	025	Burma	059	Netherlands	097
South Africa	026	Cambodia	060	Norway	098
Sudan	027	Ceylon	061	Portugal	099
Togo	028	Taiwan	062	Spain	100
Tunisia	029	Cyprus	063	Sweden	101
Uganda	030	India	064	Switzerland	102
United Arab Republic	031	Indonesia	065	Poland	103
Tanzania	032	Iran	066	United Kingdom	104
		Iraq	067	Yugoslavia	105
THE AMERICAS		Hong Kong	068		
		Israel	069	OCEANIA	
Barbados	033	Japan	070	Australia	106
Canada	034	Jordan	071	New Zealand	107
Costa Rica	035	South Korea	072		
Cuba	036	Kuwait	073	U.S.S.R.	108
		Lebanon	074		

(4) what particular variables may be identified as especially useful in explaining aggregate patterns of external economic interaction?

Construction of the Aggregate Interaction Model

Preparation of Data Matrices

The first step toward answering these questions was the massing of selected variables into two matrices, the first (A) containing information on details of total external trade, subdivisions of aggregate trade by S.I.T.C. commodity code, migration (both inflow and outflow, total and long-term) and measures of capital movement and information flow (letter and cable communication). Altogether, this table comprises 50 variables by 108 observations, thus representing 5400 pieces of information (cells in the matrix).

Similarly, a 41 x 108 Matrix (B) of attributes of hypothesized significance in the explanation of flows was assembled, on the basis of the tentative model outlined previously.

The two matrices A and B are thus the components of canonical model A~B whose function is the testing of initial hypotheses about aggregate external economic behavior of countries in the sample.

Since the data in these two matrices are almost entirely socio-economic, it is not surprising that they are skewed to a moderate extent. Consequently, because the multivariate techniques to be used require normalization of data if valid statistical inferences are to be drawn from the results, it was considered necessary to effect a normalizing transformation of original "raw" data before proceeding further.

Raw data were first subjected to common logarithmic transformation. Missing data were "screened" at this point from the distributions in which they occur, being replaced by a mean of the variable calculated over all observations for which data were available. Further preparation of basic data involved the removal of variance among distributions resulting from different scales of measurement. This was carried out by the technique of standardizing (reducing to distributions which are expressed in terms of their standard deviation and for whom the mean value ($\bar{X}$) is zero).

The log-transformed, standardized data, which may now be assumed in each case to approximate a normal distribution, were subjected to a Pearson's product-moment correlation analysis, forming triangular matrices of correlation coefficients for both A and B.

Each transformed correlation matrix formed the input data for a principal

axis factor analysis with varimax rotation,[1] giving for both attribute and interaction data a set of orthogonal (mutually perpendicular) dimensions spanning a
hyperplane in which the original variables are vectors.

The techniques of factor and principal components analysis are well
known and the mathematics of these procedures will not be discussed in detail
here.[2] In summary, the objective of factor analysis in this case was the production of unrelated (orthogonal) vectors which are linear combinations of functions of the input variables, and which lend themselves to identification in term
of basic underlying trends or patterns of variation in the original body of data.

Factor analysis further provides a set of scores for individual countrie
showing their performance on these basic, underlying dimensions, permitting
the mapping of spatial patterns of behavior on these factors. In addition, it
gives, by means of orthogonal rotation, a "simple structure" solution to the
question of intercorrelations among discrete clusters of variables, showing
those which are highly correlated with each other and with the particular factor
(such correlations being termed loadings). This is done in such a way that var
ables which are truly orthogonal may be selected for multiple regression analy
sis (where additivity [orthogonality] of independent variables is mandatory).

Only those factors considered to be significant (i. e., with eigenvalues
above 1.00) were subjected to varimax rotation in this and subsequent phases o
the study.

Output from this procedure actually incorporated in the present analysi
is in the form of factor eigenvalues, showing percent of total variance explaine
by each factor, factor loadings (the correlation of the original transformed var
ables on the new factor), and factor scores.

Interpretation of both interaction and attribute factor patterns forms a
useful prelude to the aggregate canonical analysis, which will chart empirical
relationships between formal and functional aspects of the international econom
system. These factor interpretations, together with a display of associated sp
tial patterns, are dealt with in the following two chapters, where their use as
analytical aids in this study will also be assessed.

---

[1]York University's I. B. M. 360/50 computer was used for this and all su
sequent computer analyses. The program employed was Veldfact, which deals
with a maximum of 70 input variables for unlimited observations.

[2]A detailed treatment of this family of techniques is given in: Harry
Harman, Modern Factor Analysis (Chicago: University of Chicago Press, 196
And in Rudolph Rummel, Applied Factor Analysis (Evanston: Northwestern Un
versity Press, 1970).

CHAPTER V

AGGREGATE ECONOMIC INTERACTION: INTER-

PRETATION OF FACTORIAL PATTERNS

The present chapter comprises an interpretation of underlying patterns which emerged from a principal axis factor analysis of the aggregate interaction matrix, using as evidence factor loadings for the 50 input variables, and factor scores for 108 countries in the observation set. An examination of the loadings achieved by sets of input variables on each of the interaction factors may, in the present instance, serve a number of useful purposes:

(1) it should permit a more succinct description of fundamental patterns in the network of international economic interactions;

(2) it may indicate, by means of relative size of loadings on various factors, which variables appear to be redundant as indexes of these basic dimensions of variation, and which, therefore, can be eliminated in the later dyadic phase of this study.

An examination of factor scores, which represent the behavior of individual observations with respect to the various factors, should achieve some ancillary objectives:

(1) it should permit visual confirmation of the extent to which spatial order attends the basic regularities described by the more significant factor loadings;

(2) it may aid the process of factor interpretation, by allowing certain subsystems of the world economy to be brought into sharper focus for the purpose of selecting clear illustrations of the broad regularities which the factors represent.

The use of score patterns as an interpretive device is, however, limited in this case by the likelihood of low coherence in patterns when eigenvalues are fairly small (and numbers of missing values are large). In some cases also, factor patterns are virtually reiterations of the spatial configuration of only one or a few related input variables.

Figures 11 to 14, then, provide a visual impression of the spatial patterns formed by grouped scores of sample nations on those interaction factors accounting for more than 5.00 per cent of total variance in input data. Scores are allotted to one or another of the groups shown by an objective, hierarchical grouping algorithm.[1] It should be noted here that completely distortion-free coverage of all countries was not possible in every map, as a result of the need for "screening" observations with missing input data on one or more variables Also, because the data surface is not homogeneous, i. e., because nations may be separated by oceans or seas which do not form part of the data surface, a contiguity constraint was not applied in using the grouping routine to produce the patterns shown. The groups, then, may be more accurately described as categories than as regions in the true sense, although remarkable contiguity is nevertheless displayed for some factor score groupings. Group affiliations of countries are shown by choropleth symbols or, for very small countries, by juxtaposition of the appropriate group number.

For the present purposes, factors have been ordered according to descending contribution to total variance following varimax rotation. The order in which score groupings are discussed reflects their significance and distinctiveness in the overall factor score pattern.

Principal axis factoring of the interaction matrix produced twelve factors with eigenvalues greater than 1.00, which together extracted 84.12 per cent of the variance of original input variables. Table 3 displays the loadings of interaction variables on these factors, following varimax rotation.

Interaction Factor 1: The Pattern
of Commodity Trade

The first interaction factor, on rotation, accounted for 33.81 per cent of the variance, and a full twenty five variables gained a loading on this factor exceeding $\pm$ 0.50. Highest-loading variable (0.96) was Total Imports, while an additional nine variables detailing commodity imports and exports of countries in the study sample achieved loadings in excess of $\pm$ 0.80. All loadings were positive on this factor except Ratio of Imports to Exports: Fuels, indicating the importance of fuel exports to small trading nations. Clearly, the factor describes the pattern of Commodity Trade of the sample nations, and was labeled accordingly.

---

[1] The program used was H-Group, an hierarchical profile-grouping analysis with limits of 100 variables over 100 subjects. Output includes data on cumulative information loss, permitting a "near optimal" level of grouping to be selected. The grouping algorithm uses a generalized distance function, and at each successive stage identifies groupings which minimize additional within-group variance. For a detailed description of this program see: Donald J. Veldman, Fortran Programming for the Behavioral Sciences (New York: Holt, Rinehart, and Winston, 1967), pp. 308-17.

In terms of the correspondence between individual commodity flow patterns and the aggregate flows, which clearly comprise the basic dimension, some notable differences appear. In general, commodity import patterns are more closely aligned to this dimension than exports. In both import and export components, the world trade in chemicals, out of all commodity groups, most closely indexes the pattern of aggregate trade. The pattern of exports in vegetable oils is most divergent from this basic pattern. Exports of transportation equipment likewise fail to conform closely to the dominant trading patterns, although imports of this same commodity group are quite closely aligned.

Of interest are the variables <u>Telegrams Received</u> and <u>Sent</u>, which load significantly on this factor alone, verifying the earlier-observed connection between international trade and this form of communication. (By contrast, the variables <u>Mail Received</u> and <u>Sent</u> do not load significantly here, but rather are more closely connected with long-term immigration and emigration).

Figure 11 presents the pattern of factor scores of sample nations on Interaction Factor 1: Commodity Trade. The grouping procedure was halted at six groups since this appeared to be a key point in the graph of cumulative information loss due to successive groupings (see chart accompanying Figure 11).

The first group in Figure 11 clearly picks out the great trading nations of the western world. The European Common Market, the larger British Commonwealth nations, the United States, Japan, and India are included, as are the entrepôt ports of Singapore and Hong Kong. These nations are (with the exception of India) among the most economically advanced in the contemporary world, and, as can be expected, the level of interaction among them in commodity exchange in extremely high, contributing the dominant streams of trade to the world pattern of commodity flow. The composition of imports and exports of these nations is quite complex, but heaviest contributions come from manufactures and allied sectors. Imports of raw materials are also notable for most of these countries.

Group 2 is made up of "less developed" or "developing" nations who rely fairly heavily on trade to sustain their economic structure and growth. Clearly these nations are predominantly exporters of primary produce: agricultural or pastoral commodities (as in the case of New Zealand, Argentina, Nigeria, Cuba, and Malaysia) or the produce of mines and forests (Brazil, Finland, Peru), or oil (Venezuela, Iran). They are, conversely, importers of manufactured items.

Group 3 amalgamates a number of small tropical nations, in central Africa, southeast Asia, and central America, which also are primary-exporters,

TABLE 3

AGGREGATE INTERACTION STRUCTURE AS REVEALED BY PRINCIPAL AXIS FACTOR ANALYSIS WITH VARIMAX ROTATION

Factor 1: The Pattern of Commodity Trade (33.81 per cent of total variance)	Loading > 0.4700
Exports by S.I.T.C. Category: Food	0.7252
Beverages	0.6058
Raw Materials	0.6581
Fuels	0.6074
Vegetable Oils	0.4979
Chemicals	0.7712
Manufactures	0.7694
Transportation Equipment	0.5932
Miscellaneous Manufactures	0.7424
Not Elsewhere Specified	0.4992
Total Exports	0.8370
Imports by S.I.T.C. Category: Food	0.9353
Beverages	0.7146
Raw Materials	0.9398
Fuels	0.9167
Vegetable Oils	0.9026
Chemicals	0.9557
Manufactures	0.9419
Transportation Equipment	0.9517
Miscellaneous Manufactures	0.8858
Not Elsewhere Specified	0.6295
Total Imports	0.9647
Mail Received	0.4795
Mail Sent	0.4812
Telegrams Received	0.6526
Telegrams Sent	0.6473
Ratio of Imports to Exports: Fuels	-0.5715

Factor 2: The Pattern of Capital Outflow (11.26 per cent of variance)	
Net Capital Flow (absolute)	-0.8047
Bilateral Grants	-0.8088
Bilateral Loans	-0.7818
Multilateral Transactions	-0.7726
I.B.R.D. Lenders	0.5333
Ratio of Imports to Exports: Chemicals	0.7158
Transport Equipment	0.6773

Factor 3: Long-Term Migration Pattern (5.35 per cent of variance)	
Long-term Immigration	0.7303
Long-term Emigration	0.7597
Mail Received	0.4740
Mail Sent	0.4909

TABLE 3--Continued

Factor 4: Balance of Trade in Manufactures (5.15 per cent of variance)	Loading
Ratio of Imports to Exports: Manufactures	0.7986
Miscellaneous	0.7040

Factor 5: Balance of Trade in Foodstuffs (4.95 per cent of variance)	
Exports by S.I.T.C. Category: Food	0.5129
Ratio of Imports to Exports: Food	0.7486
Beverages	0.7410
Total Ratio of Imports to Exports	-0.5498

Factor 6: Total Migration (4.23 per cent of variance)	
Total Immigration	0.8160
Total Emigration	0.7562

Factor 7: Vegetable Oil Exports (4.08 per cent of variance)	
Exports by S.I.T.C. Category: Vegetable Oils	-0.6261
Ratio of Imports to Exports: Vegetable Oils	-0.7073

Factor 8: I.B.R.D. Lenders/Industrial Exporters (3.47 per cent of variance)	
I.B.R.D. Lenders	0.4733
Ratio of Imports to Exports: Raw Materials	-0.4730
Chemicals	0.4579

Factor 9: Dealings with I.M.F. (3.18 per cent of variance)	
Drawings from I.M.F.	0.5409
Repurchases from I.M.F.	0.7755

Factor 10: Fuel/Chemical Trade (3.08 per cent of variance)	
Exports by S.I.T.C. Category: Chemicals	0.6268
Ratio of Imports to Exports: Fuels	0.6662

Factor 11: Miscellaneous Imports (2.88 per cent of variance)	
Imports by S.I.T.C. Category: Not Elsewhere Specified	0.5103
Ratio of Imports to Exports: Not Elsewhere Specified	-0.7827

Factor 12: I.B.R.D. Borrowers (2.66 per cent of variance)	
I.B.R.D. Borrowers	-0.7881

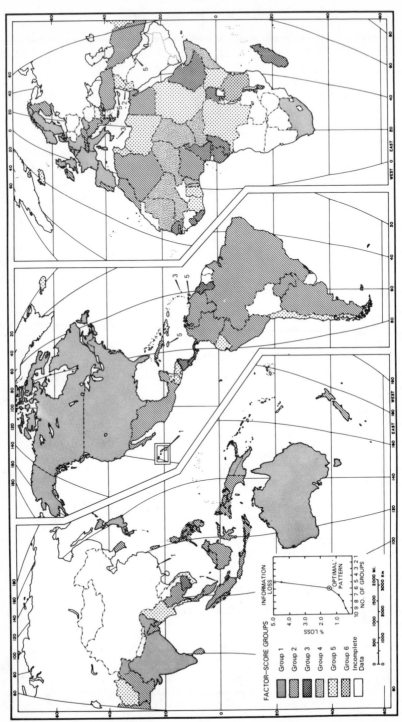

Figure 11. --Interaction Factor 1: Commodity Trade

ut which evidently have significantly different structure and volume of imports nd exports. This has caused them to remain separate from the second group. Jndoubtedly, their total volume of trade is at a markedly smaller scale, with ower contributions from the fuel and mineral sectors and proportionally greater olumes of agricultural produce. Import patterns are, however, likely to be not adically different from those obtaining in group 2.

Group 4, on the other hand, is made up of a set of contiguous states in aharan or sub-Saharan Africa and the country of Somalia in east Africa. Since 1ost of these nations are land-locked, and their commercial development is not ery far advanced, they obviously comprise a group for which the volume of rade is low (generally below $50 million [U.S.]). The structure of commodity xchange for these countries is quite distinct, since most rely heavily on exports f food, raw materials (most probably of agricultural origin) and vegetable oils which exceed 35 per cent of the exports of some nations in the group).

Group 5 is likewise mostly confined to the African continent, although utliers exist in parts of the Arab world, western Latin America, and southeast sia. This group seems to comprise nations whose exports are dominated by ne commodity category. Thus, dominance of fuel exports explains adherence f Kuwait and Libya to this group, while Chile and Congo are doubtless appended s a result of predominant mineral exports. Jordan and Ecuador, among others, ely on food exports, while Burma and South Vietnam export mainly commodities oming under the heading "raw materials."

Occupying the sixth group is the country of Tanzania, which once again is pparently too distinctive to be incorporated into the other groups at an earlier oint in the procedure. On closer examination of the trade structure of this ountry, an unusually uniform pattern of sectoral import contributions is notable, s is the fact of a large unfavorable trade balance for the period.

Interaction Factor 2: The Pattern of Capital Outflow

The second interaction factor, responsible for 11.26 per cent of the vari- nce, appears to index a pattern involving the movement of investment capital. ighest loading variable on this factor is Bilateral Grants (-0.8088); it will be oted that the group of capital-flow variables have high negative loadings on this ctor, while others, e.g., IBRD Lenders, Ratio Import/Export Chemicals, and atio Import/Export Transport Equipment, are positive.

The pattern of factor loadings may be explained in terms of the nature of associated input variables as net inflow and outflow. Outflows were negatively signed for all these variates, and formed a dominant aspect of the total capital flow pattern. The basic dimension being described by the second factor could then be labeled Capital Outflow. It is interesting that Trade Balance in Chemicals and Transport Equipment should load on this factor more highly than on Factor 1. A possible interpretation of this association is that net imports of such kinds of commodities tend to dominate total trade in parts of the underdeveloped world, to which, also, significant capital inflows are observable.

Figure 12 reveals the spatial pattern of factor score groupings for the dimension we have labeled Capital Outflow. The information-loss graph accompanying Figure 12 indicates that 5 groups yield a near-optimal classification.

The first group isolates the major capital-exporting nations of the Atlantic community, which act as the source for a considerable proportion of total flows of investment funds in the current period. The United States continues a the largest single supplier of world investment capital, exporting more than fo billion dollars each year, mostly in the form of bilateral grants, but with bilat eral loans approaching $1.5 billion per annum. A revitalized and rapidly deve oping West Germany has begun to contribute ever-increasing amounts to the fu of development capital available to underdeveloped and industrialized nations alike. Britain, France, the Netherlands, and Italy contribute considerable qua tities of investment capital, both loans and grants, although in somewhat small volumes than either the United States or West Germany.

The second group comprises mainly the smaller and newer capital-exp ing nations (Sweden, Canada, Australia, and Japan) although some nations inc porated in this group are clearly servicing previous debts by repatriating capi (e.g., Malawi, Chad, Central African Republic). The inclusion of Japan and Australia as net exporters of capital is noteworthy; both had long been recipier of not insubstantial amounts of external capital, and indeed, Australia continue to import much of its development capital from the United States, Britain, and Japan.

The third group is readily identifiable as the large capital-importing nations, dominated by India, Pakistan, and Brazil, but including also Algeria, United Arab Republic, Democratic Republic of the Congo (renamed Zaïre in October 1971), Mexico and some less populous nations. All of these nations receive considerable amounts of bilateral aid from wealthier western (and, in some cases, communist) nations, together with long-term loans from the mult lateral funding agencies. Most could be considered part of the underdeveloped

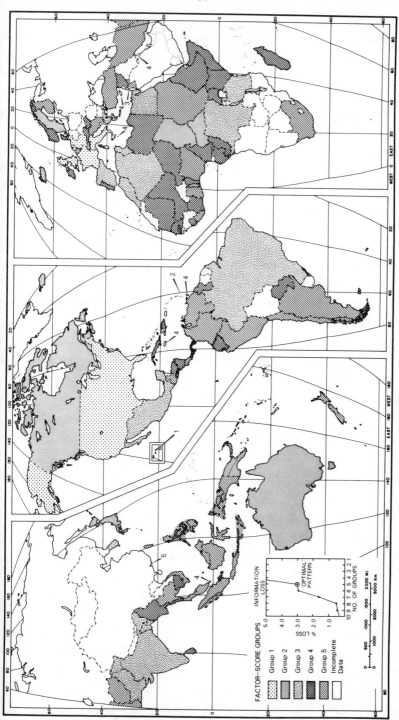

Figure 12. --Interaction Factor 2: Capital Outflow

world, although Spain, Greece, and Israel, seemingly peripheral to this category, have also been appended by the objective grouping algorithm. All of the
nations listed have more or less ambitious programs for improvement of over
head capital (hence imports of transport equipment) and expansion of commerc
agriculture (explaining imports of chemical fertilizers).

The fourth group identifies nations of the third world which receive sma
amounts of investment capital, or which, through more complex transactions,
have a small positive capital balance (as may be the case with Austria and Den
mark). The inflow of capital to these countries is generally in the form of bila
eral loans rather than direct aid from bilateral or multilateral sources (althou
a proportion of the latter is significant in some cases).

In group 5 are clustered the remaining countries of the third world who
are receiving appreciable amounts of investment capital. In some instances,
nations in this group may already be fairly high in the development spectrum (a
in the case of Republic of South Africa, Finland, and New Zealand) but their cc
tinued expansion makes them ready subjects for inputs of new foreign capital.
In other instances, the level of development is lower, but the stimulus to bilat
eral investment (in the form of accessible resources and an acceptable investment climate) evidently exists. Most countries in this group accepted signific
bilateral grants, and funds from multilateral agencies, during the period unde
review.

Interaction Factor 3: Long-Term Migration Pattern

The third factor emerging from analysis of the interaction matrix contributed 5.35 per cent to total variance, after varimax rotation. Four variabl
recorded loadings on this factor in excess of $\pm$ 0.4700. Only two of these, how
ever, are highlighted as being especially significant, these being Long-term
Immigration (loading: 0.7303) and Long-term Emigration (0.7597). The two
remaining variables indicate the association of an ancillary movement of infor
mation with the world patterns of population migration. The variables indexing
this subsidiary flow are Mails Received (loading: 0.4740) and Mails Sent (0.4

It has been noted in connection with the discussion of Trade-related flo
that Telegram patterns and Mail patterns evince quite different trends. Tele-
grams or cablegrams are evidently the primary media for relaying commerci
information, while, as the present factor pattern suggests, letter mail appear
to be the favored channel through which communication is maintained between
expatriate groups and their families in the country of origin.

The factor loadings, in this case, seem to point unequivocally toward a pattern of Long-term Migration, and this label is thus confidently affixed to Interaction Factor 3.

The factor-score pattern associated with this dimension is shown in Figure 13. A set of six groups was indicated by the information-loss graph as most appropriate in this instance. The patterns contrast sharply in some aspects to those of the previous two factors, in which groupings were, for the most part, intuitively appropriate and, hence, fairly readily interpretable. In this case, not all groups enjoy immediate intuitive acceptance. This may be due to the previously mentioned influences of missing data and disparities in official interpretation, in various countries, of the category "long-term" migration.

At first glance, for example, the association of nations such as the United States and Britain in group 1 with such intuitively dissimilar countries as Uganda, Jordan, and Malta would appear to defy rational interpretation. Close examination of the loadings for the variables associated with this factor, together with the original values for these countries in the input data set, supplies some tentative answers which, although plausible, are not without anomalous aspects.

It will be noticed, for example, that loadings for outflows of migrants and mail are somewhat larger than for inflows, leading to the not unreasonable assumption that spatial patterns of scores may be colored by this small but appreciable orientation. Examination of original data for the countries in group 1 reveals, in addition, that many have large volumes of outmigration in an absolute sense and (for almost all in this group) in relation to immigrant streams. The latter are, in many cases, likewise notably large in volume.

Comparability in mail flow patterns among these countries is obviously also infused into the factor score pattern, adding to the difficulties of clear interpretation. However, in summary, the first group may be interpreted as a clustering of nations having strong components of long-term outmigration, notwithstanding the fact that some also record considerable volumes of immigration, and that many with much lower turnover achieve rather similar balance between inward and outward streams.

The second group in Figure 13 comprises a number of third-world countries having relatively small migration turnover, but a clear dominance of emigration over immigration. Even for nations such as India and the United Arab Republic, which occur in this group, volumes of recorded turnover in long-term migrants do not exceed seven thousand per year, and the outflow greatly exceeds the inward movement in each case.

98

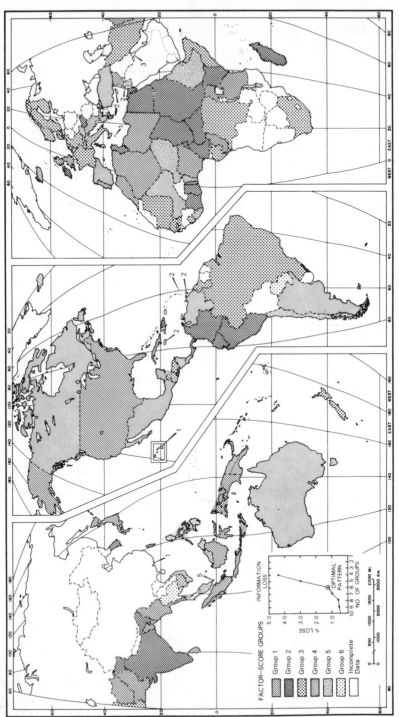

Figure 13. --Interaction Factor 3: Long-Term Migration

Significant migrant receptor nations of the new world, such as Canada and Australia, are combined in group three with other small immigrant-receiving countries such as Argentina, Venezuela, and Mexico. However, the inclusion in this group of countries such as Spain, Greece, and Turkey appears anomalous until it is realized that these, too, record appreciable inflows (composed predominantly of returning emigrants). All of these countries, in addition, are sources of moderate numbers of outmigrants. [1]

Groups 5 and 6 are very similar in their patterns of migration. Both record quite small volumes of inflow and outflow, and the incidence of missing data is higher than in other groups. Close analysis of the patterns in these two groups indicates that, by comparison with disparities between previously discussed groups, their differentiating characteristics are of minor significance.

Interaction Factor 4: Balance of
Trade in Manufactures

The fourth interaction factor, and the last for which factor score groupings have been mapped, accounts for 5.15 per cent of the total variance. Only two variables record significant loadings on this factor. These are the ratios of imports to exports in Manufactures (loading: 0.7986), and Miscellaneous Items (0.7040).

The pattern being picked out by this factor can thus be identified as Manufactured Commodities Trade Balance. Three other variables relating to trade balance in raw materials, transport equipment and aggregated or total commodity exchange achieve loadings on this factor which approach 0.40. While these are too small to be statistically significant, they may be useful in interpreting the spatial patterns of factor scores associated with this dimension. Loadings for raw material and total trade balance are negative.

The configuration of scores for Manufactured Commodities Trade Balance (Figure 14) reveals a rather indistinct pattern over six groupings, but information loss, as recorded on the accompanying graph, becomes prohibitive at successively fewer groupings.

Nations which incur quite substantial deficits in manufactures trade, and concomitantly which are large raw material exporters, dominate the first grouping in Figure 14. Thus, agricultural and mineral-exporting countries such as Australia, New Zealand, Brazil, and Republic of South Africa are included here, as are oil exporters such as Indonesia, Iran, Kuwait, and Libya.

---

[1] The inclusion of Mali in this group is the result of migration data inadequacies.

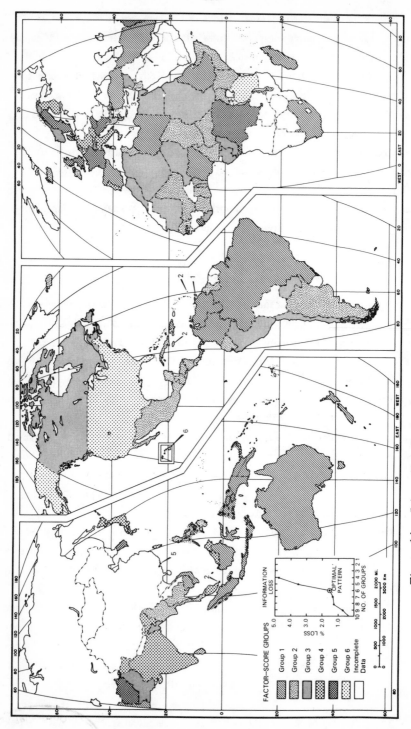

Figure 14.--Interaction Factor 4: Manufactured Commodities Trade Balance

The second group of nations includes those for which raw materials exports and manufactured-good imports are moderately important. Since most are relatively underdeveloped, and predominantly agricultural, a strong polarity is to be expected between the patterns of manufactured-good and raw material trade balance in this group. Countries in this cluster are, for the most part, drawn from tropical and subtropical areas of four continents, but some of the smaller rural nations of mid-latitude Europe (Greece, Iceland, and Ireland) are to be found in this cluster as well.

The third group comprises mainly a cluster of Moslem countries in north Africa and the Middle East, together with a number of nations in the Americas which are predominantly raw material exporting. Most of these (Canada is the rather anomalous exception) record negative trade balances (i. e., significant imports) of manufactured items. Inclusion of Canada in this group must be interpreted in terms of its similarity in trade balance for miscellaneous items, raw materials and, perhaps, aggregated commodity flow.

The fourth grouping on Factor 4 brings together several nations in Asia and Europe which share the common characteristic of moderate positive balances, during the period 1963-1965, in trade involving manufactured items. Thus, under this obviously broad rubric are grouped Japan, Taiwan, Malaysia, and India, the emerging industrial nations of non-communist Asia, and smaller advanced nations of western Europe whose trade balance, in contrast to some equally advanced neighbors, happened to be positive in the period being covered.

The fifth group, once again, enfolds seemingly disparate kinds of nations in a way that defies ready interpretation. Britain, France, Finland, and Sweden, for example, have quite large, favorable balances in manufactured items. Afghanistan, Gambia, and Yugoslavia, on the other hand, do not. However, almost all of the countries in this group recorded large total trade deficits during the period under review. Since this variable achieved a loading of almost 0.40 on this particular factor, it is not inconceivable that it has exerted some influence in causing the grouping algorithm to select these countries as a distinctive cluster.

Only two countries appear in the sixth grouping on this factor: the United States of America, and Tanzania. The joining of these two entirely dissimilar nations admits of no facile explanation. Examination of the data for both does, however, indicate a certain distinctiveness in the trading patterns of each. The United States is clearly outstanding in the size of its favorable balance on Total trade and Trade in Manufactures, while Tanzania appears quite distinctive in the relative size of its deficit on both total and manufactures trade during the period under examination. Whether or not this comparative distinctiveness has in fact contributed to the grouping of these two nations remains obscure.

Interaction Factors Accounting for Less than Five Per Cent of Total Variance

The remaining eight factors derived from the interaction matrix made contributions, after varimax rotation, of between 2 and 5 per cent of the variance contained in the original data. Very few of these highlight complex associations of variates. They are, in the main, statements indicating the orthogon positions of only one or two closely related variables in each case. As we have noted previously, interpretation of factors in such cases is a somewhat mechanical matter, devolving on the character of the one or two significant loadings. The construction of maps of factor scores in these instances would result in virtual duplication of the spatial pattern of input variables, adding no essentially new information concerning basic underlying dimensions. Thus, for the remaining interaction factors, maps of score groupings have been omitted.

The fifth factor (yielding 4.95 per cent of variance) is perhaps the most complex of those remaining. Four variables load significantly on this dimension, drawing attention to a pattern of trade in food and beverages. Highest loading variable is Ratio of Imports to Exports: Food (0.7486), followed by Ratio of Imports to Exports: Beverages (0.7410), Total Ratio of Imports to Exports (-0.5498) and Exports by S.I.T.C. Category: Food (0.5129). The factor has thus been given the label Food Trade Balance.

The pattern of trade balance in foodstuffs appears, according to this factor, to be closely aligned with simple exports of food, implying that countries exporting goods in this commodity group tend to be largely self-supporting in food. Although we may feel this conclusion is so obvious as to be trivial, such a tendency is not noticed in regard to most other commodity groups. It will not, for instance, be noticed in the case of manufactures trade balance, which reflects more evenly-matched inflow and outflow in many cases.

A further point may be made concerning food flow patterns. Since the loading for Total Ratio of Imports to Exports is negative, we may infer that countries with large positive balances in food trade do not, as a rule, enjoy favorable balances overall. This relationship may reflect the increasingly strong trend toward unfavorable terms of trade for primary producing countries

Factors 6 and 7 pick out two distinctive aspects of the complex of interactions. Factor 6, making a contribution of 4.23 per cent to total variance, highlights two variables, Total Immigration (0.8160) and Emigration (0.7562). The notable feature with regard to this dimension is its isolation from the other migration-related variables, particularly those describing long-term movements. The inclusion of short-term movements in the former measures is evidently sufficient to produce quite distinct differences in overall patterns of flow. Factor 7 (4.08 per cent of variance) depicts trade in vegetable oils as being highly distinctive. Significant variables here are Exports by S.I.T.C. Category: Vegetable Oils (loading: -0.6261) and Ratio of Imports to Exports: Vegetable Oils (-0.7073). Countries engaging in vegetable oil exports, according to this factor, are (not unexpectedly) largely self sufficient in this commodity group.

Factor 8, accounting for 3.47 per cent of total variance, is a weak pattern comprising dubiously significant loadings of three variables. These are I.B.R.D. Lenders (loading: 0.4733), Ratio of Imports to Exports: Raw Materials (-0.4730) and Ratio of Imports to Exports: Chemicals (0.4579).

The pattern revealed by this factor, although weak, does permit the formulation of a quite plausible interpretation. The International Bank for Reconstruction and Development (I.B.R.D.), as we noted in an earlier section, is an organization for dissemination of industrial and other technological aid to underdeveloped countries. Nations in a position to make contributions to the I.B.R.D., then, would be the wealthier industrial countries which might also be expected to furnish chemical (especially fertilizer) exports to needy nations. As the negative loading by Raw Material Trade Balance on this factor shows, donor countries to the International Bank for Reconstruction and Development would not be large raw material exporters, but would rather be in need of considerable imports of such materials to sustain their industrial economies.

Factor 9 (3.18 per cent of variance) lists only two significant variables: Drawings from the International Monetary Fund (loading: 0.5409) and Repurchases from International Monetary Fund (0.7755), pointing in unequivocal terms to the pattern of Financial Dealings with International Monetary Fund, which thus becomes the label given to this factor. Once again, the separation of this component of multilateral financial transaction from others, and from bilateral forms of capital flow, is noteworthy. No other variables achieved loadings of more than 0.30 on this dimension.

Factor 10 likewise picks out only two interaction variables, Exports by S.I.T.C. Category: Chemicals (loading: 0.6268), and Ratio of Imports to Exports: Fuels (0.6662). This pattern, which accounts for 3.08 per cent of total variance in the input matrix, has been entitled <u>Fuel/Chemical Trade</u>. It sustains a general trend which has been gradually emerging during this discussion of factor patterns, and which has quite important implications for this (and future) studies. This trend is an empirical refutation of the notion that patterns of aggregate trade (and, for that matter, migration and capital flow) are, in some way, monolithic entities. It suggests that aggregate flows cannot be divorced without serious disadvantage from their component subcategories in theoretical discussion of causal relationships. The essentially multidimensional nature of factor and commodity flows have, in other words, been strongly evinc by the resultant factors in this study.

The final two factors in this interaction set display very weak patterns (2.88 per cent and 2.66 per cent of total variance respectively). The nature of loadings on Factor 11 indicates that both it and Factor 12 may be dismissed as of little conceptual importance. The two significant loadings on Factor 11 are: <u>Imports Not Elsewhere Specified</u> and <u>Ratio of Imports to Exports of Goods Not Elsewhere Specified</u>. Because of the probable randomness of these variables, which are "catch-all" categories for otherwise unclassifiable trade goods, we have adequate reason to exclude this factor from further consideration. Since Factor 12 contributes even less to total variance, it may also be safely excluded

The ten factors in the Interaction matrix for which adequate interpretation has been possible will thus comprise one input matrix to the aggregate canonical correlation analysis. The second matrix in this analysis will be drawn from resultant factors which emerge from factorial reduction of the attribute matrix. A detailed interpretation of the factor output for this matrix forms the subject of the following chapter.

CHAPTER VI

NATIONAL ECONOMIC ATTRIBUTES:

INTERPRETATION OF FAC-

TORIAL PATTERNS

The objectives of the present section follow very closely those enumerated in the preceding chapter. By conducting a similarly detailed reduction of
the matrix of aggregate attribute variables, we will isolate important underlying
dimensions of variation, and pick out for subsequent elimination those variables
whose contributions to such important patterns are redundant or insignificant.
Examination of spatial patterns comprising factor score groupings will likewise
be attempted for all factors accounting for over 5.00 per cent of total variance.

The principal axis factor analysis of 41 variables relating to socio-
economic conditions of sample countries produced 10 factors, which together
extracted 78.23 per cent of the variance contained in the original input data.
Each factor made a contribution of at least 2.00 per cent to total variance, and
5 of this number contributed more than 5.00 per cent each.

Varimax rotation of the 10 attribute factors produced a "simple solution"
as shown in Table 4, which lists the factors, together with loadings of the original variables on these factors exceeding the value of 0.47.

Attribute Factor 1: Size of Economically
Active Population

The first factor, which in rotated form accounted for 19.87 per cent of
the variance, comprises a group of variables detailing the occupational structure
of the 108 sample countries but including also the total population of each country
as a significant variable. Highest loading variate is Population in Commerce,
Banking, and Insurance (loading: 0.9213), but several closely related variables,
including Population in Manufacturing, Building and Public Works, and Services
also record loadings in excess of 0.80.

Since these data are in terms of absolute numbers of workers in each
category, and in view of the close correspondence of the variables Total Econom-

TABLE 4

AGGREGATE ATTRIBUTE STRUCTURE AS SHOWN BY PRINCIPAL
AXIS FACTOR ANALYSIS WITH VARIMAX ROTATION

Factor 1: Size of Economically Active Population (19. 87 per cent of total variance)	Loading > 0. 4700
Population in Agricultural Occupations	0. 7151
Population in Extractive Occupations	0. 7946
Population in Manufacturing Occupations	0. 8327
Population in Building and Public Works	0. 9150
Population in Electricity, Water, and Gas Service	0. 7910
Population in Commerce, Banking and Insurance	0. 9213
Population in Transport and Communication	0. 7613
Population in Services	0. 9041
Population in Other Occupations	0. 4831
Total Economically-active Population	0. 7631
Total Population	0. 6649

Factor 2: Per-Capita National Income (16. 14 per cent of total variance)	
Gross National Product	0. 7455
Gross Domestic Product	0. 7739
National Income	0. 7879
Gross Fixed Capital Formation	0. 8295
Per Capita Gross National Product	0. 8969
Per Capita Gross Domestic Product	0. 9144
Per Capita National Income	0. 9250
Per Capita Fixed Capital Formation	0. 9323

Factor 3: Urban-Industrial Development (9. 43 per cent of total variance)	
Total Metropolitan-Urban Population	0. 6584
Percent Metropolitan Population	0. 7534
Contribution of Agricultural Sector to Domestic Product	-0. 8107
Contribution of Secondary Industry to Domestic Product	0. 7328
Contribution of Manufacturing to Domestic Product	0. 8085

Factor 4: Living Standard (5. 81 per cent of total variance)	
Population in Activities Not Elsewhere Specified	0. 5740
Wage Index	-0. 8803
Ratio of Living Cost Index to Wage Index	-0. 8959

Factor 5: Accessibility (5. 39 per cent of total variance)	
Contribution of Transport and Communications Sector to Domestic Product	0. 8386
Level of Urban Population Potential (Accessibility)	0. 9375
Level of Unemployment	-0. 5299

TABLE 4--Continued

Factor 6: Capital-Poor Countries (4.91 per cent of total variance)	Loading
Gold Holdings	-0.5563
Currency Reserves	-0.5781
Foreign Exchange Reserves	-0.4902
Discount Rate	0.7712
Factor 7: Trading Nations (4.50 per cent of total variance)	
Ratio of Imports to Gross National Product	0.8634
Ratio of Exports to Gross National Product	0.8934
Factor 8: Lightly-Populated Countries (4.54 per cent of total variance)	
Total Surface Area	0.8808
Population Density	-0.8622
Factor 9: Population (3.93 per cent of total variance)	
Total Population	-0.5870
Factor 10: Domestic Trade (3.70 per cent of total variance)	
Wholesale/Retail Contribution to Domestic Product	0.8607

cally Active Population (loading: 0.7631) and Total Population (0.6649), this factor may be termed Size of Economically Active Population. This interpretation is supported by the fact that loadings on industrial sector variates and on the variable Productivity of the Agricultural/Extractive Sector are positive. Inverse association would be expected here if the pattern being displayed was one which highlighted proportional significance of sectors.

Figure 15 presents the pattern of factor scores of sample nations on Attribute Factor 1. The grouping procedure, identical to that described for interaction patterns, was halted at six groups since this appeared to be a key point in the graph of cumulative information loss due to successive groupings (see chart accompanying Figure 15).

The first group picks out five countries which are identifiable as among the largest nations in the world in terms of total economically-active population. The United States, Great Britain, and Japan are, clearly, more mature industrial economies, having very high participation rates in the economically active population category. India and Brazil are not as advanced industrially, but in

108

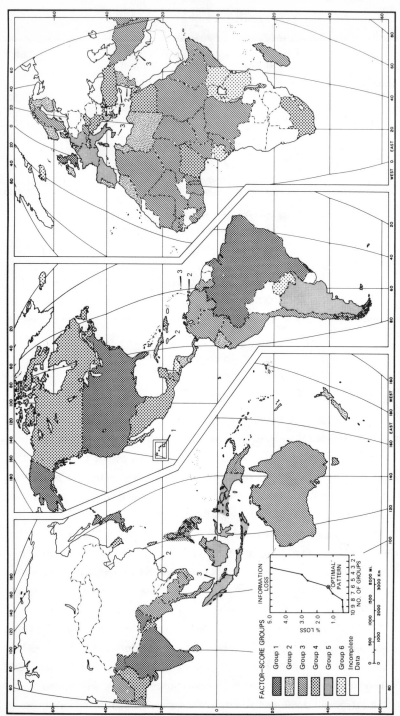

Figure 15. --Attribute Factor 1: Size of the Economically Active Population

erms of absolute numbers in various occupational categories, notably the trans-
)ortation and service sectors, they are evidently sufficiently similar to the
)ther three nations to be included by the grouping algorithm.

The second group of more numerous, moderate-sized nations clearly
dentifies countries having quite large absolute numbers in various categories of
heir economically active population. These countries have high participation
·ates in agricultural and pastoral sectors, and moderate numerical representa-
ion in industrial and service classifications. Regional groupings in this cate-
;ory are quite notable. Seven nations in this class border on the Mediterranean,
ι further six are found in central America, while several more are in maritime
·reas of Europe. For most of these 20 countries, the appellation "agriculturally
)r pastorally dominant" would be accurate, but inclusion of nations such as Hong
<ong and Switzerland serves as a reminder once again that absolute numbers,
·ather than sectoral proportionality, is the basic dimension being described here.

Group 3 comprises 50 countries drawn mainly from Africa north of the
·quator, the Middle East, southeast Asia, and western South America although
ι number of "western" nations are appended to this group as well. Again, the
ιnifying element in this group is an evident similarity in absolute size of occupa-
ional categories, notably primary and commercial. Denmark, for example, is
ncluded, drawing attention to the unusual size of the agricultural sector in this
ιighly-developed country. Other western nations in the cluster, however, are
learly not dominated by the agricultural sector. Sweden, Belgium-Luxembourg,
ιnd Australia have similar absolute numbers engaged in agricultural and total
ommercial activities to other countries in this group, but are not as reliant on
he primary sector.

The fourth grouping brings together twelve nations which have relatively
ιarge total populations and quite strong orientations toward primary production
hence large absolute numbers in primary-extractive sectors). Both relatively
·eveloped and underdeveloped nations are represented in this cluster. Canada,
he Netherlands, and Republic of South Africa are included, all of which tend to
·ely quite strongly on agricultural-extractive sectors of their economies, but
·hich have achieved high living standards by comparison with some other nations
ι this group. Examination of input variables for other nations in this class,
ιuch as Turkey, United Arab Republic, and Nigeria, reveal that agricultural
·opulation in all cases exceeds 70 per cent of total recorded economically-active
·opulation. Since the latter comprises a smaller than usual proportion of total
·opulation for these countries, however, in terms of absolute numbers they are
·vidently comparable to others in this group.

It is notable for most countries in this cluster that absolute numbers of workers in industrial sectors are larger than for most countries with strongly represented agricultural sectors. It is likely that this aspect has also featured in the isolation of these nations as a separate group.

The fifth group has brought together such seemingly dissimilar nations as France and Indonesia, Argentina, and Italy. Absolute numbers of recorded workers are, however, roughly equivalent for many of these countries in secto such as Agriculture, Extractive Industries, Commerce, Banking and Insurance Transportation and Services, and Other Activities. Total populations, howeve vary quite significantly within the group.

The sixth grouping identified on Attribute Factor 1 comprises only 7 co tries with relatively low total population and poorly-developed commercial and industrial sectors, hence low absolute numbers in many categories of gainful occupation. Three of these nations, Kenya, Uganda, and Tanzania, form a co tiguous grouping of predominantly pastoral/subsistence agricultural societies, while the remaining scattered nations rely quite heavily on agricultural-extrac occupations to support their small populations.

Attribute Factor 2: Per-Capita National Income

The second attribute factor accounts for 16.14 per cent of total varianc and reveals high loadings on a group of variables relating to total and per capit productivity. Highest loading (0.9323) is achieved by Per-capita Fixed Capita Production, but similarly high loadings are recorded also for Per-capita Natio Income (0.9250) and Per-capita Domestic Product (0.9144). Gross productivi variables rank somewhat lower on this dimension, but all loadings in this set exceed 0.70, and all are positive.

In view of the somewhat higher loadings of per-capita variables on this factor, it has been labeled Per-capita National Income.

As was mentioned when the variables ranking highly on this factor were introduced, Gross National Product and associated measures have commonly been employed as indices of the level of economic development, productivity, and general standards of living in countries. This common usage should be borne in mind in interpreting the spatial patterns of factor scores for this dim sion.

The spatial pattern of scores on Attribute Factor 2: Per-capita Nation Income is displayed in Figure 16. The information-loss chart for grouping-stages on this factor indicates that 5 groups are "near optimal" for revealing t pattern of regionalization in this case.

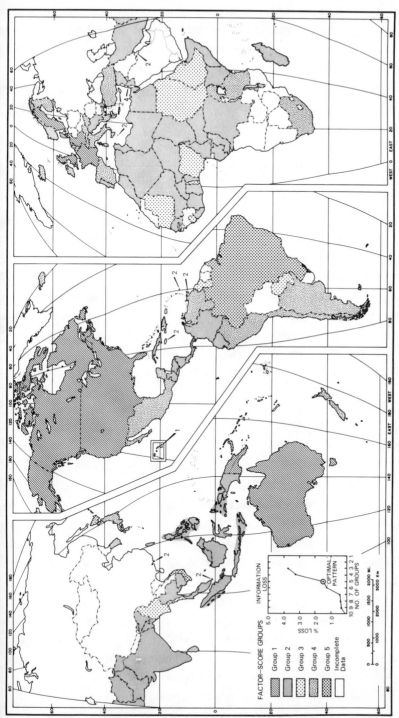

Figure 16.--Attribute Factor 2: Per-Capita National Income

The first group, which includes the United States, West Germany, Canada, Sweden, and Australia, is clearly identifiable as the high-productivity-high per-capita income nations. These have either well-developed secondary and tertiary sectors contributing to high living standards and high rates of capital accumulation, or else particularly rich resources which have contributed to the same situation (as is obviously the case for Kuwait). These nations, comprising most of the relatively advantaged part of the non-communist world, contribute the greatest amount to world productivity and investment.

The second group of countries is large, both in terms of the number of nations involved and the proportion of total global population it enfolds. The characteristic which clearly unites these nations is the quite low rate of per-capita fixed-capital formation. In most cases, also, rates of per capita Gross National Product or Gross Domestic Product are also low (even for such European nations as Norway and Portugal, which have per-capita Gross National Product figures below 400 dollars [U. S.] per year). This grouping thus comprises nations which face the greatest difficulty in effecting necessary progress toward higher levels of productivity. In the absence of a strong domestic source of investment in fixed capital, such countries are heavily dependent on external economic aid. The terms of such aid will be unlikely to emphasize the rapid amortization of private loans covering relatively short maturation periods. These are nations, in other words, whose plight is only likely to be alleviated by massive infusions of grant capital or low-interest loan capital, which can probably only be supplied by multilateral transfers or large-scale government lending by capital-rich nations.

The third group identified for <u>Attribute Factor 2</u> includes a number of underdeveloped nations in Africa, South America, and Asia, which in many ways appears similar to the nations isolated in the first group. Most have extremely low per-capita rates of fixed capital formation and other measures of productivity. Most, also, have low gross values of national income. However, in intuitive terms, there appears no radical disparity in characteristics distinguishing this and the previous group of third-world countries.

Greater disparity is, however, evident between group 3 and group 4. The latter identifies twenty-four widely scattered countries that could, for the most part, be described as moderately prosperous. These are nations which, during the period under review, achieved rates of domestic capital formulation high enough to sustain a comfortable pace of economic growth, and which enjoyed commensurate measures of per-capita and gross productivity.

Within this group, however, considerable variety is observable, such as
tween New Zealand, Italy, and Switzerland, on the one hand, and Tanzania,
anda, and Turkey on the other. Clearly the selection of the 5 group level for
rtrayal of this pattern has the disadvantage of "forced" coalescing of some
ther dissimilar groups which would undoubtedly appear separately at higher
ouping levels. Proliferation of groups, however, renders visual interpreta-
n more difficult.

The fifth group isolated from among the scores on Factor 2 comprises
ly two nations, Brazil, and South Vietnam. Investigation of input data for
ese nations indicates that they have extremely low recorded rates of per-
pita fixed capital formation. Obviously, the values for these two countries
e even too low to permit inclusion in Group 2.

Attribute Factor 3: Urban Industrial Development

The third attribute factor accounts for 9.43 per cent of the variance con-
ined in the original matrix. Highest loading (-0.8107) is for Contribution of
ricultural Sector to Domestic Product, while variables recording productivity
the Manufacturing sector, and in secondary industry generally, have loadings
ceeding 0.70. Two other significant variates aligning with this dimension are
etropolitan Urban Population (loading: 0.6584) and Percent Metropolitan Popu-
tion (0.7534).

The pattern of alignment of variables on this factor, and particularly the
gative loading of the variate showing proportional productive contribution from
riculture, suggests that the factor is describing the phenomenon of Urban-
dustrial development in sample countries, and the relative importance this has
th respect to total productivity.

The third factor, thus identified, reinforces with more rigorous empiri-
l evidence our earlier hypothesis concerning close association between urban-
ation and level of industrial development. Additional illustration of facets of
s relationship may be gleaned from the study of regional patterns of scores
this factor, as shown in Figure 17.

Problems of missing data were somewhat greater than usual for several
the input variables which form part of this factor pattern. These problems
ve, unfortunately, caused some distortions which render clear interpretation
spatial patterns difficult in certain cases.

Six groups were indicated as near optimal by the information loss graph
Figure 17.

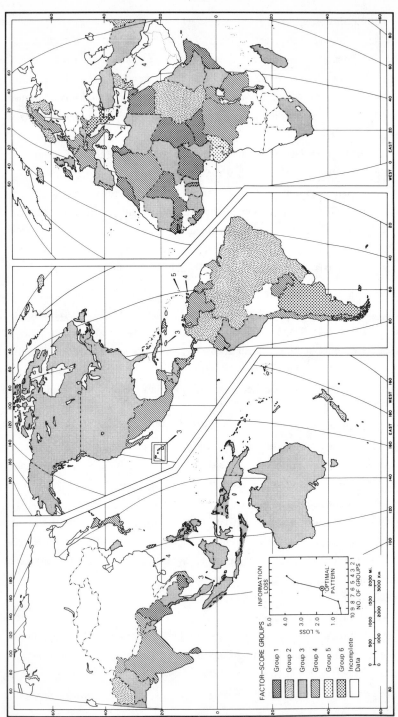

Figure 17. -- Attribute Factor 3: Urban-Industrial Development

The countries in the first group comprise a strongly regionalized set of orth African nations together with the south-east Asian countries of Ceylon, aiwan, Burma, and Cambodia. In terms of their degree of urbanization and heir profiles of agricultural, industrial, and commercial productivity, these ountries represent a fairly homogeneous and intuitively acceptable grouping. ll, for instance, have very low proportions of their total populations residing a metropolitan urban areas. All have dominant agricultural sectors in a mar- et economy which involves only a relatively small proportion of total population. he productive contributions from the "miscellaneous" category are generally igh in these countries.

The second group incorporates nations which show a predominant contri- ition of agriculture to total domestic productivity, relatively high contributions a service and miscellaneous sectors, and, for the most part, a moderate degree : urban development in proportional terms. Contributions of the industrial sec- ir in these countries is correspondingly small.

The third grouping on Factor 3 is a complex and diverse agglomeration f both well and poorly industrialized nations. For many of these countries, the ifluence of the variable Percent Metropolitan Population is visible as a factor ·ading to their inclusion in this group. Thus, the incorporation of Australia, anada, the United States, and Britain in this category is explicable in terms of iis variable. For other nations, however, such is not the case.

Perusal of sectoral productivity profiles for this group of countries indi- ites that for many of them a "mature" sectoral pattern has emerged. This pat- ·rn is characterized by higher relative productivity values in the industrial and ommercial/service sectors, and fairly small contributions from the agricul- iral/extractive sectors. For a number of countries in this grouping, unfortun- :ely, it is fairly clear that their incorporation has resulted from the data screening" process (involving replacement of missing values by means) adopted a preparing the basic attribute matrix. Thus, nations such as Ethiopia, Mala- asy, Mauritania, and Somalia, which are more than usually deficient in the inge of productivity variables, have been accorded unduly high values by the ata screening procedure.

The fourth group of nations is numerically large and embraces countries hich appear widely divergent in level of industrial-urban development. Exami- ation of input data for variables loading significantly on this factor does, how- /er, reveal some similarities in the profiles of these countries with regard to :oportional contributions of economic sectors to total productivity. Most, for

example, record high to very high percentage contributions of agricultural/ex-
tractive sectors to total productivity, and moderate contributions from the tota
industrial sector, in contrast to somewhat lower contributions from service an
commercial sectors.

However, even if we accept that primary industries are relatively the
most productive sector in this group of nations, and that appreciable industrial
productivity is also present, considerable variation on these indices still exist
within this group.

Group 5 involves only three small countries which, relative to other
nations of similar economic development status and overall size, have notably
high proportions of urban population. Both Congo (Brazzaville) and Gabon are
seriously deficient in some categories of productivity data, however. Thus,
firm interpretation of this cluster as being the result of similarity in level of
urbanization would be of dubious validity.

The sixth group, which includes Argentina, Greece, Yugoslavia, Costa
Rica, and Jordan, shows considerable internal variation in absolute and propo.
tional urban population, and in details of productivity profiles. Most countries
in this group appear to be agriculturally-oriented, moderately urbanized natio
not unlike those in group 2. The criteria for incorporation of countries in this
category appear complex and obscure.

Attribute Factor 4: Living Standard

The fourth factor makes a contribution of 5.81 per cent to total varianc
in the attribute data set. Three variables are picked out by this factor, the
highest-loading variate being Ratio of Living Cost Index to Wage Index (loading
-0.8959), with the loading for Wage Index being only slightly lower (-0.8803).
third significant variable associated with this factor, but one which loads positively in contrast to the others, is Population in Activities Not Elsewhere Spec
fied (0.5740). The implication of this association is that for countries enjoyin
relatively high living standards, proportionate membership of active populatio
in clearly definable productive categories is higher. There may be the added
implication, however, that sophisticated data collection procedures in more
advanced countries obviate the possibility of high frequencies in "catch-all"
categories such as the last-named variable represents.

The pattern which Factor 4 appears to be pointing out may be labeled
Living Standard. However, as a cautionary note, it should be reiterated that
original input data refer to straight dollar value of wages and costs of selected

ems. Weighting according to local purchasing power, and consideration of
ndigenous consumption patterns, have not been possible. Thus, some cases of
evere distortion may be produced in the pattern of "apparent" standard of liv-
ng which our variables Wage Index and Ratio of Living Cost Index to Wage Index
epresent.

The spatial pattern presented by Attribute Factor 4 is shown in Figure 18.
he accompanying graph of information loss at consecutively fewer groupings
ndicates that a six-group pattern may be "near-optimal."

The first group is largely composed of the more advanced nations whose
ving standards are quite high. Thus, Anglo-America, Britain, West Germany,
ne Scandinavian countries and Australasia are included here. All of these counries enjoy wage rates high enough to offset relatively high dollar costs of living.

The remaining countries of this group have wage rates that are, in some
ases, considerably lower. Once again, it must be borne in mind that Factor 4
 really describing a ratio of living costs to wages, permitting these less-
rosperous nations to be included in this category.

This combination of seemingly dissimilar observations evidently reflects
ne influence of the variable index of living cost, which has been incorporated in
 modified form into Factor 4. This variable is based on the costs in domestic
narkets of a broad range of items purchased by consular and embassy personnel
n the U.S. diplomatic service.

Evidence from the present grouping may support the argument that, for
ome countries, this index may not be a realistic reflection of living costs for
ne indigenous population. An entirely different basket of goods may need to be
ssembled to build an accurate index. The data actually used, however, appeared
o be the best available at the time of writing.

In the second group are a broad scatter of countries having living stan-
ards which, in the total scale of well-being of the world's population, are in the
ow-to-intermediate category. Thus, countries such as Malaysia, Hong Kong,
nd Guyana are listed here, but so, too, are decidedly more advanced nations such
s Spain, Israel, Ireland, and the Netherlands. The data for wage levels among
nese countries show, as expected, quite considerable variation, but when re-
nted to dollar costs of living in these countries, the disparities are visibly
educed.

Group 3 seems also to occupy a fairly intermediate position on the scale
f well-being of national population as measured by Factor 4. This group high-
ghts a cluster of similar nations in Mediterranean Europe, but also includes

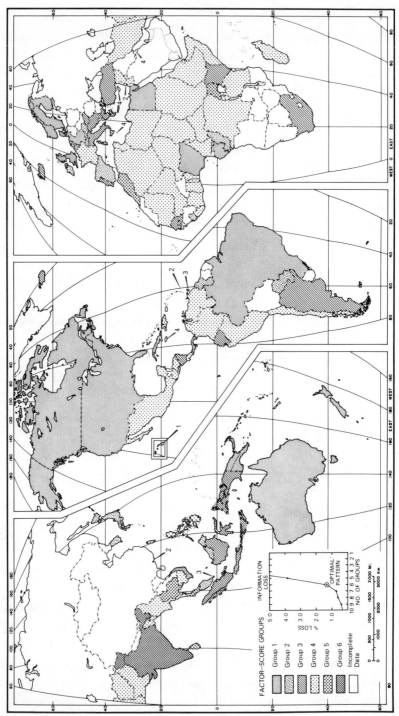

Figure 18. --Attribute Factor 4: Living Standard

ome African countries (South Africa and Tanzania), some nations in the new
orld (Argentina and Ecuador), and a few others such as Indonesia and Iceland.

The fourth group is a collection of countries having, for the most part,
uite low standards of living by comparison with western nations. Almost half
f the entire sample of nations were classified in this group. Most of the nations
f Africa, for example, are incorporated. A majority of Latin American counries, together with most of the sample countries in the Middle East and south-
ast Asia, will also be found in this category. The anomalous inclusion of
rance and Kuwait in this cluster may be traced to data deficiencies in the vari-
ble Wage Index, leading to the insertion of unrealistic values during data screen-
g.

Examination of original data for countries in this group reveals that, not
nly are wages extremely low (averaging only a few cents per hour in U.S. cur-
ency) but dollar cost of living is also very much lower for a selected list of
ommon items than in modern western countries. In some cases, the recorded
ving costs are less than a quarter of the costs obtaining in the United States.
balance, however, the relative purchasing power of the general population (in
rms of the living cost-wage ratio) is revealed as being very low for countries
this group.

The fifth cluster identified by the objective grouping procedure employed
quite small and at the intuitive level does not appear to differ greatly from
ations in group 4, although perusal of input data shows slightly higher wage
vels relative to costs of living. Group 6, on the other hand, is occupied solely
y India, pointing to the singular character of this nation with respect to the
mension of per-capita standard of living. Although prices asked for the stan-
ard basket of commodities are exceedingly low in dollar terms, the average
age paid barely reaches three U.S. cents per hour, placing India in last posi-
on in terms of our dollar-based index of living standards.

Attribute Factor 5: Accessibility

The fifth factor, and the last of the attribute set for which spatial patterns
f scores have been mapped, is a weak pattern (accounting for 5.39 per cent of
ariance) on which three variables achieved significant loadings. These are
ccessibility (urban population potential), which records the highest loading,
ontribution of Transport and Communications Sector to Domestic Product, and
evel of Unemployment. The last named variable loads negatively on this factor,
n contrast to the other two.

The underlying pattern which this dimension appears to be highlighting one involving nearness to global markets and the centers of high industrial an commercial productivity. Productivity of the internal transportation and com munications networks of these highly urbanized centers is, according to Fact correspondingly high. Areas which are peripheral to these poles of high urba industrial growth have less well-developed internal communications systems understandably enough, higher unemployment rates.

The pattern in this fifth factor, which seemingly highlights adjacency (countries to highest urban population potential, has been given the label Acces bility.

The pattern shown in Figure 19 depicts relative centrality of groups of nations with respect to world maxima of urban potential. A four-region soluti is indicated by the accompanying information-loss graph as being most appro ate in this case.

The first group includes countries which are fairly easily identifiable nations in quite close proximity to local maxima of urban population potential. Thus, the United States and adjacent large Latin American countries are inclu as are the more populous and urbanized nations of Europe, notably Britain, France, and West Germany. Outliers in this category located in southeast As and southern Africa might possibly represent localized upward flexing of the c tours of urban population potential, perhaps partly distorted by disproportiona values of unemployment or level of internal transport development.

The second group of countries embraces such nations as Australia, Ne Zealand, Chile, Argentina, and Canada, which are clearly peripheral to the major foci of world population potential. Countries such as Iran and Afghanis are likewise located in a "trough" in the urban potential surface. The develop ment of internal transportation in these nations (and other countries of group such as Spain, Guyana, and the United Arab Republic) seems in general to be relatively low, both in comparison to other groups, and in relation to other pr ductive sectors of these nations.

The third grouping comprises the densely populated nations of India an Japan, together with a tier of African states and some isolated countries in th extremities of peninsular Europe, and on the fringes of the Pacific. These nations appear to have somewhat higher levels of population potential than thos in group 2, but are lower on this scale of accessibility to urban markets than other groups. The inclusion of India in this category rather than in a high-potential group undoubtedly reflects the fact that, despite its very large popula

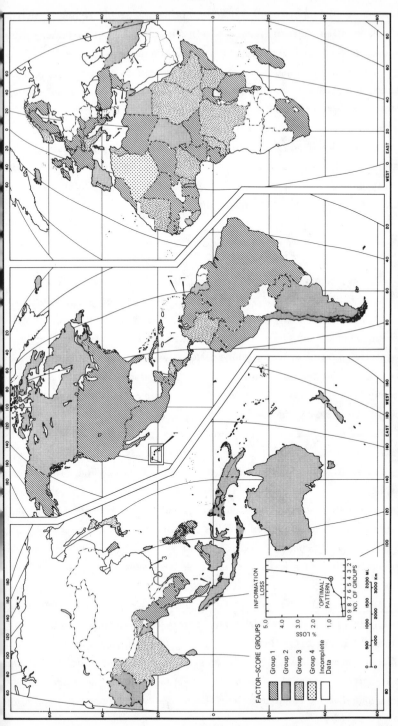

Figure 19. --Attribute Factor 5: Accessibility

tion, only a small proportion (5.1 per cent) of India's people reside in metro-politan-sized cities. Productivity levels in the internal communications secto of these nations are also generally intermediate to those in groups 1 and 2.

The fourth grouping on this dimension comprises a single nation, name Algeria. Its isolation from surrounding nations of north Africa is not explicab in terms of its value of urban population potential, nor yet in its productivity with respect to the internal communications sector. However, it records an unemployment level which in absolute terms is very much larger than surroun ing nations. Evidently, this disparity in level of unemployment has been suffi-cient to exclude Algeria from the category of nations enjoying fairly ready acc to major centers of world urban population.

Attribute Factors Contributing below
Five Per Cent to Total Variance

The five remaining factors emerging from the attribute matrix made c tributions of between 3.70 and 4.91 per cent to total variance, following rotati to "simple solution." For most of these factors, as in the case of the inter-action dimensions, only one or two variables are shown to load very highly. Consequently, plotting of factor score patterns would amount to retracing the spatial patterns of input variables. For this reason, as well as the general weakness of the variance contributions for these dimensions, no additional ma of factor scores are provided.

Factor 6, with a contribution to the aggregate variance of only slightly less than 5 per cent, is the most complex of the remaining attribute factors. Four variates align themselves significantly with this dimension. Highest loa ing among these is recorded for <u>Discount Rate</u> (0.7712), i.e., the interest rat at which the central banks of various nations make loans to private banks and finance houses. This influences more or less directly the rate of saving, inve ment, and consumer spending in these countries. The three other variables associated with this factor, in contrast to the first mentioned variate, display positive loadings that are somewhat lower.

All three of these positively-signed variables relate to the level of gold and foreign/domestic currency reserves held by banks to ensure stability in their internal and external financial dealings. The pattern which this factor illuminates, then, is one in which low reserves in a number of countries, and hence a shortage of capital for domestic investment and for the guaranteeing o foreign debts, has led to (or is at least associated with) high interest rates in

he countries concerned. Seemingly, the result of this pattern would be the
ttraction of greater domestic or foreign investment to the countries thus af-
ected. The factor describing this relationship has accordingly been given the
abel Capital-poor Countries.

Factor 7, accounting for 4.50 per cent of the total variance contained in
he input data, comprises two closely related variables with high positive load-
ngs. These are Ratio of Exports to Gross National Product (loading: 0.8934)
.nd Ratio of Imports to Gross National Product (0.8634). The pattern which this
actor appears to be pointing out is the distinctive behavior, among the attributes
f nations in the study sample, of aggregate trade as a contributor to total eco-
omic well-being.

Close positive association of both import and export ratios would indicate
hat this factor is picking out large trading nations as a distinctive dimension,
ot merely the countries for which exports comprise an important element rela-
ive to total productivity. The seventh factor has, in consequence, been given
he title Trading Nations.

The eighth factor (4.54 per cent of total variance) comprises only two
ariates, Total Surface Area (loading: 0.8808), and Population Density (-0.8622).
This simple pattern indicates clearly that countries which are large in terms of
urface area tend to be lightly populated. Of course, it is axiomatic that the con-
erse of this relationship holds equally well.

Factors 9 and 10 reveal high loadings for only a single variable each.
actor 9, with just under 4.00 per cent of total variance, shows a weak pattern
f global Population Distribution, to which are related an extensive list of other
ariables having loadings between 0.20 and 0.40, too small to be regarded as
eing individually significant in this case. The tenth factor (3.70 per cent of
ariance) comprises the single variable Contribution of the Wholesale/Retail
ector to Domestic Product (loading: 0.8607). The pattern picked out relates to
he significance of the domestic market as a contributory factor in the standard
f economic prosperity a nation enjoys. The tenth and final attribute factor has
hus been identified as Domestic Trade.

Significance of Factor Results

A brief review of the outcome of the preceding factor analyses involving
nteraction and attribute variables would be in order here. Clearly, the primary
bjective of this procedure, i.e., the identification of basic, mathematically
ndependent patterns of variation within the input data sets, has been achieved.

The identification of redundant variables is also quite clearly facilitated by the factor analysis. This point will be developed further in a later discussion of input data for the dyadic analysis.

However, the interpretation or labeling of basic dimensions has been subject to the hazards of distortion due to missing data. The use of spatial patterns of factor scores as an aid in the interpretive process has in particular been only a partial success.

In some instances, spatial subsystems or classes were quite readily identifiable. In others, the categories drawn together by the hierarchical grouping procedure defied easy interpretation.

This is not to assert that the mapping of factor scores is of little value in the task of factor analysis. It does, however, point out the added difficulties involved in such analysis when missing data are scattered through some of the input variables. Moreover, the appearance of sometimes obscure or seemingly anomalous observations in spatial classes draws attention to the need for close scrutiny of the basis for inclusion of specific input variables and their accuracy and for meticulous care in weighing the elements impinging on interpretation of underlying dimensions.

CHAPTER VII

CANONICAL ANALYSIS OF AGGREGATE

ECONOMIC FLOWS AND ATTRIBUTES

This chapter seeks two objectives. The first is a quantitative description of patterns of association among external economic dealings of countries and selected internal characteristics. The second is a probing of causal connections underlying these demonstrable associations, in the light of previously-discussed theoretical concepts and empirical findings.

The procedures for attaining these objectives are embodied in Spatial Field Theory, which, as we demonstrated in Chapter III, is made operational by the technique of Canonical Correlation. This technique permits patterns of relationship between economic flows and national economic attributes to be identified, and the strength of these relationships to be gauged.

Three steps are involved in approaching our objectives in this chapter:

(1) a review of the method of canonical correlation as it applies to our immediate objectives in this study;

(2) a description and interpretation of significant patterns of association which the canonical correlation draws from the input data;

(3) a synthesis of more significant findings, drawing together the main elements of flow-attribute relationships. This provides a fund of data about aggregate flow patterns, which will act as a backdrop to subsequent analysis at the more detailed scale of country-to-country flows.

The Objectives of Canonical Analysis

The purpose of canonical analysis in this context is the extraction of significant elements of structure within flow-attribute relationships. The input data are contained in a variance-covariance matrix of attribute and interaction factor scores, or, alternately, a correlation matrix based on these combined sets of scores which is partitioned so that within-set and between-set elements are distinguished. Canonical correlation operates on these data in a fashion analogous to factor analysis, drawing out of each set components which represent linear functions of the original variables. Pairs of components from the attribute and flow sets are combined to form canonical vectors, which can be interpreted as

125

126

statements about basic structural elements of flow-attribute relationships. The first of these vectors is obtained in such a way that the flow and attribute elements have a maximum (canonical) correlation. Each of the original variables, in this case attribute and interaction factors, has a "loading" on the canonical vector, i.e., a correlation of the original variable with the newly-formed structural dimension.

Interpretation of the underlying structural element in flow-attribute relationships (which the canonical vector represents) is in terms of the magnitude and sign of the loadings for attribute and interaction variables. Variates in both sets which load significantly on a vector thus warrant close attention in the interpretation of the basic dimension being described. Patterns <u>within</u> the attribute and interaction sets are, of course, already known, having been identified in the factor analyses of Chapter V and VI.

Subsequent canonical vectors are drawn from the input data in a fashion similar to that discussed for the first and most significant vector. The attribute and interaction components of each vector are again chosen in a way assuring maximum correlation subject to the condition that each is orthogonal to (independent of) every other vector.

In this way, the most significant patterns of association stand out from the weaker or residual patterns (their canonical correlations giving an index of significance). Complex associations of flows and attributes are, by this method amenable to fairly confident and precise interpretation.

Canonical Patterns of Flow-Attribute Association: Description and Interpretation

The results of the aggregate canonical correlation of flows and attributes displayed in Table 5, may now be more readily interpreted. The ten <u>Interaction</u> and ten <u>Attribute</u> factors (derived in Chapters V and VI), which form the input to this phase of analysis, are listed as separate sets in this table. Loadings of interaction and attribute factors on the first through tenth canonical vectors resulting from this analysis are given as ten columns of figures in Table 5. Loadings greater than $\pm$ 0.4500 have been underlined to draw attention to their significance in interpretation of vectors. The order of significance of flow-attribute associations, as stressed earlier, is indicated by the canonical correlation coefficient below each canonical vector.

The interpretation of the output of canonical correlation is perhaps even more complex a matter than the naming of factor patterns. The use of previous

AGGREGATE CANONICAL ANALYSIS*

Factors	Canonical Vectors									
	1	2	3	4	5	6	7	8	9	10
Interaction										
1. Commodity Trade	-0.6693	-0.6089	0.0609	-0.3452	0.1012	-0.1895	-0.0894	0.0398	0.0346	0.0562
2. Capital Outflow	-0.5759	0.5849	0.1626	0.0953	-0.0013	0.0171	-0.4256	-0.1698	-0.1618	-0.2425
3. Long Term Migration	-0.3154	0.2273	0.1054	0.0945	0.3606	0.2636	0.6721	0.4391	-0.0237	0.0267
4. Manuf. Trade Balance	-0.2458	-0.1690	0.0558	0.4017	-0.3604	0.2348	0.3348	-0.5776	-0.1612	0.3044
5. Food Trade Balance	-0.0448	-0.2763	-0.1788	0.1072	0.3539	0.3815	0.0218	0.2953	-0.0286	-0.7256
6. Total Migration	-0.1537	0.1479	-0.6085	-0.1693	-0.5001	-0.2633	0.3208	0.0903	0.0577	-0.3637
7. Vegetable Oil Trade	0.0378	-0.2174	0.2448	-0.0361	-0.5500	0.3768	-0.1603	0.4473	-0.4023	-0.2639
8. IBRD Lenders/Ind.Exporters	-0.1019	-0.1159	0.1046	0.6539	-0.1069	-0.1686	-0.0197	0.3321	0.6392	-0.0778
9. Dealings with IMF	-0.1002	-0.1167	-0.7192	0.3132	0.1486	0.1661	-0.3393	0.2574	-0.2725	0.2582
10. Fuel-Chemical Trade	-0.0816	0.0986	-0.1306	-0.3559	-0.1515	0.6429	-0.1389	-0.0737	0.5928	0.1722
Attributes										
1. Size of Econ. Active Popula.	-0.4941	-0.1149	-0.5988	0.4887	0.2607	-0.0593	0.0487	0.0660	0.1810	-0.1169
2. Per Capita National Income	-0.5782	0.0721	0.3036	-0.1868	0.0545	0.4947	-0.1943	-0.0189	0.4113	0.1798
3. Urban-Industrial Devel.	-0.2323	-0.3672	0.3142	-0.0686	0.4297	-0.1479	0.6284	-0.0728	-0.2462	0.1265
4. Living Standard	0.3344	-0.4925	-0.0213	0.3755	-0.0197	0.6661	0.0278	0.1356	-0.1569	0.0825
5. Accessibility	-0.0087	-0.1544	-0.1462	0.0942	-0.6711	-0.1395	0.4240	0.0043	0.3617	0.2605
6. Capital-Poor Nations	0.4143	-0.2835	0.9489	-0.0718	0.4095	-0.2136	-0.0959	-0.0371	0.7193	0.0004
7. Trading Nations	-0.0011	-0.0375	0.0012	0.3009	0.1029	-0.2441	-0.4301	-0.5609	-0.1694	0.3525
8. Surface Area	0.1559	0.1837	-0.6209	-0.4860	0.2669	0.1906	0.1048	0.0343	-0.1027	0.2763
9. Population Size	0.2253	0.6769	0.1795	0.4733	0.2301	0.1232	0.3223	0.0999	0.1425	0.1158
10. Domestic Trade	0.0745	0.0592	-0.1013	-0.0606	-0.0574	0.3136	0.2795	-0.8131	0.1044	-0.2255
CANONICAL CORRELATION	0.9046	0.7899	0.6567	0.5059	0.3232	0.2838	0.1685	0.1113	0.0667	0.0008

*Based on standardized factor scores for 108 countries. Loadings > 0.4500 underlined.

theoretical and empirical knowledge and graphic aids will be needed to reduce the possibilities of inaccuracy of description or radical misinterpretation.

In describing the results of the canonical analysis we shall want to emphasize the dominant patterns of association between sets of flows and attribute factors. Less significant or clear relationships will be sketched, appropriately with a broader brush.

Graphic displays of standardized factor scores will be used to aid the description of flow-attribute associations, in much the same way that factor score maps have been used in previous chapters. Regional groupings or classe of countries which behave similarly on these graphs may point to the underlying regularities in the mathematically-derived associations. These graphs, unfortunately, share with the factor score maps the same hazards of distortion caus by unavoidable initial data screening. A similar measure of caution must consequently attend their use.

The axes of these graphs are the attribute and interaction factors of greatest significance in the vectorial pattern under examination. Since the factor scores to be plotted are standardized (i.e., with zero mean and unit variance) the coordinates of the graphs are graduated in units of standard deviation away from the means (which become the origin of each graph).

A graphical display of factor scores has been included for all vectors with canonical correlations above 0.30. Below this level the patterns of factor scores would probably display low coherence, since the relationships they reflect would be relatively weak.

The First Canonical Vector: Relationship between Productivity and Commodity/Capital Flows

The first vector emerging from the aggregate canonical analysis[1] revea the existence of a very strong mutual influence (canonical correlation: 0.9046) linking patterns of commodity and capital flow with the development status of economies in terms of productivity per capita and structural maturity. Significant loadings on this vector are negative, indicating that countries low on trade and productivity scales are being highlighted. However, it may also be inferre that countries with vigorous trade and large capital exports will exhibit strongly developed economies with high per-capita productivity. A simple reading of thi dominant pattern might be that geographic specialization of production and con-

---

[1]The program used for this analysis was BMD-06M, which computes cor. lations and loadings for uneven-sized matrices of up to 35 variables each, for u to 9999 observations.

comitant trade do in fact promote, and are in turn influenced by, the prosperity of participating economies.

The strong empirical linkage between economic prosperity and international commerce, to which this vector very clearly points, is augmented by a number of subsidiary flow-attribute associations. Alignment with the first vector of the interaction factor Trade Balance in Manufactured Items, although weaker than the dominant commerce-productivity association, does lead to the conclusion that patterns of world prosperity are linked to foci of secondary-industrial productivity. The loading for Long-Term Migration indicates that economic motivation is a quite appreciable influence on people's decisions to change their country of permanent residence.

The moderate association of the attribute dimensions Capital-poor Nations and Living Standard, which load positively on Vector I in contrast to factors already mentioned, and Urban-industrial Development, which behaves in the same fashion as the higher-loading attributes, are readily explicable. Exports of Capital, quite expectedly, are shown by Vector I to have a recognizable relationship to the global pattern of capital deficiency. Nations poor in capital are also indicated as experiencing fairly high net outmigration, since they are for the most part countries whose rate and level of economic growth (and whose opportunities for employment) are relatively low. This interpretation is reinforced by the negative alignment of Living Standard with this dominant vectoral pattern.

An interesting facet of the pattern revealed for Vector I is the low loading of the Accessibility factor. If we were to describe the vector pattern in terms of the earlier-discussed gravity formula, we should say that, while "push-pull" elements have been stressed heavily for commodity and capital flows, the "friction" element (which Accessibility obliquely represents) is shown to have very little bearing on these forms of interaction. No other attribute or interaction factors register sufficiently strong loadings on the first vector to indicate significant association with the dominant pattern.

Pattern of Factor Scores on Vector I

Figure 20 provides an illustration of the relative positions of individual countries and groups of countries with regard to the relationships brought out in Vector I. It should be stressed again that the plotted scores shown on this graph are not mathematically-derived measures of the performance of each country on this canonical vector. They do not, in other words, result from the canonical correlation. They are standardized scores of sample countries on each of two

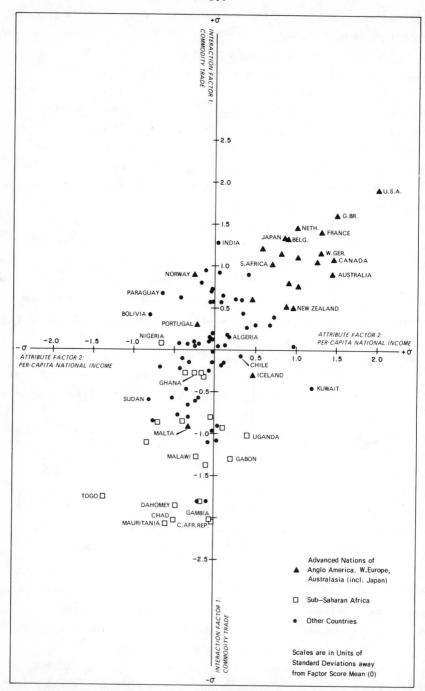

Figure 20.--Representative Factor Pattern for Aggregate Canonical Vector I: Commodity Trade and Per-Capita National Income.

representative factors, one each from the attribute and interaction sets, which
best describe the basic flow-attribute association outlined by the first vector.
The factors forming the axes of the graph in Figure 20, i. e., which were chosen
as representative in this case, are <u>Commodity Trade</u> and <u>Per-Capita National</u>
<u>ncome.</u> The basis for choosing these factors is their high loading on the vector
n question.

The graph reveals a relatively tight, noticeably linear pattern of factor
scores with a positive orientation, indicating the fairly close correlation of commerce and productivity patterns. The phenomenon of regionalization, noted in
connection with patterns of economic development by earlier writers, [1] is also
generally evident in Figure 20. Nations of sub-Saharan Africa, for example,
crowd toward the lower end of this scatter of points, with such west African
states as Chad, Gambia and Togo forming a sub-set of very poor, economically
ntrospective countries.

Some African nations, despite low per-capita productivity, have apparently established quite appreciable volumes of external economic communication.
Nigeria is in this position, as are some of the other large African states such as
Ghana, Congo, and Kenya which form a tight cluster close to the origin of the
graph.

Latin American countries, Asian nations, and Communist states mainly
occupy the middle ground on this graph. They tend to have generally higher com-
mitments to international commerce than the African states, although in many
cases they are not noticeably better placed in terms of per capita prosperity. A
few European nations are found in this intermediate group as well, with Malta,
Portugal, and Norway being similar in per capita income but quite disparately
active in trade. Iceland, conversely, has considerably higher standards of prosperity. But it has lower involvement in trade than either Norway or Portugal.

The upper end of the scatter of points in Figure 20 is occupied, not unexpectedly, by the relatively advanced nations of western Europe, Anglo America,
and the Pacific. The United States enjoys a singularly high position on both trade
and productivity scales. Some distance behind is Great Britain, then France and
West Germany, then a close grouping of the more prosperous countries of the
new and the old world. South Africa and Japan are both included in this cluster.

---

[1]See Brian J. L. Berry, "An Inductive Approach to Regionalization of Economic Development, " in Essays on Geography and Economic Development, ed.
N. S. Ginsburg (Research Paper No. 62; Chicago: University of Chicago, Department of Geography, 1960), pp. 93-99.

The Second Canonical Vector: Relationships between
Population Size and Trade/Capital Flows

Although the flow-attribute association for canonical Vector 2 is strong (canonical correlation: 0.79), the pattern revealed is less straightforward and less clear than that displayed on Vector 1. Several overlapping sets of inter-relationships, involving facets of trade and factor flow particularly, can be distinguished in the pattern for this vector.

The second vector shows as its clearest pattern that the size of a nation population has considerable bearing on its position with regard to global flows c investment capital. A country with large population, in other words, is unlikel to occupy the "middle ground" in the scale of financial donations or receipts. I such a country is wealthy, it is likely that outflows of capital from this country will be correspondingly large. If a populous nation is poor, massive influxes i aid will (at least in the present period) be in evidence. The United States and India represent the obvious polar extremes in this particular relationship.

The size of a country's population is also indicated by Vector 2 as being related to volume of trade, but in an inverse fashion. Large countries, especially those with low living standards, seem to place less emphasis on international trade. Less populous nations may be inferred to place greater emphas on trade, and (judging from the loadings on Food Trade Balance and Long-Tern Migration) to export more food than they import, and take volumes of immigran which are large in absolute terms.

Looking at the loadings within the attribute set for this second vector, w see that size of population is also weakly associated with living standard and urban industrial development. In smaller countries, both of these characteristics seem to be proportionally higher. It follows here, as in the first vector, that world foci of industrial productivity will be connected to patterns of disbur ment of the fruits of productivity, namely, commodities and investment capital

Patterns of Factor Scores on Vector 2

The pair of factors chosen as representative of the attribute-interaction relationship described by Vector 2 are Capital Outflow and Population Size. Fi ure 21 displays a plotting of scores for 108 sample nations with these dimensio as the axes of the graph.

It is important to note that, because of the inverse sign of the loadings these two factors, populations larger than the sample mean are recorded as ne tive plottings while large capital outflows are positive.

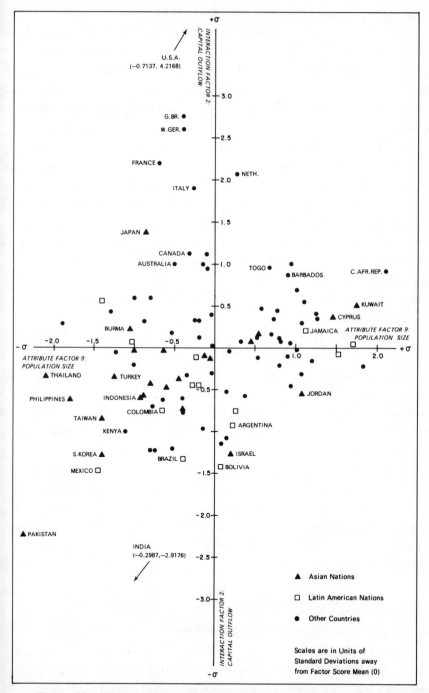

Figure 21.--Representative Factor Pattern for Aggregate Canonical Vec-
or 2: Capital Outflow and Population Size.

The point pattern for this vector, as can be expected from the number o
factors with at least moderate loadings and from the admixture of congruent an
inverse associations, is rather amorphous. Regional clusters are not nearly a
compact or coherent as on Vector 1, and the graph is of little use as a general
aid to interpretation of the second vector. Loss of clarity in the graphic patter
is also undoubtedly due to the fact that the dimension Population Size was one o
the weakest in the attribute set, and its pattern of factor scores may not be as
meaningful as would be the case for a strong factor pattern.

It is possible, however, to determine some loose regional groupings in
the graph for Vector 2. Nations in the "recipient" group for capital outflows ar
clearly dominated by the more densely populated nations of Asia and Latin Ame
ica. India and Pakistan absorb very large quantities of aid and loan capital,
while other large non-communist Asian nations such as South Korea, Philippine
Indonesia, and Taiwan are quite closely clustered on the graph in the "large
population-large capital receipts" quadrant. In the Latin American realm, recipients of heavy capital infusions include Mexico, Brazil, Colombia, Bolivia,
and Argentina.

Some of the larger African countries, and a few of the less-developed
nations of Europe, also appear to draw large amounts of capital, as do some
relatively small and quite prosperous nations such as Israel. Most of the smal
nations of the world, as the graph indicates, are only moderate importers of
capital. The occasional case of the receipt of higher amounts is usually an ind
cation of traditional or colonial ties, e.g., British West Indies, French West
Africa.

Once again, the nations of Europe and the new world are separated from
the cluster at the upper end of the capital outflow scale, in a rather attenuated
pattern which sees the United States occupying a position of unique importance.
Great Britain and West Germany are next in order, followed by a trio of other
common-market countries, and then the newer capital exporters such as Japan,
Sweden, and Australia.

The Third Canonical Vector: Relationship between
Size of Productive Sector and Volume of
Productive-Factor Movement

The third canonical vector points to a relationship between a facet of
associated productive factor movement (represented by the dimensions Total
Migration and Dealings with the International Monetary Fund), and the size of
the economically active population in nations which are potential exporters or

mporters of migrating personnel. Although small countries are highlighted on his vector, the association being described is assumed to cover large countries s well. Thus, a greater volume of personnel movement is indicated as taking lace where countries of origin and destination comprise large and productive growth-poles," whose very size and maturity of occupational structure will act s stimuli to interchange.

Countries with high levels of migration, and incurring large transactions vith the International Monetary Fund, are, according to Vector 3, also likely to e large in physical extent. This association may at first seem rather enigmatic, lthough if we accept the previously suggested notion that size can be an index of esource potential, it becomes less puzzling. A tentative interpretation of this spect might be that it is pointing out a general pattern of attraction of mobile abor and certain forms of capital to countries richly endowed with resources.

It will be noted that a number of other attribute factors are weakly asso-iated with this flow-attribute pattern, particularly dimensions of <u>Per-capita</u> <u>Iational Income</u> and <u>Urban Industrial Development</u>. Their positive association 'ith this vector (in contrast to the negative loadings of the interactions which his vector highlights) may indicate that nations with large drawings from the . M. F., or large outmigrations, have smaller degrees of urban-industrial devel-pment and less impressive levels of gross or per-capita income.

<u>Patterns of Factor Scores on Vector 3</u>

The two factors selected as representative of the association highlighted y Vector 3 are <u>Surface Area</u> and <u>Dealings with I. M. F.</u> The pattern of scores lotted on a graph with these factors as coordinates is shown in Figure 22. Since oth factors are positively-signed, the scales of size in land area and dealings vith the I. M. F. increase in the fashion normal for a cartesian coordinate system.

The graph displays a loose but appreciable association between a nation's erritorial extent and the degree to which it makes use of the currency-stabiliz-ng and loan-guaranteeing services of the International Monetary Fund. The osition of Canada, the largest non-communist nation in terms of territory and ne of the six principal countries in terms of I. M. F. quotas, is quite notable on his graph. Brazil and India are also relatively extensive territories, and their ositions with respect to quota size in the Fund are 14 and 5 respectively. The nclusion of the Soviet Union close to the "median" position in the cluster of arge countries must be given an explanation. Although it was a party to dis-ussions in 1946 aimed at setting up the I. M. F., the U. S. S. R. refused to ratify

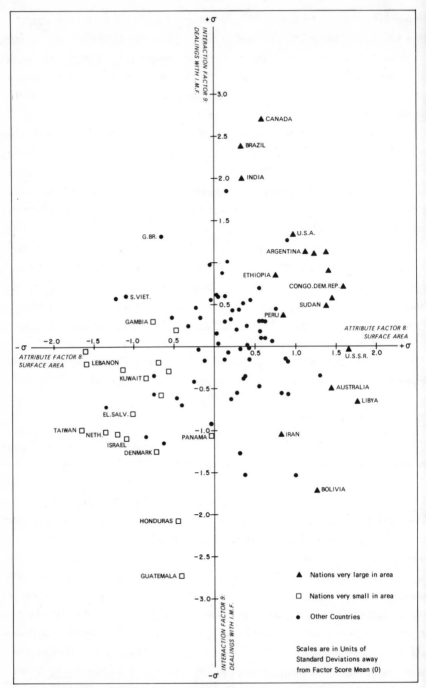

Figure 22.--Representative Factor Pattern for Aggregate Canonical Ve
tor 3: Dealings with I.M.F. and Surface Area.

he articles of agreement decided upon by the majority of the nations involved, nd consequently has never applied for admission to the Fund. Its position on his graph may be ascribed to other elements in the variable set which underlie he factor Dealings with I. M. F.

Most of the larger nations of the world, as the graph suggests, share as . common characteristic the need for large quantities of investment capital. Although the International Monetary Fund does not supply direct loan or grant capital itself, it does act as a mechanism whereby nations may attract loans from ·ther sources, and import needed commodities to sustain development, through ts ability to guarantee domestic currency stability and alleviate balance of payments difficulties. It is thus a strong indirect stimulus to investment in new esource-rich nations, or even in less well-endowed nations such as India which re struggling to maintain a positive rate of economic growth. Some not-so-arge countries also make extensive use of the services of this organization. ·or example, Great Britain, which had been experiencing balance of payment ·roblems during the period under review, occupies a rather prominent position n the graph.

The very small nations of the world comprise a diffuse pattern at the ·pposite end of the galaxy of points. Outstandingly low on this scale are several ·ations from central America, while the smaller countries of the middle East ·nd Europe also tend to occupy the lower end of the cluster. Some of these, such ·s Denmark, Israel, the Netherlands, and Kuwait, are comparatively wealthy ·nd have quite extensive sources of capital for domestic investment. Others, ·owever, are relatively poor and their ability to attract needed investment funds ·s, probably, correspondingly low.

The Fourth Canonical Vector: Relationship between Size of Productive Population and Dealings with the International Bank for Reconstruction and Development

The picture presented by Vector 4 is not one in which strong and clearly ·dentifiable flow-attribute associations are brought into sharp focus (the canon-cal correlation is a bare 0. 51). Rather, it is a more impressionistic sketch of · complex pattern in which trade in industrial raw-materials and manufactures ·nd dealings with the I. B. R. D. are "mapped" into an appropriate configuration ·f occupational and demographic characteristics (Size of Economically Active Population, Population Size, Living Standard) and a surrogate for national re-·source potential (viz., Surface Area of national units).

Some tentative interpretations of elements in this complex pattern are, however, possible. One fairly clear association is that between the size of the productive sector of a country's population and its power to contribute to the work of the International Bank for Reconstruction and Development. Countries with relatively strong and productive economies, such as nations in the Atlantic community, will obviously be in a position to contribute technical and financial aid in considerable quantities. Such countries are also likely to be large export ers of industrial products, as the loading on the Factor <u>Manufactures Trade Ba ance</u> seems to imply, and to have high <u>Living Standards</u> (as the loading on this attribute factor bears out). It would seem, also, that the larger "land-rich" nations are the recipients of this aid from the International Bank for Reconstruc tion and Development (I. B. R. D.), rather than donors of such aid. The negative sign of the loading for this factor tends to offer empirical support for this inter pretation.

Patterns of Factor Scores on Vector 4

Once again, the relatively low loadings of the sets of attribute and inter action factors are reflected in a score distribution that lacks any coherent trend when plotted on a graph using the representative factors <u>Size of Economically Active Population</u> and <u>I. B. R. D. Lenders</u> as x and y coordinates. The useful ness of this graph as an interpretive aid is therefore limited.

The fourteen principal I. B. R. D. member countries[1] have been picked out on this graph, and convey an impression of a relatively weak association between the size of total population and number of gainfully employed on the one hand, and size of subscription to I. B. R. D. capital stock on the other.

Again the group of Atlantic Community nations emerges as the mainstay of the international capital market, with the United States taking the burden of supplying capital for multilateral lending. This country, in fact, is responsible for 30 per cent of total subscriptions to capital stock of the I. B. R. D. The United Kingdom contributes 12 per cent, and West Germany 5 per cent. Considerable quantities of private loan capital are acquired by the Bank for its development loan program, coming from traditional sources of high-interest seeking capital in western Europe and North America. Loans from the I. B. R. D. are usually for a 25-year term, with a 5-year "period of grace" before repayments are required

---

[1] As at June 30, 1965. Ranking is in terms of number of $100,000 dollar shares, as given in van Meerhaeghe, <u>op. cit.</u>, p. 123.

[2] <u>Ibid.</u>, p. 129.

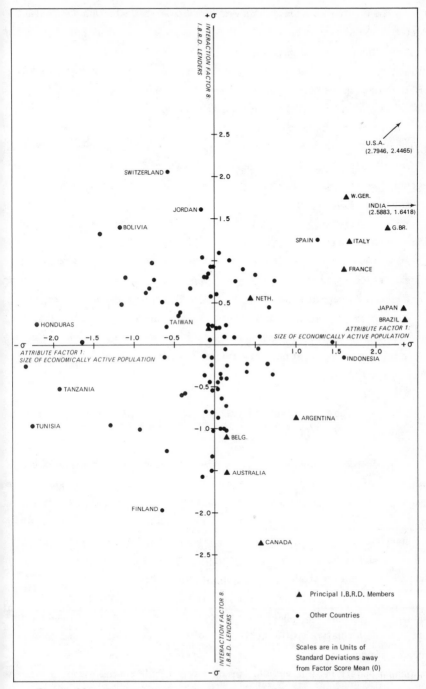

Figure 23.--Representative Factor Pattern for Aggregate Canonical Vector 4: I.B.R.D. Lenders and Size of Economically-Active Population.

The position of India on this graph obviously indicates the degree to which this nation is making use of I. B. R. D. capital. The situations of some of the large "land-rich" nations in the New World are also noteworthy. These nations, particularly Canada and Australia, had only minor dealings with the I. B. R. D. during the period under review.

An element contributing to relative positions of countries on this graph, and which must not be overlooked in interpretation of patterns, is the fact that the variable Exports of Manufactured Goods loaded quite significantly on the factor we called I. B. R. D. Lenders/Industrial Exporters. When this is taken into account, the low position of raw material exporting members of the I. B. R. D. is somewhat more understandable.

Apart from the countries mentioned above, there are few others which stand out in the overall pattern of points in Figure 23. The traditional capital-exporting country of Switzerland is one exception. So, too, are Tanzania and Tunisia, which appear to comprise polar opposites to those previously discussed in the pattern of capital loans from the I. B. R. D. Most other nations tend to cluster in proximity to and oriented with, the y coordinate, indicating that for these nations no appreciable relationship exists between size of economically active population and level of interaction with multilateral loan capital administered by the I. B. R. D.

The Fifth Canonical Vector: Relationship between Aggregate Migration and Closeness to World Centers of Urban Population

In Vector 5, which has a canonical correlation of 0. 32 between interaction and attribute components, we observe that Accessibility emerges for the first time as a significant factor. It is associated with the interaction factors Total Migration and Trade in Vegetable-oil Products. Some discussion of the late appearance of Accessibility as a significant factor in the canonical analysis of flows would be pertinent here, especially in view of the emphasis given to this "friction" variable in theoretical models of interaction.

It is quite evident that, in the patterns of flow-attribute relationships discussed to this point, the "push-pull" factors have been accorded overriding importance, with relative spatial positioning of countries being rejected as of no strong empirical significance. We might conclude from this that the distance component underlying this variable produces negligible spatial order in patterns of international interaction. Such a conclusion at this point, however, would ignore the fact that we are dealing only with broad aggregate relationships, and

using only one particular measure of the relative spatial positioning of countries
(i. e., nearness to metropolitan clusters). Closer analysis of dyadic patterns,
and perhaps the use of other measures of distance or contiguity among countries,
may yield an entirely different conclusion concerning the role of space in producing regularity among flows dealt with to this point.

The most notable effect of accessibility to urban population centers, as
Vector 5 reveals, is to regulate the size of total migrant streams moving among
various origins and destinations. As we mentioned previously in discussing the
dimension Total Migration, this factor indexes aggregate flows of personnel
among countries, not solely the long-term type of migration. Vector 5 tells us,
in effect, that as accessibility improves (i. e., as closeness to major foci of
urban population increases) the flow of personnel between countries so oppor-
tunely placed is correspondingly enlarged. We might say that the denominator of
the gravity model, the friction of distance, is thus shown to have a relatively high
"coefficient" in this model of total international migrant flows.

A curiosity of this pattern displayed in Vector 5 is the similarity in behavior of Total Migration and Trade in Vegetable Oils Products. The latter form
of commodity flow is, obviously, also very strongly influenced by the factor of
accessibility. This suggests that the perishable qualities of this distinctive commodity type may influence its patterns of production, distribution and marketing
at the international level.

The Pattern of Factor Scores on Vector 5

The factors selected as representative of the relationships empirically
evidenced in Vector 5 are Accessibility, and Total Migration. The pattern of
scores on these factors for the 108 nations in the study sample is shown in Figure 24.

The pattern shown for this relationship is somewhat more compact than
those discussed for previous vectors. However, visual inspection of the trend of
the scatter of dots leads to the conclusion that, since it is oriented very closely
with the y coordinate, the significance of the relationship may be low. It will be
noted that since the loading for Accessibility is negative, high values will have
negative rather than positive signs.

By picking out the nations of the world with high proportions of urban population, some interesting facets of this (admittedly loose) association between population movements and accessibility emerge. The nations identified as urban-
oriented which occupy positions below the abscissa seem to represent local max-

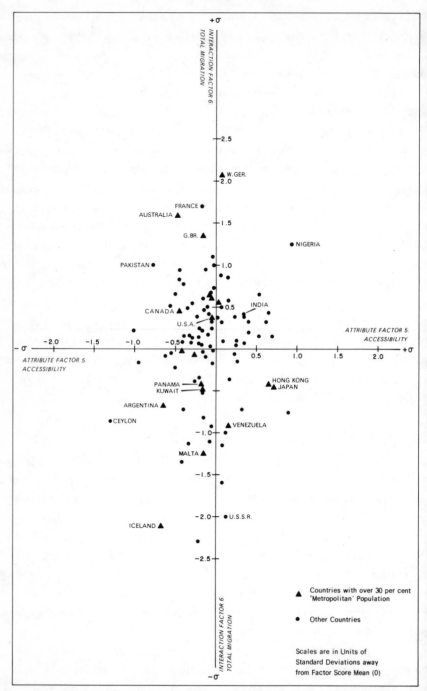

Figure 24.--Representative Factor Pattern for Aggregate Canonical Vector 5: Total Migration and Accessibility.

ma of urban population potential. They are, for the most part, in areas relaively remote from the main centers of global potential, which focus on the North
Atlantic Community. These areas record small amounts of migration relative
o the major world patterns. In contrast, nations above the abscissa, particu-
arly those with accessibility scores that are negative rather than positive,
record high migration figures and (for those close to the ordinate) relatively
high values of accessibility to the global hub of urban population.

Thus, although Australia and Pakistan are peripheral to the world urban
potential foci, they record quite strong currents of migration. The flows in
Australia's case are inward, while those for Pakistan were, in the study period,
mainly outward, with Britain as a major destination point. West Germany, the
United Kingdom, France, Scandinavia and the United States are revealed on this
graph as being both foci of urban population potential and generators of large
volumes of population movement. Around the latter countries are a tight cluster
of nations enjoying fairly close proximity to these poles of human interaction,
and mostly comprising a crescent of European, Middle Eastern, and African
nations.

Canonical Vectors with Correlation
Coefficients below 0.30

Vectors 6 through 10 achieved canonical correlation coefficients of less
han 0.30, but despite this indication of relative weakness of the attribute-interaction systems described by these vectors, examination of their loading patterns
reveals some interesting features. A brief discussion of salient features associated with each vector may be illuminating.

Vector 6: Relationship between Living Standard and Resource Exploitation

A correlation coefficient of 0.28 is given for the attribute and interaction
components of Vector 6. In each factor set there is only one high loading. The
relevant factor in the interaction set is Fuel-Chemical Trade, while Living Standard obtains the highest loading among attribute factors. Loadings in both cases
are positive.

One aspect of the pattern revealed by this vector is a fairly clear causal
connection between the ability of some countries to exploit their oil, gas, and
coal resources and their standards of living. Attention to this particular relationship has already been drawn in earlier chapters. An associated feature,

however, is the trade pattern in chemicals, which also tends to affect favorably the wage levels of those nations involved.

It will be noted that the pattern of trade in chemicals and fuels corresponds in a general fashion to food and vegetable oil trade patterns, and that countries engaging in such forms of trade are not generally found among the large trading nations (if we judge by the weak negative loading of Attribute Factor 7).

Vector 7: Relationship between Long-Term Migration and Degree of Urban Industrial Development

The correlation coefficient for Vector 7 is relatively weak (0.18), so that any interpretation of the association between flows and attributes registering high loadings on this vector must be treated with due caution.

Dealing first with the relationship between the two highest-loading factors (Long-term Migration and Urban-Industrial Development), we observe that high levels of migration are empirically matched with patterns of advanced urban industrial development. This would tend to indicate that motivation for migration is more strongly conditioned by considerations of the scope of employment opportunity and the attractiveness of the urban life style than simply wage level or a sense of the general per-capita productivity of a country. The latter attributes may be more closely connected in many countries with agricultural or extractive occupations, offering relatively few opportunities for large numbers of foreign immigrants. On the other hand, urbanization, as we have intimated earlier, is a crucible for rapid expansion of secondary and tertiary activities which constitute an effective lure for immigrants, whether from international or interregional origins.

As the loading for the factor Accessibility indicates, volume of long-term migration is associated to a moderate degree with distance from major urban clusters. However, the importance of the distance factor is not as marked as in the case of Total Migration discussed earlier. Decisions to change country of permanent residence, we might conclude, appear to weigh more heavily the nature of urban employment opportunities in the destination country, rather than the cost-distance to be overcome in effecting permanent relocation. The latter factor, however, does play an appreciable although not dominant role in determining migration patterns.

Another facet of the pattern revealed by Vector 7 bears some comment. Since the loadings for Commodity Trade and Capital Outflow have a negative sign heir patterns of movement clearly bear an inverse relationship to the pattern of ong-term migration. Large exporters of trade goods and investment capital, hen, are usually importers of long-term migrant labor, and conversely. However, it would be straining the slender empirical evidence for this relationship oo far to infer from this that mobile labor acts as a substitute for, or is replaced by, flows of goods and investment capital. This broad inverse pattern an, however, certainly be borne in mind in the analysis of more detailed dyadic patterns which follows in subsequent chapters.

Vector 8: Relationship between internal and External Trade

The pattern of factor loadings for the eighth canonical vector reflects a return to the theme of trade flows and their economic context. Yet another aspect of the global trade pattern is evidenced here. The highest-loading interaction variable in this case is Manufactures Trade Balance, while in the attribute set maximum loadings are recorded for Domestic Trade and Trading Nations.

Similarity in sign of all three high loading dimensions suggests that nations with highly productive domestic (wholesale-retail) trade sectors are also nations which engage in significant volumes of international trade. Such countries, according to the evidence provided by this factor, are likely to export (and import) mainly manufactured products.

As a corollary, we may make the generalization that the pattern of aggregate commodity flow at the international level may be validly indexed by the pattern of movement of manufactured commodities. Industrial flows, in other words, are "typical" international flows.

Perusal of other loadings in the interaction set indicates several more associations that provide additional "feedback" to patterns already discussed. The most significant of these is probably the inverse relationship of Long-term Migration with the dominant pattern revealed by this vector, which reinforces the association evidenced by Vector 7.

Vectors 9 and 10: Residual Patterns

The remaining two vectors to emerge from the canonical correlation of flows and economic attributes evince very weak coefficients of association, indicating that detailed scrutiny may not be a profitable exercise. The pattern of association in Vector 9 seems to be a sketch of the environment in which trade in industrial raw materials and fuels, and capital flows, behave as alternate or perhaps joint responses. In this environment are embraced the capital-hungry developing nations who are attempting to finance their growth with export of their mineral wealth, and the partners in such a venture, the capital exporting, industrial-trading nations whose incomes are, of course, relatively high.

The tenth and final vector comprises a very faint pattern surrounding the Balance of Trade in Foodstuffs, and not even a tentative interpretation of this weak pattern would seem to be possible.

Results of the Aggregate Canonical
Analysis: A Synthesis

This chapter has sought to describe and interpret salient relationships among aggregate flows and national economic attributes. Our aim has been to shed light on the extent to which empirical patterns reflect theoretically-derived generalizations concerning economic flows. The need for rigor in description of flow-attribute associations has prompted the use of canonical correlation in this instance. This technique has permitted the extraction of dominant and well-defined structural elements (vectors) from the matrix of relationships uniting flows and assemblages of economic characteristics. Interpretation of these vectors, employing a priori knowledge of factor patterns and graphic displays of factor scores, has resulted in identification of the specific environments surrounding certain classes and combinations of flows. The strength of the flow-attribute associations has been indexed by a canonical correlation coefficient for each defined relationship. Spatial and taxonomic patterns have in some cases been revealed by the factor score graphs, and used to confirm our interpretation of vectorial associations.

Summary of Flow-Attribute Relationships

The strongest patterns of association among external forms of interaction and internal characteristics are undoubtedly those surrounding commodity and capital flows. The first vector loadings, and the plotted factor scores in Figure 20, reveal very clearly the importance of the global pattern of per capita productivity to an understanding of these flows. The degree of economic prosperity was revealed by the same vector as being particularly related to trade in manufactured commodities. Also, a fairly clear causal link was indicated (Vector 6) between the standard of living in some nations and their ability to derive trade earnings from exports of natural resources. Vector 8 pointed to a weak but clear relationship between volume of external trade and the development of domestic trade sectors.

Demographic and occupational structures of nations are also shown to ave strong bearing on patterns of trade and capital movement. The less-developed, heavily populated countries are highlighted in Vector 2 as being at the ocus of a global pattern of capital movement involving combined bilateral and multilateral flows. The pattern on Vector 4 tends to reinforce aspects of this omplex relationship.

The evidence we have examined in this chapter points to the overriding mportance of stimuli (e.g., conditions engendering high productivity and strong emand) in the environment surrounding trade and capital flows. Measures of riction against movement (as indexed by the factor of Accessibility), are not rominent. In terms of our earlier theoretical discussions, we might infer that form of comparative advantage or potential complementarity dominates the set f factors "explaining" trade and capital flow.

Aggregate movements of the productive factors (total and long-term igration, and multilateral capital) display affinity with an economic environment differing substantially from that of international trade. Our interpretaions of Vectors 3, 5, and 7 suggest that degree of urban development and resource potential may be stronger inducements to migration of labor and multiateral development capital than simply the economic status of nations in gross r per-capita productivity terms. Moreover, the factor of Accessibility (proxmity to major world foci of urban population) is shown to have a strong association with international movements of population. The importance of this surroate for the frictional effects of distance in relation to migratory movements ontrasts with its low relevance to commodity flow patterns.

The results of the canonical analysis, in short, lead us to conclude that ystems of commodity trade and migration, at an aggregate scale, are relaively independent. They behave, in other words, as if they are neither strongly omplementary nor clearly substitutive. On the other hand, the behavior of apital flows suggests weak complementarity with commodity trade and also (in he form of multilateral loans) with migration. This dichotomous behavior indiates the complexity of phenomena gathered under the rubric of "capital moveent," and also the disparate relevance of different economic environments to arious classes of capital transaction. Multilateral loans, for example, seem ommonly to involve the smaller developing nations whose economies are hungry r productive-factor inputs. Trade-related capital flows, on the other hand, enter on the more highly productive economies, and appear to comprise more ilateral, high interest-seeking investments.

Implications of Aggregate Results
for the Analysis of Pairwise Flows

As summarized above, the results of the aggregate canonical correlati
are useful in highlighting broad relationships between formal and functional ele
ments of the international economy. While demonstration of these aggregate
regularities has been a primary goal of this chapter, a major ancillary goal is
the exploitation of its potential usefulness as a source of guidance in the finer
and more complex analysis of country-to-country flows.

That such a detailed analysis is necessary for a full understanding of
flow patterns can be demonstrated by reviewing the limitations of the foregoing
aggregate study. The main disadvantages of this scale of analysis, i.e., the
obliteration of fine but important detail, and the inconclusiveness of interpreta
tions based on broad but hazy patterns, can be overcome by study of country-t
country flows. Where clear patterns of flow-attribute association characteriz
particular subsets of the sample of national economies, these can be highlight
by detailed analysis, whereas they are obscured and diluted by aggregation.
Constraints on the use of variables important to flow study, which are impose
by the very nature of aggregate analysis, can also be removed. The use of su
rogates (e.g., Accessibility as a measure of distance effects) is reduced, per
mitting more definitive and conclusive analysis of relevant factors impinging
flows.

More practical implications concerning pairwise flow study may be
gleaned from the results of the aggregate analysis. The limited usefulness of
factor score displays as aids to an understanding of basic relationships is a pe
suasive argument for using representative variables, rather than the factors
themselves, in the dyadic canonical analysis. Reduced coherence of spatial p
terns and relationships, a partial result of missing values in original data,
underscores the need for careful trimming of the observation set to minimize
such effects. Reexamination of the set of input variables, and closer attentio
to the question of accuracy in interpretation of structural patterns in these va
ables, are also suggested.

The flow attribute relationships evinced at the aggregate level of analy
may very well be reflected in detailed dyadic flows among individual countrie
We may anticipate, however, that at least some of these general trends will d
appear, to be replaced at the detailed level by different associations. Aggreg
level findings should, in any case, provide a useful frame of reference for int
preting such detailed patterns. In the chapters that follow, these findings wil
be used as a guide for choosing procedural steps, refining original hypothese
and testing them in an empirical model of pairwise economic interaction.

CHAPTER VIII

PAIR-WISE ECONOMIC INTERACTION: DATA
AND STRUCTURE OF A CANONICAL MODEL

The task to be essayed in the next two chapters is the development of a model to replicate factor and commodity flow complexes in a framework of interconnected dyads. Attention thus shifts from the level of gross and net flows of nations to that of specific pair-wise interactions. The present chapter will draw on ideas of flow theory contained in Chapter II and utilize empirical evidence gleaned from the aggregate-level analysis of flows in Chapters IV to VII. However, it will introduce some important new dimensions. Specific attention will be paid in this chapter to:

(1) relevant theoretical aspects of dyadic interrelationships,

(2) appropriate structuring of the dyadic flow model, and

(3) determination of variables influencing propensities for dyadic interchange.

Theoretical Aspects of Dyadic Interaction

Our discussion of the theoretical underpinnings of economic flow analysis in Chapter II provided a set of concepts which should prove useful in the present context. Obviously, the basic principles of interaction may be safely considered applicable to the more specific case of dyadic interchange.

(1) The axiom of mutual interdependence of flows and attributes in the world economy continues to hold at the dyadic level. Volumetric and compositional aspects of flows may still be assumed explicable in terms of characteristics of national economies that can be identified and measured.

(2) The theorem of partial substitutability of factor and commodity movements remains valid, once again, under conditions of common economic stimuli and universal operation of non-prohibitive frictions.

(3) Also applicable at the dyadic level is the notion that, for any particular kind of flow, volume (relative to that of competing kinds of flow) is regulated by the nature and relative severity of frictions applying to each kind of movement.

(4) The concept of multilateral influences shaping "mixes" of flow continues to apply at the disaggregated as well as at the aggregated level, and likewise indicates the need for a compromise in specification of variables for the model, whose basic data are, in strict terms, "bilateral" or dyadic.

149

The Basis for Comparison of
Dyadic Attributes and Interactions

Although analysis of interaction and attribute matrices will, in the pres
ent phase of the study, utilize canonical correlation in much the same fashion a
in the aggregate phase, the use of this structure for dyadic data is based on
acceptance of an assumption not applicable in the previous analysis. This assumption states that attribute dyads, or pair-wise differentials in national economic characteristics, have conceptual relevance in the explanation of empiri-
cally-measured pair-wise interaction among nations. Since the bases for this
assumption are by no means self-evident, some further discussion of this aspe
of the dyadic model may be enlightening.

In essence, the use of attribute dyads implies that, in the multidimensional space comprising the attribute variable set, the degree of "closeness" o
individual points can be ascertained. The economic or socio-political "distanc
between pairs of points in the attribute space is, then, supposed to form a mutually-reinforcing relationship with the "mix" and volume of interaction betwee
those points.

If the analogy between this abstract attribute space and real (geographic
space is taken further, certain additional working hypotheses may be added. V
may, for example, postulate that close "neighbors" in economic or political
space (i.e., countries whose stage of development and whose administrative
complexions are similar) will experience greater volumes of interaction than
pairs occupying polar extremes in our abstract space. It is not difficult to find
instances where this hypothesis applies. Earlier empirical evidence in this
study indicates that movements of automobiles and other sophisticated manufac
tures commonly take place in greatest volume between countries of similar ecc
nomic development status. Frequently (as with automobiles) the same commod
ity will move in both directions between particular countries, appearing, at a
superficial level, to contravene the notion of comparative advantage. Similari
in cultural characteristics may also explain specific high-volume flows among
nations (as for example in the rice trade of Southeast Asia). In short, it may
not be unrealistic to hypothesize the existence of a "distance decay" effect, wh
operation in some abstract spaces is essentially isomorphic with the effect sho
to operate in geographic space.

However, it would be useful to point out that important exceptions to thi
hypothesized direct relationship between propinquity and volume of interaction
are, perhaps, just as easy to find. Flows of some primary raw materials, fo

example, exhibit a pattern involving origin and destination countries occupying widely disparate positions on the scale of industrial development. Multilateral capital flows, and movements of some classes of labor, likewise take place across substantial "distances" in their respective abstract spaces. In a model which attempts to integrate major forms of economic interaction, then, a sensitivity to this dichotomy between "neighborhood" and "polarizing" effects in various dimensions of the attribute space would appear to be very important.

The disentangling of such effects, at least in the present context, is a task that may best be approached inductively. For the immediate purpose of structuring the dyadic model, however, it will be possible to dispense with statements concerning the direction of relationships between dyadic distances in socioeconomic attributes and volumes of interaction. These will come into play in a later phase of interpretation and evaluation of model output. We need only assert here that complementarity, as a basis for pair-wise interaction, implies a consistent effect of dyadic attribute differentials, but not necessarily a "neighborhood effect," nor conversely a "polarity" in economic characteristics.

Structuring the Dyadic Flow Model

The model structure in this phase of the study is, in its more general aspects, identical to that employed in the aggregate-level study. Matrices of attributes and interactions will be "mapped" into each other by the canonical correlation algorithm, giving successive pairs of vectors from each matrix, between which a maximum correlation is assured.

However, a dilemma of a mechanical nature arises if asymmetric values (e.g., unidirectional flows) occupy one matrix and symmetrical dyadic values occupy the second. The matrix with symmetrical values is triangular, since each i — j dyadic value has a mirror-image j — i value across the main diagonal. The matrix with one-way flows is, on the other hand, a square matrix, since $i \rightarrow j$ flows are not necessarily equivalent to $j \rightarrow i$ movements. Correlation of these matrices as they stand would yield distorted and practically useless results.[1]

A solution to the problem is suggested, however, by our earlier discussion of symmetry in dyadic models.[2] If specific "push" and "pull" values can be

---

[1] This dilemma was recognized by Berry in his study of commodity flows in India. He proposes no formal solution, but adopts the practical expedient of matching triangular elements of attribute and interaction matrices above and below the diagonal respectively. See: Berry, op. cit., p. 200.

[2] See Chapter III, pp. 55-56.

identified and measured for each point in the population, a square rather than triangular attribute matrix will result since measures of stimulus for dyad i — may not be the same as for j — i. Correlation of such a matrix with an inter-action space comprising one-way flows would pose no mechanical problems.

Alternately, where only the same gross scalars are available to measu propensities for interchange at both i and j, the model should, by our previous argument, apply to flow balance or turnover between pairs of points in the pop lation. In this case, both attribute and interaction matrices will be triangular and correlation is, again, quite feasible.

The relevance of these deliberations to the present model should now b apparent. Since, in this study, only the broadest of scalar variables have bee available with suitable reliability and completeness, symmetrical dyads will occupy cells in the attribute matrix. If symmetrical dyadic values are likewis to occupy the interaction matrix, our choice of an approach to flow analysis appears constrained to the examination of trade, migration, and investment fl turnover between pairs of countries.

Variables Measuring Flow Turnover and
Propensity for Dyadic Interaction

The need for data in symmetrical dyadic form as input variables in the present phase of analysis suggests that review of the data set previously em-ployed may be desirable. In this process of review, several points will be emphasized:

(1) our discussion of the theoretical bases of flow analysis, and our experi ence with the aggregate study, should provide guidance in the selection of suitable variables. In particular, examination of intercorrelations, and explanatory "payoff" of variables in the aggregate phase of this stu should permit screening or elimination of redundant variates as well a those of little explanatory power;

(2) we should once again be able to identify variables with "general" or "specific" applicability vis-a-vis the kinds of flows to be examined;

(3) we may be able to identify other variables whose nature precluded thei use in the aggregate study, but which may have theoretical applicabilit in the present dyadic analysis;

(4) we shall have to consider the constraints imposed on variable selectior by the sheer size of the dyadic data sets relative to the limitations on capacity of available computational facilities.

As before, variables are classified in the present phase under the rub of "attribute" or "interaction" measures, but specific variables classified in t "interaction" category in the aggregate analysis will not necessarily remain ir this category in the present section. In effect, both aggregate attributes and

teractions can be thought of as generators of, or propensities for, dyadic interchange among countries, and thus most of the original variables retained for use
a this dyadic phase are categorized here as "attribute" measures. A new inter-
ction matrix has thus to be constructed.

The Dyadic Interaction Matrix

The interaction matrix for this phase of the analysis is composed of only
three variates. These are measures of the volume of total two-way movement
f (1) commodities, (2) long-term migration, and (3) investment capital between
ll pairs of countries in a sample of contemporary nations.

Pair-wise Trade

The source of data for dyadic trade is the same as for the variable Total
Trade discussed in connection with the setting up of the aggregate model.[1] The
values given for pair-wise trade are, as with aggregate trade, based on estimated U.S. dollar value of all goods moving between specific countries of provenance and destination. The original data, when formed into a matrix with
origin countries as rows and destinations as columns, yields an export matrix
(below the main diagonal) and import matrix (above the diagonal) involving each
pair of nations in the sample twice. A measure of trade turnover between pairs
f countries, which is required by the stance we have adopted on the form of the
dyadic model, is then computed by summation of unidirectional elements $i \rightarrow j$
nd $j \rightarrow i$ for each i, j. This yields a flow matrix, with elements displaying the
required bilateral symmetry, for inclusion in the canonical model.

Pair-wise Migration

The matrix of migration flows between pairs of countries, as intimated in
the discussion of data sources for the aggregate model,[2] has been assembled
from numerous sources, predominantly national statistical abstracts and yearbooks. Data are for long-term migrants entering a particular country, who have
given a specific foreign country as place of origin. As was pointed out earlier,
some inconsistencies and discrepancies have been unavoidable in compiling this
matrix, since national definitions of "long term" as against "short term" or
temporary" are occasionally found to differ. Similarly, where some nations

[1] See Chapter I, p. 5.　　[2] See Chapter IV, pp. 72-74.

have not collected data on immigrants arriving from certain other countries, emigration figures from these origin countries to the particular destinations in question have been employed. Once again, these may, in a number of instances be somewhat less reliable than immigration statistics, for reasons cited earlier

Migration turnover between pairs of countries will be the second input variable to the dyadic canonical model. Computation of turnover in this variate is, of course, identical to that discussed for pair-wise Trade.

Pair-wise Capital Flow

The nature and sources of data for the third flow matrix, dyadic capital flows, have not previously been discussed in this study. These data are in the form of U.S. dollar value of bilateral loans, of a long-term nature, made by countries who are members of the Organization for Economic Cooperation and Development (O. E. C. D.). [2] The actual statistical source of the data is the Geographical Distribution of Financial Flows to Less Developed Countries 1960-1964, published by the O. E. C. D. at its headquarters in Brussels. Since the most recent year for which statistics were available was 1964, only the 1963 and 1964 data have been employed in this instance. The two-year mean constitutes an unavoidable departure from our practice of taking a mean for the period 1960-1965 inclusive as the standard time-slice for all data in this study.

It is acknowledged that this abbreviation of the time period may affect comparability of data to the extent of inducing some bias in the results of the analysis, although it is felt that this would not by itself be of radical consequence or cast serious doubt on the validity of major conclusions. A further shortcoming of this data must, however, be noted. Although the majority of capital-exporting western nations are included in the list of donor countries for which data are available, the command economies of the Soviet bloc are once again excluded. In addition, flows of capital among the donor countries themselves,

---

[1] See p. 74.

[2] The O. E. C. D. is an organization of some 20 member nations whose objectives are generally embodied in its title: it aims at promotion of sound and continued economic growth of member nations and also the furnishing of aid to developing economies. This organization is an outgrowth of the older Organization for European Economic Cooperation (O. E. E. C.) which became defunct following the rise of the Common Market in Europe. The growth of new economic problems at the global level and the need for aid to those nations struggling to achieve economic take-off led to renovation of the parent organization as a technical aid source and an investment capital administrator with a major new role of growth promotion in the less-developed world.

hich are likely to be appreciable, are also excluded. This latter fact does con-
train the generality of our conclusions concerning factors surrounding capital
lows, and consequently our conclusions regarding such flows must be made with
ue caution. Despite the shortcomings of these data, they comprise perhaps the
1ost comprehensive, reliable and most readily available body of statistics on
isaggregated, dyadic movements of international investment capital. Their use
ill, it is hoped, vindicate the belief that empirical knowledge of the geographic
ehavior of investment capital, albeit imperfect and incomplete, will be of value
n unraveling the complex interrelationships between economic flows in general
nd economic characteristics of nations which generate them.

he Dyadic Attribute Matrix

In view of our assertion that both aggregate interaction variables and
.ttributes of nations together influence propensities for individual country-to-
:ountry movements, the ideal input into the new attribute matrix would com-
rise in total 91 variables used in the aggregate phase (50 interaction, 41 attri-
ute). However, where 108 countries are included in the sample of observations,
he matrix for each of these 91 variables comprises 108^2 - 108 or 11,556 pieces
f dyadic information. For 91 such matrices, storage and manipulation of these
lata involve enormous amounts of computer storage, far more, in fact, than was
vailable to the author.[1]

The need for parsimony in the selection of dyadic data for the attribute
natrix thus carries the added force of an imposed upper limit on available com-
uter storage. This has necessitated the utilization of procedural steps in prep-
ration of this data matrix that would have been regarded otherwise as unnecessary and perhaps even undesirable. Reduction in the number of sample observa-
ions is the first such step which was found to be necessary.

he Observation Set

For the second time in this study it was found that a compromise had to
e reached between the need for comprehensiveness and completeness, in terms
of the number and nature of suitable input variables, and universality in terms
of the number of observations which could be included. In the aggregate phase
of analysis, the problem of missing data emerged as the main arbiter in deciding

---

[1]Maximum available capacity under normal operating conditions on York
University's I. B. M. 360/50 was 300k or approximately 200,000 bytes.

the outcome of this compromise. Those variables for which inordinately large gaps appeared in the overall distribution were excluded, and those countries which consistently failed to supply data over a wide range of variables were likwise screened from the observation set.

The problem of missing data becomes even more of a dilemma in this dyadic phase of analysis. Each single missing value in the aggregate matrix now becomes magnified to the extent of the total number of dyads in which the country with deficient data is involved. Where even a few variables are affecte in this way for a particular country, very large gaps open up in the dyadic input matrices.

Minimizing these gaps obviously involves removal of offending observations, and consequent further reduction in universality of analytical results. However, this step was taken in conjunction with a review of the group of theoretically-relevant input variables, and a final observation set of 74 nations resulted. The nations included on this list are displayed in Table 6.

Further positive and negative consequences in this reduction of the obse vation set must be noted. On the positive side is the fact that, in terms of avai able computer storage, fewer observations allowed inclusion of more useful variables, and reduction of missing data greatly strengthened any conclusions about the variables involved. On the negative side, however, is the fact of a stronger bias in the final sample toward better-developed nations in the noncommunist world, and a consequent reduction in the generality of any conclusions reached.

It follows, of course, that the observation set of 74 nations must apply t both attribute and interaction matrices. The final input matrix of interaction variables thus comprises, in this dyadic analysis, $(74^2 - 74) \times 3$ separate recorded interactions. The procedure adopted to select final variables for the canonical correlation analysis is shown in the stages enumerated below.

Identification of Underlying Dimensions in Monadic Attribute Variables

Since all 91 monadic variables could clearly not be used in the final mod the expedient of "screening" redundant variables was utilized in conjunction wit reduction in the observation set. This involved (1) reexamination of the factor output from the aggregate phase, and the correlation matrices associated with preliminary manipulation of aggregate data, to eliminate variables which displayed low explanatory power vis-a-vis important flow patterns, or high inter-

TABLE 6

THE DYADIC STUDY: SAMPLE NATIONS

Country No.	Country	Country No.	Country
1	Congo (Zaïre)	38	Indonesia
2	Ethiopia	39	Iran
3	Ghana	40	Hong Kong
4	Kenya	41	Israel
5	Morocco	42	Japan
6	Nigeria	43	Jordan
7	Senegal	44	South Korea
8	South Africa	45	Kuwait
9	Sudan	46	Malaysia
10	Tunisia	47	Pakistan
11	Uganda	48	Philippines
12	United Arab Republic	49	Singapore
13	Canada	50	Syria
14	Costa Rica	51	Thailand
15	El Salvador	52	Turkey
16	Guatemala	53	South Vietnam
17	Honduras	54	Austria
18	Jamaica	55	Belgium-Luxembourg
19	Mexico	56	Denmark
20	Nicaragua	57	Finland
21	Panama	58	France
22	Trinidad and Tobago	59	West Germany
23	U.S.A.	60	Greece
24	Argentina	61	Hungary
25	Brazil	62	Iceland
26	Chile	63	Ireland
27	Colombia	64	Italy
28	Ecuador	65	Netherlands
29	Guyana	66	Norway
30	Peru	67	Portugal
31	Venezuela	68	Spain
32	Afghanistan	69	Sweden
33	Burma	70	Switzerland
34	Ceylon	71	United Kingdom
35	Taiwan	72	Yugoslavia
36	Cyprus	73	Australia
37	India	74	New Zealand

correlation with more potent, theoretically relevant variables; (2) factor analysis of remaining, preselected variables to determine the basic dimensions of variation in the data set, and to permit final selection of highly independent attribute variables.

The output of the first of these two steps comprised 59 monadic variables, representing a fairly subjective quotient of theoretically more relevant and em-

TABLE 7

THE DYADIC ATTRIBUTE MATRIX: VARIABLES
RETAINED FROM AGGREGATE STUDY

Variable No.	Variable Name
1	Total Net Capital Flow
2	Multilateral Capital Flow
3	Discount Rate
4	Wage Index
5	Long Term Immigration
6	Long Term Emigration
7	Total Population Density
8	Per Capita Gross National Product
9	Per Capita Gross Domestic Product
10	Per Capita Fixed Capital
11	Metropolitan Population
12	Percent Metropolitan Population
13	Ratio of Imports to Gross National Product
14	Ratio of Exports to Gross National Product
15	Accessibility
16	Unemployment
17	Area of Land Surface
18	Total Population
19	Mail Received
20	Mail Sent
21	Telegrams Received
22	Telegrams Sent
23	Drawings from International Monetary Fund
24	Repurchases from International Monetary Fund
25	Gold Holdings
26	Foreign Exchange Holdings
27	Living Cost
28	Gross National Product
29	Gross Domestic Product
30	Gross Fixed Capital Formation
31	Exports by S.I.T.C. Category: Food
32	Exports by S.I.T.C. Category: Raw Materials
33	Exports by S.I.T.C. Category: Fuel
34	Exports by S.I.T.C. Category: Chemicals
35	Exports by S.I.T.C. Category: Manufactures
36	Exports by S.I.T.C. Category: Transportation Equipment
37	Total Exports
38	Imports by S.I.T.C. Category: Food
39	Imports by S.I.T.C. Category: Raw Materials
40	Imports by S.I.T.C. Category: Fuel
41	Imports by S.I.T.C. Category: Chemicals
42	Imports by S.I.T.C. Category: Manufactures
43	Imports by S.I.T.C. Category: Transport Equipment
44	Total Imports
45	Economically Active Population in Agriculture
46	Economically Active Population in Manufacturing
47	Economically Active Population in Building and Public Wor'

TABLE 7--Continued

Variable No.	Variable Name
48	Economically Active Population in Commerce, Banking and Insurance
49	Economically Active Population in Transportation and Communication
50	Total Economically Active Population
51	Proportion of Domestic Product from Agriculture
52	Proportion of Domestic Product from Industry
53	Proportion of Domestic Product from Manufacturing
54	Proportion of Domestic Product from Construction
55	Proportion of Domestic Product from Transport/Communications
56	Proportion of Domestic Product from Wholesale/Retail Trade
57	Trade Balance in S. I. T. C. Categories: Food
58	Trade Balance in S. I. T. C. Categories: Manufactures
59	Trade Balance in S. I. T. C. Categories: Fuels

irically more significant measures of national economic characteristics. These variables are displayed in Table 7.

Once again, on this table, attributes which apply generally as stimuli to all three flows can be distinguished, after the fashion described in the aggregate study. Alternately, of the old interaction variables included in this table, obviously such measures as total imports and exports relate quite specifically to the pattern of dyadic trade, whereas total long-term immigration and emigration, and multilateral capital flow relate respectively to pair-wise flows of migrants and investment funds. Some other aggregate interaction variables, however, may be more general in their relationships with dyadic flows. For instance, imports and exports of raw materials may be associated with flows of capital and labor, total receipts of mail might index a propensity for commodity and labor movement (although the results of the aggregate study indicate a closer relationship with migration than with trade).

Of the 32 variables rejected as a result of this screening procedure, roughly half were eliminated because of inordinately high intercorrelation with other, more potent variables or variable clusters. Thus, the variables Bilateral Grants and Loans were eliminated because they had lower loading values than Multilateral Capital Flows, which, in conjunction with Total Net Capital Flows, seemed to contain most of the relevant information on movement of investment funds. In the same fashion, National Income, as distinguished from Gross National Product (G. N. P.), seemed to be less powerful as an explanatory variable, but nevertheless duplicative of the information given by G. N. P.

Other variables were eliminated as a result of the low explanatory value they displayed in the aggregate phase. In this class are the "Miscellaneous" or "Other" categories used in productivity, employment and trade variable sets.

Factor Reduction of Combined Aggregate Data Sets

The second step in final selection of input variables for the attribute matrix entailed subjection of the 59 preselected variates (log-transformed and standardized, and with missing data replaced, as previously, with mean values to principal axis factor analysis with varimax rotation. The results of this analysis indicated that thirteen factors with eigenvalues > 1.00 essentially described the dimensions of variation in the original set.

Amalgamation of variables from both attribute and interaction matrice in the aggregate study naturally led to the emergence of a somewhat different group of factors, but, as will be seen, maintenance of many of the original factor patterns is a noteworthy feature of the new factor output. However, it is nc our intention to give detailed interpretations of individual factors at this point since this would be largely repetitive of the discussions in Chapters V and VI. We shall, however, wish to consider relevant general features of the new patterns, in an appropriately broad fashion.

Factor loadings for the 59 input variables on the resultant 13 factors are shown in Table 8. The highest-loading variables on the seven most significant factors are underlined to identify them as input variates to the dyadic attri bute matrix.

Although the primary objective of this factoring procedure has been the identification of statistically-independent variables (i. e., those loading most significantly on each separate factor) for use in the canonical model, a number of other interesting facets are revealed from a perusal of the factor loading patterns. It will be useful to touch upon these aspects here.

It has been noted, for example, that some factors comprise very similar sets of high-loading variables to those in the aggregate study (as is only to be expected). Thus Factor 3 (9.6 per cent of total variance) essentially duplicates aggregate Factor 1 described in Chapter VI, being an identification of a pattern involving demographic/occupational structure of the countries in the sample. Highest loading variable on this factor was Percent of Active Population in Commerce, Banking, and Insurance.

Factor 4 (6.59 per cent of variance) is likewise a repetition of another factor in the aggregate phase of this study, pointing to the phenomenon of relative urban industrial development. Highest loading variable is Percent Metropolitan Population (0.8295), while other significant loadings are recorded for Industrial Output as Percent of Domestic Product (loading: 0.7089), Manufacturing Output and Agricultural Output as Percent of Domestic Product (with loadings of 0.5294 and -0.5078 respectively).

Factor 5, which contributes 4.54 per cent to total variance, reveals high loadings by the two variables Mail Received (0.8290) and Mail Sent (0.8119), and picks out a roughly similar pattern to a factor in the aggregate attribute matrix. This earlier pattern showed that mail flows were allied to flows of long-term migrants. (Here, the variables Long-term Immigrants and Emigrants have loadings of 0.3069 and 0.3695 respectively on Factor 13.)

A number of other factors in Table 8 tend to bear out some conclusions more precisely drawn in the aggregate canonical analysis. Thus, Factor 2 (10.2 per cent of variance) points to a group of measures which describe the income or productivity of countries and relate this to the importance of external trade as a contributory element in total productivity. Thus, variables such as Gross or Per-Capita National Product figure prominently in this factor pattern, but highest loading is achieved by the variable Ratio of Imports to G.N.P.

Factor 8 displays a pattern reminiscent of another of the canonical variates in the aggregate study, detailing a relationship between the flow variables Long-term Immigration and Emigration and the attribute of Accessibility (Urban Population Potential). The latter variable loaded most significantly on this new factor.

Yet other factor patterns reveal new or altered combinations of input variables as compared with the corresponding aggregate factor study. Factor 1, for instance, explains nearly 26 per cent of total variance, and picks out a group of high-loading variates which include demographic, monetary, and productivity characteristics of countries as well as aspects of their trade dealings with the rest of the world. The pattern which this factor seems to be highlighting is one which surrounds contemporary commodity interchange. It suggests that large trading nations are also nations with high productivity, with a predominantly urban and industrial orientation. They demonstrate propensities for importing and exporting the necessities for maintaining industrialized economies as well as the products of these economies. The highest loading variable on this factor is Chemical Imports (0.9187).

TABLE 8

FACTOR ANALYSIS OF COMBINED ATTRIBUTE
AND INTERACTION VARIABLES
(Variables Selected for Dyadic Model Are Underlined)

Variable No.	Variable Name	Loading >0.4700

Factor 1
(25.95 per cent of variance)

Variable No.	Variable Name	Loading
<u>41</u>	Imports by S.I.T.C. Category: Chemicals	0.9187
<u>44</u>	Total Imports	0.9154
43	Imports by S.I.T.C. Category: Transport Equipment	0.9074
37	Total Exports	0.9020
42	Imports by S.I.T.C. Category: Manufactures	0.8960
39	Imports by S.I.T.C. Category: Raw Materials	0.8705
35	Exports by S.I.T.C. Category: Manufactures	0.8505
40	Imports by S.I.T.C. Category: Fuel	0.8393
38	Imports by S.I.T.C. Category: Food	0.8354
34	Exports by S.I.T.C. Category: Chemicals	0.7950
11	Metropolitan Population	0.7803
32	Exports by S.I.T.C. Category: Raw Materials	0.7387
31	Exports by S.I.T.C. Category: Food	0.7196
53	Contribution of Manufacturing Sector to Tot. Domes. Prod.	0.6302
29	G.D.P.	0.6123
28	G.N.P.	0.6051
18	Total Population	0.6012
30	Gross Fixed Capital Formation	0.5990
51	Contribution of Agricultural Sector to Tot. Domes. Product	-0.5946
52	Contribution of Industry to Domestic Product	0.5289
26	Foreign Exchange Reserves	0.5252
23	Drawings from I.M.F.	0.5189

Factor 2
(10.25 per cent of variance)

Variable No.	Variable Name	Loading
<u>13</u>	Ratio of Imports to G.N.P.	0.9093
<u>14</u>	Ratio of Exports to G.N.P.	0.8809
9	Per Capita G.N.P.	0.8528
10	Per Capita Fixed Capital	0.8354
8	Per Capita G.N.P.	0.8039
30	Gross Fixed Capital Formation	0.7195
29	G.D.P.	0.7086
28	G.N.P.	0.6918

Factor 3
(9.63 per cent of variance)

Variable No.	Variable Name	Loading
<u>48</u>	Economically Active Pop. in Commerce, Banking, and Ins.	0.8876
<u>47</u>	Economically Active Pop. in Building and Public Works	0.8586
45	Economically Active Population in Agriculture	0.7747
50	Total Economically Active Population	0.7721
49	Economically Active Pop. in Transportation/Communication	0.7546
46	Economically Active Population in Manufacturing	0.7203
18	Total Population	0.5313
11	Metropolitan Population	0.4928

TABLE 8--Continued

Variable No.	Variable Name	Loading >0.4700
	Factor 4 (6.59 per cent of variance)	
12	Percent Metropolitan Population	0.8295
52	Contribution of Industry to Domestic Product	0.7089
53	Contribution of Manufacturing to Domestic Product	0.5294
51	Contribution of Agriculture to Domestic Product	-0.5078
	Factor 5 (4.54 per cent of variance)	
19	Mail Received	0.8290
20	Mail Sent	0.8119
	Factor 6 (4.31 per cent of variance)	
2	Aggregate Multilateral Capital Flow	0.5990
59	Fuel Trade Balance	-0.5787
3	Discount Rate	0.5548
	Factor 7 (3.67 per cent of variance)	
55	Contribution of Transport/Commun. Sector to Domes. Prod.	0.8259
54	Contribution of Construction Sector to Domestic Product	0.5806
	Factor 8 (3.66 per cent of variance)	
15	Accessibility	0.7629
5	Long Term Immigration	0.5682
6	Long Term Emigration	0.5434
	Factor 9 (3.58 per cent of variance)	
7	Population Density	0.8888
17	Total Land Area	-0.7661
	Factor 10 (3.30 per cent of variance)	
56	Contribution of Wholesale/Retail Trade to Domestic Product	0.8356
27	Living Costs	0.5962
16	Unemployment Level	-0.5070
	Factor 11 (3.04 per cent of variance)	
23	I.M.F. Repurchases	-0.7864
26	Foreign Exchange Reserves	-0.5501

TABLE 8--Continued

Variable No.	Variable Name	Loading >0.4700
	Factor 12 (2.79 per cent of variance)	
57	Trade Balance in Food	0.8596
31	Exports by S.I.T.C. Category: Food	0.6198
	Factor 13 (2.46 per cent of variance)	
58	Trade Balance in Manufacturing	0.6911
33	Exports by S.I.T.C. Category: Food	0.6075

Note: Factors are listed in descending order of contribution to total variance f
lowing Varimax Rotation.

Factor 9 is also a new pattern, but contributes little (3.58 per cent) to total variance and reveals only two high-loading variables: Population Density (0.8888) and Surface Area (-0.7661). The label for this factor can clearly be taken from its highest loading variate.

Factor 6 contributes more (4.3 per cent) to total variance, and reveals three prominent variables: Aggregate Flow of Multilateral Capital (0.5990), Discount Rate (0.5548), and Fuel Trade Balance (-0.5787). The relationship between the first two variables is logical and clear. In the present context, thi factor seems obviously to provide a measure of the likelihood that capital trans fers will take place between various pairs of countries. The association of Fue Trade Balance with this factor is not, however, entirely self-explanatory. Sta ing this association in a naive form, it appears that nations with positive trade balance in fuels (greater exports than imports) tend also to have lower discount rates and lower levels of capital transaction with multilateral lending agencies. This may be interpreted as an interesting sidelight of the more general pattern of aggregate capital flow, perhaps one to be borne in mind in later interpretatio of canonically-derived patterns of attributes and flows.

Factor 7 (3.67 per cent of variance) shows only two significant loadings These are contributed by Transport and Communications Output as Percent of Domestic Product (0.8259), and Construction Industry Output as Percent of Domestic Product (0.5806). This factor provides a perspective on some aspec of the internal organization of nations that could prove useful to understanding volumes of flows to and from countries. The internal communications of a nati

and the degree to which this contributes to total productivity, as well as the relative productivity of the construction industry, could both be thought of as indices of the rate of development of a country. They point specifically to those nations whose economies are just experiencing the phase of rapid "drive to maturity," featuring rapid development of systems of social overhead capital.

Factors 8 through 13 contribute less than 4 per cent each to total variance contained in the original 59 variates. None of these were consequently considered for inclusion, through the medium of a highest-loading variable, in the canonical model of dyadic interaction. Of these five factors, No. 8 contributed most to total variance, and its highest loading variable (accessibility) would have been chosen to represent this dimension had the contribution of this factor to total variance been slightly more significant.

The seven variables selected from the factor analysis are thus, in a sense, representative of seven clusters of high-loading variables which comprised the bulk of the 59 input variates. At the same time, they form surrogates for the considerable number of original aggregate variables which, because of high intercorrelation, were screened in the preliminary review of potential input data. The high loadings of the selected variates on their respective orthogonal dimensions ensures maximum independence of attributes in the canonical model.

Transformation of Monadic to Dyadic Variates

The seven variates which emerged from the principal axis factoring procedure had yet to be transformed into pair-wise differentials as demanded by our hypothesis concerning operation of the "distance" effect in the socioeconomic "space." This step was performed by simply entering the absolute difference between the values (standardized and log-transformed) in a matrix of pair-wise economic differentials. The resultant matrix was then conserved as the major part of the Dyadic Attribute Matrix which will form an input to the canonical model.

New Dyadic Variables

A number of other attributes of nations exist as possibly significant influences on patterns of economic interaction but which, because of their peculiarly dyadic nature, could not be included in the aggregate study. Four such variables will be considered for inclusion in the present model. Two of these relate to economic/political relationships between individual countries which on empirical

grounds must be considered important potential moderators of trade and factor-
flow volume. These are Tariff Agreements, and Date of Independence. Two
others express relationships between nations in geographic space which conceiv
ably could affect volumes of interaction. These are Distance (shortest angular
distance between urban population centers of nations[1]), and Contiguity. An
explanation of the nature of these variables, the empirical measures selected to
represent them in the model, and the way in which they might theoretically
explain aspects of economic interaction, now follows.

Tariff Agreements

The unhindered development of geographic specialization in production is
according to the comparative advantage theory of trade, supposed to promote
mutual benefit and prosperity in trading partners. However, deliberate hindrance of trade has long been in use as a weapon by which nations attempt to
conserve what they perceive as their own economic advantage. The most commonly applied impediments to completely free interchange are import duties
and quotas. Others (export duties, embargoes, exchange restrictions) also
exist, but are perhaps less general in their effect.

Tariffs or customs duties have several objectives, which may variously
result in the imposition of moderately light to quite prohibitive restrictions on
trade. One of the primary objectives of non-prohibitive tariffs is the raising of
revenue for the destination country of goods shipments (an import duty) or the
origin country (export duty). A second important function of tariffs is the protection of domestic industry, which, according to the standard argument, would
be unable to germinate (in the case of infant industries) or maintain adequate
growth (in the case of "developing" industries) if unrestricted imports of competing products were permitted. Import duties, or quotas, are thus the mechan
isms whereby local commodities are permitted to compete with imports on the
domestic market. Alternately, export duties or restrictions for some commod
ities have the effect of increasing their supply and lowering their price on the
domestic market (since a foreign outlet for the product is denied), thus stimulating home consumption.

The imposition of tariffs or duties on imports may vary quite significantly in a nation's dealings with others. This will depend on numerous political, strategic, and economic factors such as traditional attitudes and relation-

[1] See explanation of the derivation of this variable on pp. 80-81.

ships, formal economic treaties, or the possibility of retaliatory counter-measures which might retard exports to a country against whose own goods an import duty is contemplated.

Assembly of data on tariff agreements for the present phase of this study involved a choice between several alternative ways of measuring and classifying relationships. It would have been possible, as in some previous studies, to use dummy or nominal variables for recording participation or non-participation in bilateral (or, for that matter, multilateral) trade agreements. There were two arguments against employing a series of dummy variables, however. The first of these was the previously discussed imperative of a computational limitation on the number of variables that may be included. The second was the conviction that propensity for trade between one country and another might vary with, and thus be indexed by, the kind of trade agreements which bound those particular trading partners. Thus, a rough ordinal scheme might prove more useful for expression of trade-pact influences than simply a series of nominal indices. The scheme ultimately devised for use in this study is shown in Table 9.

TABLE 9

MEMBERSHIP OF PARTNER COUNTRIES IN
FORMAL TRADE AGREEMENTS

	No Trade Agreement	Bilateral	Multilateral		
			Member-ship in GATT	Customs Union Free-Trade Area	Semi-Political and Other
Index Value	0	1	2	3	4

This scheme implies that multilateral trade agreements of a semi-political nature, or of the customs-union or free-trade-area variety are a more influential regulator of propensities for high-volume trade among partner nations than simply membership in the General Agreement on Tariffs and Trade (GATT), [1]

---

[1] As of June 1, 1966, sixty-eight nations were members of the General Agreement on Tariffs and Trade. This agreement, which came into being in 1947, has the objective of substantially reducing tariffs and similar impediments to trade among member nations, as well as the aim of eliminating discrimination against exports of these countries. A secondary objective is the promotion of stable commodity prices and improved access to world markets for under-developed countries.

and that multilateral agreements as a whole are more potent that simple bilateral agreements or no formal trade ties at all.

Traditional Political/Economic Ties

Students of international trade have frequently pointed to the obvious importance of cultural/political ties among nations as a regulator of volume of trade in the contemporary world. Indeed, it is apparent that the old argument about "trade following the flag" enjoys considerable empirical verification. The same, of course, may be demonstrated for movement of labor and capital.

The nature of such economic/political ties varies, but it is probably safe to assume that in most nations patterns of livelihood reflect a certain degree of inheritance from a past period when the political and economic system was dominated by some outside nation or culture. In very many instances, this relationship of dominance and subservience was clearly of a type we should call "colonial." Where a country had been under colonial rule for an appreciable time, its economy would, in the normal course of events, become deeply integrated with that of the "mother" country, and it would be natural to expect that a residual effect of economic domination might linger after the granting (or even seizure) of independence, to the extent that certain patterns of external economic relations might still be observed. In other cases, where the domination from outside may have taken the form of a relatively brief occupation, or a subordination of an already advanced economy, the strength and longevity of residual patterns of interaction might be expected to be considerably smaller. The strength of any past political effects in present-day economic patterns would also intuitively depend on the relative recency with which a nation gained political independence.

These considerations have been incorporated into the present study in the variable Year of Independence/Nationhood, which shows for a particular nation the date at which it obtained recognized legal existence as a state, and the country which most recently exerted dominance over it for a period of more than 5 years. Nations which have been fortunate enough not to have experienced domination by an outside political power are represented in this set of observations by the year of attainment of legal (i.e., internationally recognized) nationhood. Countries which have been dominated by more than one external power for greater than five years at a time have this fact recorded in terms of the year in which the external control was removed in each case.

Distance and Contiguity

The method by which the Dyadic Distance between consecutive pairs of countries has been calculated was discussed in detail in Chapter IV. It should be stressed again that the distance measure being employed is actually angular rather than linear distance or cost or time equivalents. The use of this measure has been prompted by the greater facility it offers in calculating locational differentials and making comparisons of these, and also because of the nature of angular measure as a transformation which "damps down" skewness in linear distance.

The variable Contiguity has been included to take account of the special opportunities for interaction among countries which share common borders. In selecting an empirical measure to represent this contiguity effect, we have made the assumption that, ceteris paribus, the probability of interaction between a country and its immediate neighbors is some function of the length of common boundaries. The values of contiguity used, then, are approximate lengths of international land boundaries obtained by tracing the borders from relatively small-scale, conic-projection maps in the Rand McNally International Atlas.

Completion of Dyadic Attribute Matrix

Completion of the attribute matrix could now be achieved by selection of variates from among this set of four intrinsically dyadic attribute variables, which practical necessity decreed should be dealt with separately in the initial stages of preparing data for testing our model. These four variables, pair-wise distance, tariff agreements, date of independence, and length of common land boundary, were subjected to principal axis factoring in a fashion identical to that used for the 59 variables previously discussed. The results of this process consisted in two factors, indicating that two of the four variables adequately explained the total variance in the set.

The first factor accounted for 33.32 per cent of total variance, and the variables loading on this dimension were Pair-wise Distance and Length of Common Land Boundary. The pattern described by this factor, then, could be interpreted as a measure of the "nearness" or "propinquity" of nations in geographic space. Loadings by both variates were almost identical, with Distance recording a slightly higher coefficient. Consequently, this variable was selected to be placed in the dyadic attribute matrix. This measure will, in fact, perform in some ways as a more suitable replacement for the variable Accessibility, which was screened from the attribute set due to the (admittedly narrow) failure of

Factor 8 to contribute a sufficiently high percentage of total variance.

The second factor, contributing 26.23 per cent of the variance, comprises the remaining two variates in this group, Tariff Agreements (loading: 0.7361) and Date of Nationhood/Independence (loading: 0.7110). This factor could thus be labeled Political/Economic Ties, and its highest-loading variable Tariff Agreements, complements the group of nine variables which constitute our dyadic attribute set.

The attribute and interaction matrices, comprising sets of symmetrical dyadic values for 74^2 - 74 different pairs of countries, were then subjected to canonical analysis. A description of the procedure and results of the dyadic analysis, and an appraisal of the worth of the canonical model employed, form the subject matter of the following chapter.

CHAPTER IX

CANONICAL ANALYSIS OF COUNTRY-TO-COUNTRY
FLOWS AND ECONOMIC ATTRIBUTES

In this chapter we shall apply to empirical data the canonical attribute-interaction model whose structure and input variables were discussed in Chapter VIII. This model, as explained earlier, envisages that volumes of commodity exchange, labor migration and capital flow between pairs of countries both affect and are affected by disparities in selected economic characteristics of countries. The degree of disparity is hypothesized to act as an index of the strength of incentives as well as impediments to the particular forms of interaction being analysed. Canonical correlation is applied, as before, with the objective of facilitating precise identification and interpretation of flow-attribute relationships.

In structuring the dyadic model, we have attempted to draw as much as possible on experience gained in the aggregate phase of this study. The model used in that phase has, indeed, provided both technical and conceptual input to the proposed dyadic construct. The technical contributions have been mainly in the area of data selection, enabling us to pick out of a welter of potentially useful variables a small group of independent variates which index deep-seated, complex patterns of variation. The conceptual input to the present model includes the furnishing of empirical verification for the hypothesized broad relationships among flows and attributes which have guided the structuring of the dyadic-level model.

This chapter will, to some degree, act as an extension of the aggregate study, but in other important ways it represents an attack on quite separate and distinctive dimensions of flow analysis. Our goals in the present instance will, then, be the provision of answers to the following questions about country-to-country flows:

(1) what are the patterns of relationships between dyadic flows and economic characteristics of nations?

(2) to what extent is it possible to determine the effects of degrees of similarity (neighborhood) or marked discrepancy (polarity) in economic characteristics on volumes and "mixes" of flows?

171

(3) which flows appear to be complementary and which are mutually substitutive?

In treating these questions concerning dyadic flows we will need to give conside ation also to the following two questions:

(4) to what extent does the friction of distance affect specific flows and thei complementary or substitutionary relationships with other forms of inter action?

(5) in what ways do the results of this dyadic study reinforce or contradict the results of the aggregate analysis?

Identification of Dyadic Flow-Attribute Relationships through Application of Canonical Correlation

Answers to these questions concerning dyadic flow-attribute relationships are contained in the results of a canonical analysis, displayed in Table 10 Input data for this analysis comprised the 3 interaction and 9 attribute variables discussed in the previous chapter, covering the $(\frac{74^2 - 74}{2})$ dyads in the study sample. Three canonical vectors emerged from this analysis, representing three basically different dimensions or patterns of relationship in the set of attribute and flow variates. Interpretation of these vectors, as in the aggregate model, is in terms of the size and sign of loadings of input variates on the individual vectors.

By comparison with the results of the aggregate canonical model, the vectorial patterns of relationship in this dyadic analysis are quite weak (the highest canonical correlation is only 0.32). A reason for this could be the greater amount of randomness or "noise" inherent in disaggregated data of this sort, an effect which our reduction of sample size attempted to minimize, but which apparently is still disappointingly large. Notwithstanding this fact, a detailed examination of the loadings of dyadic flow and attribute variates on the three resultant vectors shows some readily interpretable and theoretically significant relationships, which suggest appropriate answers to the questions we are seeking to resolve in this chapter.

In using dyadic variates in the interpretation of vector patterns, however we should bear in mind that these variates were expressly chosen to represent more complex factor patterns. The larger number of original variables making up these factors were displayed in Table 8, Chapter VIII. It is appropriate that, in our interpretation of relationships, we look not only at the associated variables themselves, but beyond them to the basic factor patterns which they index.

TABLE 10

DYADIC CANONICAL ANALYSIS

Variates	Canonical Vectors (Loadings)		
	Vector 1	Vector 2	Vector 3
Interaction			
1. Pairwise Trade	0.9648	-0.2915	-0.0579
2. Pairwise Migration	0.1739	0.9295	-0.3652
3. Pairwise Capital Flow	0.0246	0.2350	0.9875
Attribute			
1. Multilateral Capital	-0.2250	0.3389	-0.4195
2. Percent Metropolitan Population	-0.0189	0.0189	0.2082
3. Ratio of Imports to G.N.P.	-0.1049	0.1072	-0.2200
4. Mail Received	0.1806	-0.2024	0.3439
5. Chemical Imports	0.3042	-0.1260	-0.6268
6. Employment in Commerce, Banking and Insurance	0.3177	-0.1866	0.2214
7. Employment in Transport and Communications	-0.0777	-0.0178	-0.1988
8. Dyadic Distance	-0.4680	-0.1714	0.6230
9. Political/Economic Ties	0.4404	0.7560	0.4006
Canonical Correlation	0.3227	0.2579	0.0653

Vector 1: Relationships of Pairwise Trade to
Physical and Economic "Distance"

The dominant flow-attribute relationship revealed by the first dyadic vector is an inverse association (canonical correlation: 0.32) linking the volume of
commodity flow between pairs of countries and the distance which separates them.
Because this is an inverse association, we may say that close neighbors tend to
experience high volumes of commodity interchange, while countries separated
by greater physical distance record correspondingly smaller flows of trade.
Since the distance variable was employed in this study as a surrogate for contiguity of nations as well, it might be legitimate to infer that the existence of long
common boundaries between nations is a relatively powerful inducement to commodity interaction.

This empirical relationship between distance and trade is highly significant in the present study, impinging on the basic theoretical underpinnings of
flow theory, and pointing up some differences in the role of this variable as an
influence on individual as against aggregate flows. Closer analysis of this relationship in a comparative context (incorporating relative significance of distance

to various flow complexes) is certainly desirable, and will be undertaken in a later section of this chapter.

A second interesting relationship revealed by the first vector involves the variable Political/Economic Ties, which is shown to have a moderately strong influence on volumes of dyadic trade. In interpreting this relationship, we must keep in mind that the measure of political/economic association is based on trade and tariff agreements among countries, and is an ordinal measure rather than a "distance" measure as in the case of most other attribute variables employed. Thus, a higher degree of "connectedness" of countries in multilateral or bilateral trade pacts is recorded in this ordinal scheme by higher scalar values.

Hence, the positive loading of this variate on Vector 1 indicates that closeness of nations through political/economic trade ties has a decided bearing on the volumes of trade moving between partner countries. Those nations conjoined in traditional, semi-political relationships with other countries, or in economic unions of the common-market or free-trade area type tend, as one would expect, to record highest volumes of inter-group trade flow. Membership in GATT tends to engender volumes of flow which generally exceed those between countries of our sample not participating in multilateral commodity agreements, but somewhat less than nations which have entered into closer economic or political association with others.

While it is clear, from the evidence presented, that the granting of trade preferences has bearing on the way in which a country's trade volume is concentrated or dispersed among its trading partners, it would be taking this evidence perhaps too far to conclude that trade agreements actually determine total volumes emanating from or terminating in a particular country. It may be, in other words, that tariff agreements have a trade diverting, rather than trade generating role. It is not feasible, from our data, to distinguish confidently which is the more likely of the two possibilities.

Other associations which might be pointed out in the loading pattern for Vector 1 are those involving the disparity of commercial development in trading partners and of behavior in respect of chemical importation. In both cases, to obtain the full significance of the recorded association, our interpretation should take into account the factorial pattern which each variable was chosen to represent, and not merely the specific connotations of the variates themselves.

Thus, the variable Employment in Commerce, Banking, and Insurance, as we saw earlier, is the highest loading (and therefore representative) variable

f Factor 3 in the combined factor analysis of aggregate flow-attribute variables
Table 8). This variable thus indexes a complex pattern surrounding the size of
ne economically active population of countries (since a majority of variables
ealing with this aspect of a nation's economic structure load heavily on this fac-
or).

The interpretation which appears to be suggested by this specific associa-
ion (bearing in mind the underlying factor patterns) is that economies which are
issimilar in structure, and hence in size of various sectors, tend to experience
orrespondingly large volumes of commodity interchange. In more concrete
erms, trade appears to be stimulated where pairs of countries are markedly
issimilar in the size of their commercial and manufacturing sectors (as sug-
ested by the positive loading of Employment in Commerce, Banking and Insur-
nce, and the prominence of industrial sectors in Dyadic Factor 3). The stimu-
us in this case is a "polar" rather than "neighborhood" effect, since large
ather than small disparities are indicated by the positive loadings. A rather
acile (although probably permissible) general interpretation might be that this
attern verifies the operation of some form of comparative advantage among
rading partners. The comparative advantage, in this case, seems to be re-
lected in fairly strong geographic specialization in output from different produc-
ive sectors, calling forth large volumes of commodity interchange between
ations with appropriate "complementarity."

Polarization with respect to a facet of total import propensity is also evi-
enced by the loading for Chemical Imports. This variable, as Factor 1 in
Table 8 shows, is representative of a cluster of variables detailing a nation's
ropensities[1] for trade and level of productive output in terms of the absolute
ize of its economy. The variable Total Imports, it will be noted, is only slightly
ess correlated with this underlying dimension. The relationship of this factor
attern, as indexed by Chemical Imports, with the dyadic trade variate is cer-
ainly worthy of an explanation.

However, clear and unequivocal interpretation of this association is diffi-
ult, since several possible alternate explanations can be put forward. What the
loadings for Trade and Chemical Imports appear to indicate is that the volume of
trade between two countries is larger, the greater the absolute difference between their respective propensities for importing commodities. From this we

---

[1] It will be recalled that, in Chapter VIII, aggregate data were selected for
inclusion in the dyadic model as measures of the propensities of countries for
specific forms of pairwise interaction.

could infer, for example, that countries of vastly different size experience heaviest volumes of dyadic trade.

Yet, this interpretation seems incongruous, since we would expect large trading partners to have greatest trade volumes. And indeed, if we assume that the larger the absolute size of a country's propensities for trade, the greater will be its absolute disparity in this regard with respect to all other (including large) countries, the latter interpretation is possible in this case, and the form may be discarded. Very large countries, in other words, although relatively similar to each other in size, may have greater absolute disparities in propensity for imports than much smaller (albeit relatively dissimilar) nations.

Another interpretation of this "polar" effect in relation to volume of trade is possible, in view of the nature of the relevant attribute variable as an index for a pattern of trade which has been aggregated with respect to commodity composition. Thus, the index we are using (disparity in propensity for chemical imports) may be replicating a comparative advantage effect for production and consumption not only of this commodity group, but also for other components of total trade such as food, raw materials, and fuels. In all of these groups, propensities for importation would be greatly disparate among trading partners, since one partner would record strong positive trade balances for the commodity and the other a strong negative balance. Admittedly, this pattern does not seem to hold in the case of manufactures trade, for which the variable we employed is also an index. However, it is conceivable that, for all commodity sectors taken together, a large disparity in the propensity for importation really expresses the individual polarized elements of demand for specific commodity groups. If this were the case, the positive association of dyadic trade volume and size of the disparity in propensity for total (and chemical) imports would not be incongruous.

The remaining variable loadings on Vector 1 were not sufficiently strong to warrant a detailed attempt at interpreting underlying patterns of association.

Vector 2: Relationship of Labor Mobility and Political/Economic Integration

In the second vector the interaction-attribute relationship is dominated by Pairwise Migration and Political-economic Ties. The relationship is clear but has a correlation coefficient of only 0.26. The high positive loadings of both the migration variable, and the variable describing degree of formal economic ties among interacting economies, lead to the interpretation of this vectorial pat tern as a description of close economic and political integration as an environment most strongly conducive to labor mobility.

Indeed, the degree of integration among nations appears significantly more effectual in the stimulation of labor flows than even in the inducement of trade, at least when viewed against relative effects of other stimuli.

Thus, in the period under review, relatively free movement of persons among ex-colonial and metropolitan countries of the British and French communities (and lesser erstwhile colonial associations) seems to have been more enhanced by the existence of these supranational affiliations than have the flows of trade. The common market and free-trade areas, in the same fashion, appear to have experienced large exchanges of labor as a consequence of their formal provisions for free movement of persons, and the prohibition of job discrimination against migrant workers. The inducements to movement of labor, in other words, seem to be psychological (in the sense that similarities in language and customs are seen by prospective migrants as positive advantages in selecting closely affiliated countries) as well as purely economic.

Among the remaining attribute variables which seemingly draw forth high levels of migration, the loading for multilateral capital dealings indicates that it is the next most influential. Its positive loading implies that this variable acts on dyadic labor flow through a "polar" rather than "neighborhood" effect. In other words, greater discrepancies between partner nations in total capital dealings with the International Monetary Fund and International Bank for Reconstruction and Development are related to larger volumes of migration.

The factor for which this variable is intended as an index (see Table 8) also shows a high loading for the variable Discount Rate. This leads to the supposition that migratory movement may be taking place in greatest volume between origin countries having scarce capital and low rate of growth (high discount rate) and destinations where the rate of development is faster and capital for investment in new domestic (and foreign) enterprise is more plentiful. Countries where growth rates are lower, whether this be through chronic underproductivity or through anti-inflationary monetary measures, are likely to have high rates of unemployment, which could negatively act as a stimulus to outmigration. This interpretation, however, is rather speculative, and the low loadings revealed for Multilateral Capital do not warrant further probing of this tentative hypothesis.

Loadings for other attribute variates on this vector are too weak to provide more than a tentative trend pattern. We may say, in general, that migration tends to be larger in volume between nations having relatively similar economic structure and whose economies (in terms of population actively employed are likewise not highly disparate. Larger volumes of migration also tend to take place between countries whose degree of urban development is widely different, and whose reliance on trade as a contributory element in maintaining high living standards is also comparatively dissimilar.

Vector 3: Relationship of Capital Flows and
Disparity in Economic Development

Three variables load quite highly on Vector 3. These are the interaction variate Dyadic Capital Flow and the attributes Chemical Imports and Dyadic Distance. The canonical correlation of interactions and attributes is very weak indeed for this vector, which displays a coefficient of only 0.065. Any interpretation of the relationships in this instance, therefore, must be regarded with reserve.

In treating the association between capital movement and chemical imports, we should once again bear in mind that the latter is being used to index a complex pattern surrounding a nation's propensities for importing the necessities of an expanding but as yet immature economy. Thus, to extend our earlier discussion of this factor pattern, we can conclude that we are dealing with an environment in which the need of interacting partners for importation of such items as chemicals (for agricultural fertilizers, most probably), transport equipment (for integrating an expanding domestic space-economy), as well as manufactured goods, are widely different. To put this pattern even more simply the loadings on Vector 3 tell us that capital flows are moving between developed and underdeveloped countries.

This association, however, should come as no surprise, in view of the nature of the O. E. C. D. data employed in this phase of the study. What does seem to be rather unusual, in contrast, is the high positive association of the distance variable on this vector pattern. What this association says, in effect, is that greater volumes of capital flow take place over greater distances, in apparent negation of the concept of friction of distance.

To explain this particular pattern, we will need to draw the variable Political/Economic Ties into the discussion as well. The moderate, positive loading of this variable indicates that affiliation of ex-colonies with metropolitan countries in the O. E. C. D. tends to influence the particular orientation of capital flows. For the most part, ex-colonies of nations such as Britain, France, Belgium and Holland are quite remote from the "mother" countries. Also, nations

n greatest need of capital infusion are clearly the relatively under-developed
and peripheral areas of the third world (as the loading on <u>Chemical Imports</u>
implies). Bearing these observations in mind, it is fairly easy to appreciate
why capital flows are shown on vector 3 as having the only pattern of the three
forms of interaction which is not sensitive to the <u>frictional</u> effects of distance.

Other loading patterns on this third vector are of minor significance, and
do not warrant discussion.

Comparative Analysis of Vector Patterns

As a corollary and synthesis of the foregoing detailed analysis of specific
associations on each separate vector, it might be profitable to examine some
broader relationships involving comparison of all three vectors taken simultane-
ously. We will specifically want to examine the nature of relationships among
the flows themselves, since we are interested in determining the degree to which
these may be considered complementary or substitutive. We shall also need to
give specific attention to the role of the distance variable as an element in the
environment of dyadic flows of labor, capital, and commodities.

Trade and Factor Flows: Substitutive or Complementary?

The loading patterns for flows of pair-wise trade, migration, and capital,
as shown in Table 10, dispel any notions that these flows are either strongly
complementary or are effective substitutes for each other under the conditions
we have examined. They appear, indeed, to have fairly individual patterns of
behavior, with only relatively small correspondence being evident between different types of movement. In all three environmental contexts revealed by the
canonical correlation as having some bearing on volume and mix of flows, only
one interaction variable loaded significantly each time. Where loadings appre-
ciably different from zero were achieved by the other flow variates on a particular vector, these did not display consistent patterns of association vis-a-vis
their relationships on other vectors.

In the environment represented by Vector 1, the loadings of all three
flow variates were positive, indicating that all three are induced conjointly by
the type of dyadic situation described by attribute variates on Vector 1. In other
words, since no form of interaction is actively <u>discouraged</u> under these conditions, and no other flow must then substitute for the "undesirable" flow, we may
interpret the environmental conditions in Vector 1 as those under which all three

forms of interaction are weakly complementary.

Thus, where countries are relatively closely juxtaposed in a physical sense, and where ties of a semi-political or traditional-economic nature bind the economies of countries, the climate is favorable for joint movement of commodities, labor, and capital. The closer the nations in geographic space, as the strong association of Trade and Distance on Vector 1 indicates, the more commodity flow will dominate this complementary interaction mix.

However, where traditional or formal economic associations among countries are very strong, the movement of labor tends to show the greatest response with the friction of distance forming only a relatively minor brake on volume of interaction (as appears the case in Vector 2). Thus, where the distance is large but the economic ties nevertheless strong (as in ex-colonial associations) movement of personnel (and, to a lesser extent, capital) seem to be substituted for commodity trade, which is shown by its negative loading on Vector 2 to be discouraged by such an environment.

Interpretation of this environment as of the "colonial" type is reinforced by the polarity in multilateral capital dealings, urbanization, and economic reliance on trade (all registering low positive loadings on Vector 2, Table 10), which would plausibly differ quite considerably between metropolitan nations and most former colonies. However, it must be noted that, under these circumstances, the substitution relationship between factor movements and trade is relatively weak, as revealed by the small loadings of Trade and Capital Flow on this vector and the low canonical correlation value recorded for the entire flow-attribute association.

Wide disparity in productivity, incomes, and relative physical location among potentially-interacting nations constitutes an environment, as Vector 3 indicates, for substitution of capital flows for both trade and labor movement. these disparate nations are part of a traditional (e.g., colonial) economic association, the flows of capital will be commensurately stronger. In general, we may say that capital tends to move in place of commodities or labor between the highly-developed, productive and prosperous nations of the western world and underdeveloped countries of the relatively remote third world, whose economies are not trade-oriented and whose population structures comprise relatively few people in a financial position to emigrate.

A cautionary note should be sounded in connection with relationships involving capital flow. As mentioned previously, the O.E.C.D. data employed represent a somewhat biased sample of the world configuration of capital movement

ent, although the component represented is undoubtedly an important one. It
ould be noted that too firm a statement about general substitution relationships
volving this capital-flow pattern is not possible, since more comprehensive
ta may reveal somewhat different over-all trends.

low Relationships and the
e Friction of Distance

An initial reading of the pattern of loadings for Dyadic Distance in Table
0 gives the impression that factor flows (and particularly capital movements)
re far less subject to the frictional effects of distance than commodity trade.
his might be construed, in the absence of qualifying evidence, as meaning that
roductive factors are more mobile than trade goods, in exact opposition to the
asic tenets of established Trade Theory. This, however, would be an unfortun-
tely hasty conclusion, since it ignores the (seemingly contradictory) evidence
resented in the aggregate model, and the nature of ancillary attribute variables
1 the dyadic model of interaction.

In the aggregate model, variables relating to commodity trade were
hown to have far lower association with the variable Accessibility (used as a
easure of relative distance from important urban clusters) than the variables
etailing total personnel movement. As a subset of total migratory movement,
owever, the aggregate flow of long-term migration was considerably less influ-
nced by relative distance, and this trend is reflected in the dyadic pattern of
igration, which uses the same variable (Long-term Migration) in a disaggre-
ated form.

The evidence provided by other input variables in both levels of analysis
uggest a possible explanation for the lack of sensitivity of long-term migration
o distance. In the real world, the psychological frictions operating against relo-
ation of personnel, hypothesized earlier as being closely related to distance,
learly do not display empirical evidence of such a relationship. Similarities in
anguage, culture, and administrative systems, which have been hypothesized as
egulating the psychological preparedness of laborers to select new countries of
ermanent residence, and which underly the variable Political/Economic Ties,
how a pattern quite unrelated to distance separating interacting partners.

Thus, in ex-colonial associations of nations, strong movements of labor
re observable despite vast distances separating the countries concerned. These
atterns, however, would probably be far more closely aligned with the distance
ariable if total migration (short-term and seasonal movement as well as per-
anent migration) were to be subjected to dyadic flow analysis.

182

Résumé

The dyadic model of international flows produced three separate pattern of flow-attribute associations which, although less pronounced and clear-cut than the stronger aggregate results, did point out a number of significant facet of the complex international economy.

The first and strongest pattern of association, centering on dyadic trade flows, revealed the significant braking effect exerted by physical distance on volumes of commodity interchange. Economic/political integration (through trade ties), and dissimilarity in productivity structure and specific propensitie for trade, were revealed as significant stimuli to dyadic commodity flow.

The second of the three patterns of association highlighted in this chapt outlined the environment surrounding labor migration. It pointed to strong tra tional political/economic ties as the main stimulus, and to urbanization/labor-market variables as secondary stimuli, which override the mild influence of di tance as a deterrent to labor movements.

The third relationship brought out in this dyadic analysis highlighted the environment of important capital flows. Featured in this pattern was the deper dency of remote, underdeveloped ex-colonies on their former "mother countrie the capital rich North Atlantic nations.

Perhaps the most important result of this disaggregated analysis was th indication that movement of commodities, labor, and capital are quite distincti in their relationships with sets of dyadic attributes. Only slight substitution effects and complementarity are observable among flows as particular combina tions of dyadic variables wax more important, and others less so, in the three basic flow "environments" represented by the three canonical vectors.

The relevance of these empirical findings to the field of economic flow theory must now be demonstrated. This task is undertaken in the following cha ter, which places the present study in its theoretical context and draws some conclusions concerning current and future research in the field of flow analysis

CHAPTER X

ECONOMIC FLOW THEORY AND EMPIRICAL EVIDENCE:
SOME CONCLUDING OBSERVATIONS

This study has focused on the building and application of inductive models of international economic interaction stressing the relationship of patterns of flow and selected internal economic attributes of nations. Patterns and relationships among flows have been identified and analysed in the light of current theoretical understanding of causal interconnections embracing individual flow types and specific stimuli and impediments. Relevant theoretical notions were set out in Chapter II as a series of alternative propositions governing abstract relationships among economic flows. These propositions covered the diffuse strands of preexisting theory on economic interaction, and our objective was to draw these together into an integrated framework on which to base empirical analysis of flows. As a conclusion to this study, it would be appropriate to review the implications of our empirical results for some of the more important of these deductive generalizations concerning economic flows, and to place our study in its relevant conceptual context.

Such a review will serve a number of important and related purposes. It will permit us to evaluate the success of our own models, using theoretical and other empirical studies as a frame of reference. It may also allow us to reevaluate some preexisting theoretical notions concerning international flows in the light of empirical evidence. In addition, it should permit us to speculate on future lines of research into areas of present weakness or uncertainty, pointing to ways of extending the frontiers of geographic analysis of international economic interaction.

The Multidimensional Nature of Flows:
Theoretical Implications

The data presented in this study have pointed in unequivocal fashion to the need for a flow theory which explicitly accepts the multi-faceted nature of economic interaction and which, in particular, acknowledges the role of mobile productive factors. In this regard, however, our study has simply served to rein

force previous calls for a review of the assumptions of established trade theor

which relate to comparative mobility of productive factors vis-a-vis trade goo

and the sets of conditions which might impinge on this mobility. The patently

unrealistic nature of the "classical" assumptions regarding factor immobility

have, in other words, been clearly underscored in this analysis.

The empirical evidence presented has likewise shown that the antithesi

of complete factor immobility (i.e., unrestricted flows of factors as well as

trade) is equally unrealistic. The complex combinations seen to exist among

stimuli and deterrents to trade and factor flows certainly ensure that these are

not, in any important sense, "freely interchangeable" responses to given eco-

nomic conditions (an alternative earlier proposed as a theoretical possibility).

Reality, as is usually the case, lies somewhere in the "gray area" between the

two extremes of complete immobility and complete mobility of productive factc

and commodities.

Before we attempted to analyse the conditions under which trade and fa

tor flows might complement, or substitute for one another, we found it impera

tive to consider the theoretical underpinnings of individual flow analysis, as

embodied in the largely separate established theories of trade, international

human migration, and capital movement. Our empirical analysis has produce

some results which have bearing on aspects of these theories, and a brief reca

pitulation of these results may be appropriate.

Upon consideration of theoretical constructs formulated to explain trad

volumes, it was found necessary to classify deductive frameworks into those

which considered primarily only the stimuli to interaction (e.g., the compara-

tive advantage model) and those which paid due attention to the effects of fric-

tions acting against movement (i.e., those operationalized in the form of gravi

or Pareto models). The dyadic model presented in the current study included

weak canonical pattern between trade volume and polarity in economic structur

of trading partners, which could be taken as evidence (although far less than c

clusive) for the operation of comparative advantage. However, quite contrasti

evidence was also discovered in both the aggregate and dyadic phases of the

study, which pointed to close similarity in important economic characteristics

(e.g., urban-industrial development) as a stimulus to trade.

The conclusion suggested by this contradictory evidence was that trade

(and, indeed, migration and capital) could not be regarded as a monolithic enti

for which one fixed set of universally-applicable determinants existed. Thus,

hile geographic specialization of production may explain some forms of trade
s, for example, between raw material-rich countries and manufacturing-
riented nations), it may be quite inapplicable in the case of other forms of com-
odity exchange (e. g., flows between highly industrialized nations), where phe-
omena such as risk-spreading, cultural or traditional consumer preferences,
nd competitive behavior among international companies would seem to have
ore relevance.

The effect of the friction of distance on commodity trade was shown to be
ppreciable but <u>relatively</u> small in the case of aggregate trade, but quite strong
the dyadic model. Moreover, it was clear from the evidence presented that
ertain commodity groups responded far more closely to increased distance (or
elative positioning with respect to world urban foci, in the aggregate model)
an did other kinds of commodities. As a general conclusion, it would be legiti-
ate to assert that omission of some measure of the friction of distance (whether
bsolute or relative) in trade flow models would be a quite serious deficiency.

Our study also has implications for theoretical frameworks relating to
ersonnel movement among countries. Here, also, the distance variable was
hown to have appreciable explanatory power, particularly where flows com-
rised long <u>and</u> short-term movements of migrants. The aggregate model, for
xample, revealed quite close correspondence between patterns of total migra-
on and the global configuration of urban population potential, thus confirming
e results of previous general interaction studies. With regard to long-term
igration, the intervention of an additional element was observed to cause a dis-
rtion of the effect of distance. This element was the psychologically-based
version of people to relocation in an unfamiliar culture or political system, an
fluence which was encountered in an inverted form under the guise of the dyadic
ariable <u>Political/Economic Ties</u>. The behavior of the migration data with re-
pect to this variable lent credence to the idea that "colony-motherland" relation-
hips had the effect of "stretching" migration over greater distances than would
therwise be expected. The economic effect of distance, in the form of transfer
osts, did not appear to be very significant in the explanation of patterns of per-
onnel movement, either at the aggregate or dyadic levels of analysis.

In terms of stimuli to migration, empirical evidence was shown to exist
or the effect of urbanization as a strong "pull" on prospective emigrants. Other
nducements to migrate proposed in previous studies, such as disparity in wage-
evels, per-capita G. N. P., or unemployment, did not emerge as empirically
ignificant influences on long-term population movements. We might conclude

that cultural similarity, the anticipated enjoyment of an urban life style, as we
as a choice of urban employment opportunities in the destination country, are
the major inducements to quasi-permanent migration. Such stimuli are not no
bly discounted by greater intervening distances between countries of provenanc
and destination.

The psychological constraints which impinge on migration are also revealed by our aggregate and dyadic studies to be applicable in the case of capit
flows. Here, again, traditional colonial ties seem to create a "funnel" for cap
tal movement in which the friction of distance is minimal. At the aggregate
level, the pattern of capital flow appeared strongly related to the same environ
mental conditions that influenced commodity trade (highly industrialized countries were the main source areas for both). However, at the level of country-
country flows, in which movement between developed and less-developed natio
was depicted, the capital flow-inducing environment was distinctively different
It is probable, however, that the patterns shown give only a partial view of the
total configuration of global investment flows. Still, it would appear that the
statement by Iversen (discussed in Chapter II) concerning psychological influences on decisions to invest in other countries is given some empirical suppor
by the results of our study.

Trade-Factor Substitution:
Environmental Conditions

Although most trade theorists currently subscribe to explanatory frame
works which aknowledge the mobility of productive factors, there is, as we hav
seen, some divergence in theoretical explanation of the conditions under which
factor flows may be substituted for, or may complement trade. The neoclassi
and modern theories of trade hold, in effect, that commodity movement is clea
predominant, since it comprises an adequate response to disparities in produc
factor prices in two countries (comparative cost doctrine) or in relative factor
endowments in two nations (modern theory). In both cases, factor flows are
seen as theoretically possible but unnecessary. On the other hand, as Mundell
shows, trade may be seen to be quite imperfect as a substitute for migration o
capital flow under certain market conditions and in the face of some impedime
to commodity movement. It is possible to demonstrate, in other words, certa
conditions in which capital and labor movement will replace trade. The eviden
in this study has pointed to sets of environmental conditions (embracing both
"polar" and "neighborhood" effects) under which factor flows appear to respon

ositively and strongly, as well as situations in which trade definitely appears
 dominate. It seems that empirical support is indicated (although it is by no
 eans conclusive) for the notion of relatively high mobility of productive factors
 s-a-vis trade under specific conditions.

An Evaluation of the Canonical Flow Models

The two canonical models of international flows presented in this study
ave demonstrated the existence of empirical evidence for regularity in patterns
f flow-attribute relationships, as well as for recognizable substitutive relations
etween factor movements and commodity transactions. In doing so they have
mployed a model form based on Field Theory, and used an appropriate tech-
ique, Canonical Correlation, which place stress on _mutual_ interconnections
ather than unidirectional causal relationships, overcoming what may be con-
idered a theoretical shortcoming of previous flow models. However this study,
lso, may be shown to have unfortunate deficiencies, and a full evaluation of its
fficacy must include a discussion of these.

In terms of the approach adopted in this study, it must be noted that a
tatic, rather than dynamic model has been constructed--only a single time-
lice was taken, and data for this period have been averaged to give a general
icture of interaction and attribute patterns at one arbitrary point in time. Thus,
mportant phenomena such as rates of change of relevant conditions, temporal
ause-effect cycles, and other dynamic features of possible significance to the
nderstanding of economic flow patterns could not be analysed.

This deficiency could, of course, be overcome by such techniques as are
mployed in comparative statics, in which a series of "slices" are taken at inter-
als of time and causal connections in a simulated time dimension may be more
eadily analysed. In view of data problems and computational difficulties entailed,
owever, the use of such techniques was considered beyond the scope of the pres-
nt study.

A second area in which the present study may be considered somewhat
ess than satisfactory involves the complex problem of data selection. This prob-
em has already been described at some length, particularly with respect to the
ifficulties caused by data omissions for some variables in less-developed and
entrally-planned economies, and the need for reduction of sample size com-
ined with "screening" procedures. As previously noted, the results of these
teps have been lower degrees of accuracy and comprehensiveness than would
therwise have been the case.

A few other shortcomings of the model are worthy of some discussion. One of these is a side-effect of the objective techniques used to select, as parsimoniously as possible, the final variates for inclusion in the model. Although maximum independence of variables was achieved in this way, there is no automatic guarantee that the variables selected had the highest explanatory power in terms of their contribution to understanding the variance patterns of individual flows. Refinements to our theoretical understanding of basic flow influences, well as more painstaking but time-consuming calibration of the models, might have resulted in a set of variates with somewhat greater explanatory power.

Avenues for Further Research

In this study we have broached a subject which can only be described as enormous, and which lies at the interface of the disciplines of Geography, Economics, and Political Science, from all of which research contributions are being, and will doubtless continue to be, made. The approach we have adopted has emphasized the analysis of very broad patterns of relationship, but it also lends itself to analysis of far more detailed facets of this topic than we have attempted here. For example, separation of theoretically-relevant variables governing, respectively, supply and demand for goods, labor, and capital, would permit parallel analysis of patterns of imports and exports, as well as inflow and outflow of labor and capital. Such studies could be made to yield much useful information concerning the operation of the international economy. In the same fashion, studies at interregional rather than global scale might very well use the model format employed here to advantage. Berry's analysis of commodity flows in India is an example of such a finely-drawn study and an illustration of the usefulness of canonical models for understanding detailed aspects of economic regionalization.

Further work needs to be done also in the deductive analysis of flows, incorporating more realistic assumptions regarding the relationships among flows themselves, and perhaps providing a formal mathematical framework in which interactions and attributes are satisfactorily integrated. Although the contributions from geographers in this field have been relatively few to date, it is to be hoped that researchers in the geographic discipline will increasingly turn their attention and their abilities to analysis of this important field of international economic interaction.

APPENDIX

DATA SOURCES

Sources Used in Compilation of Trade Data

International Monetary Fund. Direction of Trade: A Supplement to International Financial Statistics. Washington: International Monetary Fund and International Bank for Reconstruction and Development, January-December, 1967.

United Nations Statistical Office. Yearbook of International Trade Statistics, 1966. New York: United Nations, Department of Economic and Social Affairs, 1968.

Sources Used in Compilation of Migration Data

Australia. Commonwealth Bureau of Census and Statistics. Quarterly Summary of Australian Statistics: March-December, 1966. Canberra: Government Printing Office, December, 1966.

Belgium. Ministère des Affaires Economiques. Annuaire statistique de la Belgique. Brussels: Institut National de Statistique, 1966.

Canada. Dominion Bureau of Statistics. Canada Yearbook 1967. Ottawa: Queen's Printer, March, 1967.

Costa Rica. Ministerio de Economía y Hacienda. Anuario estadístico de Costa Rica 1963. San José: Dirección General de Estadística y Censos, 1964.

Cyprus. Statistics and Research Department, Ministry of Finance. Statistical Abstract, 1965. Nicosia: Printing Office of the Republic of Cyprus, January, 1967.

Dominican Republic. Oficina Nacional de Estadística. Estadística demográfica 1963. Santo Domingo: Dirección General de Estadística y Censos, 1967.

Denmark. Danmarks Statistik. Statistisk Arbog 1963, 1964, 1965. Copenhagen: Det Statistiske Departement, 1965, 1966, 1967.

Finland. Central Statistical Office. Statistical Yearbook of Finland, 1966. Helsinki: Valtion painatus keskus, 1967.

France. Ministère de l'Economie et des Finances. Annuaire statistique de la France, 1966. Paris: Institut National de la Statistique et des Etudes Economiques, 1967.

190

Germany, Federal Republic. Statistisches Bundesamt. Statistisches Jahrbuc für die Bundesrepublik Deutschland 1965. Stuttgart and Mainz: Kohlhammer, 1965.

Great Britain. Central Statistical Office. Annual Abstract of Statistics, 1965 London: Her Majesty's Stationery Office, 1965.

The Intergovernmental Committee for European Migration. International Migi tion. Vols. III, IV, and V. 1965, 1966, 1967.

Ireland. Central Statistical Office. Irish Trade Journal and Statistical Bullet Dublin: Stationery Office, 1967.

Italy. Istituto Centrale di Statistica. Annuario statistico italiano, 1965, 1966 Rome: Istituto Centrale di Statistica, 1965, 1966.

Jamaica. Department of Statistics. Annual Abstract of Statistics, 1967. Kin ton: Government Printer, 1967.

Korea. Economic Planning Board. Korea Statistical Yearbook, 1964, 1965, 1966, 1967. Seoul: Economic Planning Board, 1964, 1965, 1966, 1967

Malta. Director of Statistics. Demographic Review of the Maltese Islands for the Year 1965. Malta: Central Office of Statistics, 1965.

Netherlands. De Directeur-General van de Statistiek. Jaarcijfers voor Neder land 1963-1964. Hilversum: Centraal Bureau voor de Statistiek, 1966.

New Zealand. Department of Statistics. Monthly Abstract of Statistics, July 1966. Wellington: Government Printing Office, 1966.

Norway. Norges Offisielle Statistikk. Statistisk Årbok, 1963, 1964, 1965. Oslo: Statistisk Sentralbyra, 1965, 1966, 1967.

Organization for Economic Cooperation and Development. Labour Force Stati tics. 1956-1966. Paris: Bureau of Publications, 1968.

Portugal. Instituto Nacional de Estatística. Anuário demográfico 1963, 1964, 1965. Lisbon: Direccão Geral de Estatística, 1964, 1965, 1966.

Spain. Instituto Nacional de Estadística. Anuario estadístico de España, 1964 1965, 1966. Madrid: Dirección General de Estadística, 1965, 1966, 1

South Africa. Bureau of Statistics. Statistical Yearbook 1965. Pretoria: Gov ernment Printing Office, 1965.

Sweden. Statistiska Centralbyran. Statistisk Arsbok for Sverige. Stockholm: Norstedt, 1966.

Switzerland. Bureau Fédéral de Statistique. Annuaire statistique de la Suisse Basel: Birkhauser, 1967.

United States of America. Department of Commerce. Statistical Abstract of the United States, 1967. Washington: Government Printing Office, 196

nited States of America. Department of Labor. Labor Developments Abroad, 1965, 1966, 1967. Washington: Government Printing Office, 1965, 1966, 1967.

enezuela. Ministerio de Fomento. Anuario estadístico de Venezuela. Caracas: Dirección General de Estadística y Censos Nacionales, 1966.

Sources Used in Compilation of Capital Flow Data

)rganization for Economic Cooperation and Development. Geographical Distribution of Financial Flows to Less Developed Countries, 1961-1965. Paris: Bureau of Publications, 1967.

Jnited Nations Statistical Office. International Flow of Long-Term Capital and Official Donations: 1961-1965. New York: United Nations, Department of Economic and Social Affairs, 1966.

Sources Used in Compiling Data on
National Economic Characteristics

nternational Monetary Fund, Statistics Bureau. International Financial Statistics. Washington, D.C.: International Monetary Fund, January-December, 1967.

Jnited Nations Statistical Office. Yearbook of National Accounts Statistics, 1963, 1964, 1965. New York: United Nations, Department of Economic and Social Affairs, 1964, 1965, 1966.

_____. Statistical Yearbook, 1966. New York: United Nations Department of Economic and Social Affairs, 1967.

_____. Demographic Yearbook, 1966. New York: United Nations, Department of Economic and Social Affairs, 1967.

SELECTED BIBLIOGRAPHY

International Flows: General Relationships

Anderson, Theodore R. "Potential Models and the Spatial Distribution of Population." Papers and Proceedings of the Regional Science Association, II (1956), 175-82.

Arrow, Kenneth J.; Chenery, H. B.; Minhas, B. S.; and Solow, R. M. "Capital Labor Substitution and Economic Efficiency." Review of Economics and Statistics, XLIII (August, 1961), 225-50.

Bickel, Gary W. Factor Proportions and Relative Price under C. E. S. Production Functions: An Empirical Study of Japanese-United States Comparative Advantage. Technical Report No. 148. Stanford, Calif.: Institute for Mathematical Studies in the Social Sciences, December, 1966.

Byé, M. "Internal Structural Changes Required by Growth and Changes in International Trade." International Trade Theory in a Developing World. Edited by Roy Harrod and Douglas Hague. London: Macmillan, 1963. Pp. 141-72.

Cairnes, John. Some Leading Principles of Political Economy Newly Expounded. New York: Harper & Bros., 1874.

Carrothers, Gerald A. P. "The Gravity and Potential Concepts of Human Interaction--A Select Bibliography." Journal of American Institute of Planners, XXXII, No. 2 (Spring, 1956), 100-102.

Elliot, G. A. Tariff Procedures and Trade Barriers. Toronto: University of Toronto Press, 1955.

Ginsburg, Norton S., ed. Atlas of Economic Development. Chicago: University of Chicago Press, 1960.

Haavelmo, Triegve. A Study in the Theory of Economic Evolution. Amsterdam: North Holland Publishing Company, 1954.

Hultman, Charles W. Factor Migration: Trade Theory and Growth Centers. Research Paper No. 29. Lexington: University of Kentucky, Program on the Role of Growth Centers, 1970.

Isard, Walter, and Peck, M. J. "Location Theory and International and Interregional Trade Theory." Quarterly Journal of Economics, LXVIII (February, 1954), 97-114.

Johnson, Harry G. "Effects of Changes in Comparative Costs as Influenced by Technical Change." International Trade Theory in a Developing World. Edited by Roy Harrod and Douglas Hague. London: Macmillan, 1963. Pp. 96-112.

_____. Money, Trade and Economic Growth. London: Allen & Unwin, 196

Keeble, D. E. "Models of Economic Development." Socio-Economic Models i Geography. Edited by Richard J. Chorley and Peter Haggett. London: Methuen, University Paperbacks, 1968.

LaFave, W. R., and Hay, P. International Trade, Investment, and Organiza-tion. Urbana, Ill.: University of Illinois Press, 1967.

Leontief, Wassily W. "Domestic Production and Foreign Trade: The America Capital Position Re-examined." Proceedings of the American Philosop cal Society, XCVII (September, 1953), 331-49.

_____. "Factor Proportions and the Structure of American Trade: Further Theoretical and Empirical Analysis." Review of Economics and Statis-tics, XXXVIII (November, 1956), 386-407.

Lerner, Abba P. "Factor Prices and International Trade." Economica, XIX (February, 1952), 1-18.

Mackintosh, W. A. "Innis on Canadian Economic Development." Journal of Political Economy, LXI (1953), 185-94.

Van Meerhaeghe, M. A. G. International Economic Institutions. New York: Wiley, 1966.

Minhas, B. S. "The Homohypallagic Production Function, Factor Intensity Reversals, and the Heckscher-Ohlin Theorem." Journal of Political Economy, LXX (April, 1962), 138-56.

Mundell, Robert A. International Economics. New York: Macmillan, 1968.

_____. "International Trade and Factor Mobility." American Economic Review, XLVII, No. 3 (June, 1957), 321-35.

Myint, H. "Infant Industry Arguments for Assistance to Industries in the Settin of Dynamic Trade Theory." International Trade Theory in a Developing World. Edited by Roy Harrod and Douglas Hague. London: Macmillan, 1963. Pp. 173-93.

Myrdal, Gunnar. An International Economy: Problems and Prospects. New York: Harper and Brothers, 1956.

Olsson, Gunnar. Distance and Human Interaction: A Review and Bibliography. Bibliography Series, No. 2. Philadelphia: Regional Science Research Institute, 1965.

Pearce, I. F. "A Further Note on Factor-Commodity Price Relationships." Economic Journal, LXIX (December, 1959), 725-32.

Robinson, Romney. "Factor Proportions and Comparative Advantage, Part I." Quarterly Journal of Economics, LXX (May, 1956), 169-92.

_____. "Factor Proportions and Comparative Advantage, Part II." Quarterly Journal of Economics, LXX (August, 1956), 346-63.

Russett, Bruce, et al. World Handbook of Political and Social Indicators. New Haven: Yale University Press, 1964.

Rybczynski, T. M. "Factor Endowment and Relative Commodity Prices." Economica, XXII (November, 1955), 336-41.

Samuelson, Paul A. "Prices of Factors and Goods in General Equilibrium." Review of Economic Studies, XXI (1953-54), 1-21.

Samuelson, Paul A., and Stolper, W. "Protection and Real Wages." Review of Economic Studies, IX (1941), 58-73.

Stewart, J. Q. "Empirical Mathematical Rules Governing the Distribution and Equilibrium of Population." Geographical Review, XXXVII (1947), 473-75.

Tarshis, Lorie. "Factor Inputs and International Price Comparisons." The Allocation of Economic Resources: Essays in Honour of Bernard Francis Haley. By Abramovitz et al. Palo Alto: Stanford University Press, 1959. Pp. 236-44.

Tinbergen, Jan. Shaping the World Economy. New York: Twentieth Century Fund, 1962.

Valavanis-Vail, S. "Leontief's Scarce Factor Paradox." Journal of Political Economy, LXII (December, 1954), 523-28.

Warntz, William. Macrogeography and Income Fronts. Monograph Series No. 3. Philadelphia: Regional Science Research Institute, 1965.

International Trade

Alexander, John W. "International Trade: Selected Types of World Regions." Economic Geography, XXXVI (April, 1960), 95-115.

Beckerman, W. "Distance and the Pattern of Intra-European Trade." Review of Economics and Statistics, XXXVIII (1956), 31-40.

Berry, Brian J. L. Essays on Commodity Flows and the Spatial Structure of the Indian Economy. Research Paper No. 111. Chicago: University of Chicago, Department of Geography, 1966.

Bhagwati, Jagdish. "The Pure Theory of International Trade: A Survey." Economic Journal, LXXIV (March, 1964), 1-84.

_____. International Trade. Middlesex, England: Penguin Books, 1969.

Caves, R. E. Trade and Economic Structure: Models and Methods. Cambridge: Harvard University Press, 1963.

Chipman, John. "A Survey of the Theory of International Trade." Econometric XXXIII, No. 3 (1965), 477-519.

_____. "A Survey of the Theory of International Trade." Econometrica, XXXIII, No. 4 (1965), 685-760.

_____. "A Survey of the Theory of International Trade." Econometrica, XXXIV, No. 1 (1966), 1-76.

Contracting Parties to the General Agreement on Tariffs and Trade. The Activi ties of GATT. Geneva: GATT Publications, 1962.

Corden, William M. Recent Developments in the Theory of International Trade Special Paper in International Economics, No. 7. Princeton, N.J.: Princeton University, Department of Economics, March, 1965.

Ford, John L. The Ohlin-Heckscher Theory of the Basis and Effects of Com- modity Trade. New York: Asia Publishing House, 1965.

Grotewold, Andreas. "The Growth of Industrial Core Areas and Patterns of World Trade." Annals of the Association of American Geographers, LXI, No. 2 (June, 1971), 361-70.

Grotewold, Andreas, and Grotewold, Lois. "Some Geographic Aspects of Inter national Trade." Economic Geography, XXXIII (July, 1957), 257-66.

Haberler, Gottfried. A Survey of International Trade. Special Papers in Inter- national Economics, No. 1. Princeton: Princeton University, July, 196

Harrod, Roy, and Hague, Douglas, eds. International Trade Theory in a Devel oping World. London: Macmillan, 1963.

Johnson, Harry G. International Trade and Economic Growth. Cambridge: Harvard University Press, 1958.

Lancaster, K. "The Heckscher-Ohlin Trade Model: A Geometric Treatment." Economica, XXIV (February, 1957), 19-39.

Leighton, Richard I. Economics of International Trade. New York: McGraw- Hill, 1970.

Liesner, H. H. "Regional Free Trade: Trade-Creating and Trade-Diverting Effects of Political Commercial and Monetary Areas." International Trade Theory in a Developing World. Edited by Roy Harrod and Douglas Hague. London: Macmillan, 1963. Pp. 194-204.

Linnemann, Hans. An Econometric Study of International Trade Flows. Amste dam: North Holland Publishing Co., 1966.

MacDougall, G. D. A. "British and American Exports: A Study Suggested by the Theory of Comparative Costs, Part I." Economic Journal, LXI (December, 1951), 707-8.

Meade, J. E. Trade and Welfare. Oxford, England: Oxford University Press, 1955.

Metzler, Lloyd. "Tariffs, the Terms of Trade and the Distribution of National Income." Journal of Political Economy, LVII (February, 1949), 1-29.

Moroney, John R., and Walker, James M. "A Regional Test of the Heckscher-Ohlin Hypothesis." Journal of Political Economy, LXXIV (1966), 573-86.

Michaely, Michael. "Factor Proportions in International Trade: Current State of the Theory." Kyklos, XVII (1964), 529-50.

Mikesell, R. F. "The Theory of Common Markets as Applied to Regional Arrangements among Developing Countries." International Trade Theory in a Developing World. Edited by Roy Harrod and Douglas Hague. London: Macmillan, 1963. Pp. 205-29.

Ohlin, Bertil. Interregional and International Trade. Cambridge, Mass.: Harvard University Press, 1933.

Samuelson, Paul A. "International Trade and the Equalization of Factor Prices." Economic Journal, LVIII (June, 1948), 163-84.

Slater, David W. World Trade and Economic Growth: Trends and Prospects with Applications to Canada. Toronto: University of Toronto Press, 1968.

Thoman, Richard S., and Conkling, Edgar. Geography of International Trade. Englewood Cliffs: Prentice Hall, 1967.

United Nations. "Trade Expansion and Regional Groupings." Trade and Development, VI (1965), 82-83.

Viner, Jacob. International Trade and Economic Development. Glencoe, Ill.: The Free Press, 1952.

Williams, John. "The Theory of International Trade Reconsidered." Economic Journal, XXXIX (1929), 195-209.

International Productive Factor Flows

Adler, John H., ed. Capital Movements and Economic Development. New York: St. Martin's Press, 1967.

Ajo, Reino. Contributions to Social Physics. Lund Studies in Geography, Series B, No. 11. Lund, Sweden: C. W. K. Gleerup, 1953.

Balassa, Bela. "The Capital Needs of the Developing Countries." Kyklos, XVII (1964), 197-206.

Berry, Brian J. L., and Schwind, Paul J. "Information and Entropy in Migrant Flows." Geographic Analysis, I, No. 1 (1969), 5-14.

Bogue, Donald J., and Thompson, W. S. "Migration and Distance." American Sociological Review, XIV (1949), 236-44.

Bouscaren, Anthony T. International Migration since 1945. New York: Frederick A. Praeger, 1963.

Bright, Margaret J., and Thomas, Dorothy S. "Interstate Migration and Inter-vening Opportunities." American Sociological Review, VI (December, 1941), 773-85.

Carey, Henry. Principles of Social Science. Philadelphia: J. Lippincott, 185‎

Harrod, Roy F. "Desirable International Movements of Capital in Relation to Growth of Borrowers and Lenders and Growth of Markets." Internation: Trade Theory in a Developing World. Edited by Roy Harrod and Dougla‎ Hague. London: Macmillan, 1963. Pp. 113-41.

International Labour Office. International Migration. New York: Gordon and Breach, 1969.

Isaac, Julius. Economics of Migration. London: Kegan Paul, 1947.

Isard, Walter, et al. Methods of Regional Analysis. Cambridge: The M.I.T. Press, 1960.

Iversen, Carl. Aspects of the Theory of International Capital Movements. New York: Augustus M. Kelley, 1967.

Kindleberger, C. P. International Short-term Capital Movements. New York, 1937.

Lovgren, Esse. "The Geographical Mobility of Labor." Geografiska Annaler, XXXVIII, No. 4 (1956), 344-94.

Makower, R.; Marschak, J.; and Robinson, H. W. "Studies in Mobility of Labour." Oxford Economic Papers, I (1938), 83-123.

Miernyk, William H. "Labor Mobility and Regional Growth." Economic Geogra-phy, XXXI (1955), 321-30.

Missionaries of St. Charles. International Migration Digest, I, No. 1 (Spring, 1964).

Nelson, Phillip. "Migration, Real Income, and Information." Journal of Re-gional Science, I, No. 2 (Spring, 1959), 43-74.

Parsons, E. C. "Capital Flows to Underdeveloped Countries." European Year-book 1961. The Hague: Council of Europe, 1962. Pp. 102-15.

Pincus, John. Economic Aid and International Cost Sharing. Baltimore: Johns Hopkins Press, 1965.

Porter, R. "Approach to Migration through Its Mechanism." Geografiska Annaler, XXXVIII, No. 4 (1956), 317-43.

Raimon, Robert L. "Interstate Migration and Wage Theory." Review of Eco-nomics and Statistics, LIV (1962), 428-38.

Ravenstein, Ernest G. "The Laws of Migration." Journal of the Royal Statisti-cal Society, XLVIII (1885), 167-235.

Ravenstein, Ernest G. "The Laws of Migration." Journal of the Royal Statistical Society, LII (1889), 241-305.

Schwind, Paul J. Migration and Regional Development in the United States. Research Paper No. 133. Chicago: University of Chicago, Department of Geography, 1971.

Stewart, C. T. "Migration as a Function of Population and Distance." American Sociological Review, XXV (1960), 347-56.

Stouffer, Samuel A. "Intervening Opportunities and Competing Migrants." Journal of Regional Science, II, No. 1 (Spring, 1960), 1-26.

Thomas, Brinley. "International Movements of Capital and Labour since 1946." International Labour Review, LXXXIV, No. 3 (September, 1956), 3-16.

_____. Economics of International Migration. London: Macmillan, 1958.

_____. "Migration and Economic Growth, A Study of Great Britain and the Atlantic Economy." Economic Geography, XXXII (1956), 87-88.

United Nations Statistical Office. International Migration Statistics. Statistical Papers, Series M, No. 20. New York: U.N. Department of Economic Affairs, 1953.

Velikonji, Joseph. "Postwar Population Movements in Europe." Annals of the Association of American Geographers, XLVIII (1958), 458-71.

Wendel, Bertel. A Migration Schema: Theories and Observations. Lund Studies in Geography, Series B, No. 9. Lund, Sweden: C. W. K. Gleerup, 1953.

Zipf, George K. Human Behaviour and the Principle of Least Effort. Cambridge: Harvard University Press, 1949.

Methodology

Anderson, Theodore W. Introduction to Multivariate Statistical Analysis. New York: Wiley, 1958.

Adelman, Irma, and Morris, Cynthia T. Society, Politics and Economic Development: A Quantitative Approach. Baltimore: Johns Hopkins Press, 1967.

Bartlett, M. S. "The Statistical Significance of Canonical Correlations." Biometrica, XXXII (1940), 29-38.

Berry, Brian J. L. "A Method of Deriving Multifactor Uniform Regions." Przeglad Geograficzny, XXXIII (1961), 263-82.

_____. "A Synthesis of Formal and Functional Regions Using a General Field Theory of Spatial Behavior." Spatial Analysis: A Reader in Statistical Geography. Edited by Brian J. L. Berry and Duane F. Marble. Englewood Cliffs: Prentice-Hall, 1968. Pp. 419-30.

Berry, Brian J. L. "An Inductive Approach to the Regionalization of Economic Development." Essays on Geography and Economic Development. Edit by Norton Ginsburg. Research Paper No. 62. Chicago: University of Chicago, Department of Geography, 1960. Pp. 78-107.

Blalock, Hubert M. Social Statistics. New York: McGraw-Hill, 1960.

Cooley, William W., and Lohnes, Paul R. Multivariate Procedures for the Behavioral Sciences. New York: Wiley, 1962.

Duncan, Otis D. Metropolis and Region. Baltimore: Johns Hopkins Press, 19

Gauthier, Howard L. "Transportation and the Growth of the Sao Paulo Econom; Journal of Regional Science, VIII, No. 1 (1968), 77-94.

Hagood, Margaret. "Statistical Methods for the Delineation of Regions Applied to Data on Agriculture and Population." Social Forces, XXI (1943), 287

Hagood, Margaret; Davilevsky, N.; and Geum, Corlin O. "An Examination of the Use of Factor Analysis in the Problem of Sub-Regional Delineation.' Rural Sociology, III (1941), 216-34.

Harris, Chauncy D. "The Market as a Factor in the Localization of Industry in the U.S." Annals of the Association of American Geographers, XLIV (1954), 315-48.

Hotelling, Harold. "Analysis of a Complex of Statistical Variables into Princip Components." Journal of Educational Psychology, XXIV (1933), 417-41 and 498-520.

_____. "Relations Between Two Sets of Variates." Biometrika, XXVIII (1936), 321-77.

Kendall, M. G. A Course in Multivariate Analysis. London: Charles Griffin, 1957.

Kemeny, John G. Mathematical Models in the Social Sciences. Boston, Ginn, 1962.

King, Leslie J. Statistical Analysis in Geography. Englewood Cliffs, N.J.: Prentice-Hall, 1969.

Lewin, Kurt. Field Theory in Social Science. New York: Harper Torchbooks, 1951.

Lowry, Ira S. "A Short Course in Model Design." Journal of the American Institute of Planners, XXXI, No. 2 (May, 1965), 158-65.

Morrison, Donald F. Multivariate Statistical Methods. New York: McGraw-Hill, 1967.

Prais, S. J. "Econometric Research in International Trade: A Review." Kyklos, XV (1962), 560-79.

Rao, Calyampudi R. "On the Distance between Two Populations." Sankhya, IX (1949), 246-48.

Rao, Calyampudi R. Linear Statistical Inference and Its Applications. New York: Wiley, 1965.

Ray, Michael D., and Lohnes, Paul R. "Canonical Correlation in Geographical Analysis." Unpublished Research Paper, State University of New York at Buffalo, November, 1970.

Rummel, Rudolph. Applied Factor Analysis. Evanston, Ill.: Northwestern University Press, 1970.

Russett, Bruce. International Regions and the International System. Chicago: Rand McNally, 1967.

Smith, Robert H. T. "Toward a Measure of Complementarity." Economic Geography, XL, No. 1 (1964), 1-8.

Smith, Robert H. T., and Gould, Peter R. "Method in Commodity Flow Studies." Australian Geographer, VIII (1961), 73-77.

Tintner, Gerhard. "Some Applications of Multivariate Analysis to Economic Data." Journal of American Statistical Society, XLI (1946), 472-500.

Ullman, Edward L. "The Role of Transportation and the Bases for Interaction." Man's Role in Changing the Face of the Earth. Edited by William L. Thomas, Jr. Chicago: University of Chicago Press, 1956. Pp. 862-80.

Warntz, William. Toward a Geography of Price: A Study in Geo-Econometrics. Philadelphia: Regional Science Research Institute, 1959.

THE UNIVERSITY OF CHICAGO
DEPARTMENT OF GEOGRAPHY
RESEARCH PAPERS (Lithographed, 6×9 Inches)

(Available from Department of Geography, The University of Chicago, 5828 S. University Chicago, Illinois 60637. Price: $5.00 each; by series subscription, $4.00 each.)

48. BOXER, BARUCH. *Israeli Shipping and Foreign Trade* 1957. 176 pp.
53. ACKERMAN, EDWARD A. *Geography as a Fundamental Research Discipline* 1958. 40 pp. $1.00
56. MURPHY, FRANCIS C. *Regulating Flood-Plain Development* 1958. 216 pp.
61. PLATT, ROBERT S. *Field Study in American Geography* 1959. 408 pp.
62. GINSBURG, NORTON, editor. *Essays on Geography and Economic Development* 1960. 196 pp.
71. GILBERT, E. W. *The University Town in England and West Germany*
    1961. 79 pp. 4 plates. 30 maps and diagrams. (Free to new subscribers)
72. BOXER, BARUCH. *Ocean Shipping in the Evolution of Hong Kong* 1961. 108 pp.
74. TROTTER, JOHN E. *State Park System in Illinois* 1962. 152 pp.
79. HUDSON, JAMES. *Irrigation Water Use in the Utah Valley, Utah* 1962. 249 pp.
84. KANSKY, K. J. *Structure of Transportation Networks: Relationships between Network Geo and Regional Characteristics* 1963. 155 pp.
91. HILL, A. DAVID. *The Changing Landscape of a Mexican Municipio, Villa Las Rosas, Chiap* NAS-NRC Foreign Field Research Program Report No. 26. 1964. 121 pp.
94. MC MANIS, DOUGLAS R. *The Initial Evaluation and Utilization of the Illinois Prairies, 1815–* 1964. 109 pp.
97. BOWDEN, LEONARD W. *Diffusion of the Decision To Irrigate: Simulation of the Spread of a Resource Management Practice in the Colorado Northern High Plains* 1965. 146 pp.
98. KATES, ROBERT W. *Industrial Flood Losses: Damage Estimation in the Lehigh Valley* 1965. 76 pp.
102. AHMAD, QAZI. *Indian Cities: Characteristics and Correlates* 1965. 184 pp.
103. BARNUM, H. GARDINER. *Market Centers and Hinterlands in Baden-Württemberg* 1966. 172
105. SEWELL, W. R. DERRICK, *et al. Human Dimensions of Weather Modification* 1966. 423 pp.
106. SAARINEN, THOMAS F. *Perception of the Drought Hazard on the Great Plains* 1966. 183 pp.
107. SOLZMAN, DAVID M. *Waterway Industrial Sites: A Chicago Case Study* 1967. 138 pp.
108. KASPERSON, ROGER E. *The Dodecanese: Diversity and Unity in Island Politics* 1967. 184 pp.
109. LOWENTHAL, DAVID, editor. *Environmental Perception and Behavior* 1967. 88 pp.
110. REED, WALLACE E. *Areal Interaction in India: Commodity Flows of the Bengal-Bihar Ind. Area* 1967. 210 pp.
112. BOURNE, LARRY S. *Private Redevelopment of the Central City: Spatial Processes of Stru Change in the City of Toronto* 1967. 199 pp.
113. BRUSH, JOHN E., and GAUTHIER, HOWARD L., JR. *Service Centers and Consumer Trips: S on the Philadelphia Metropolitan Fringe* 1968. 182 pp.
114. CLARKSON, JAMES D. *The Cultural Ecology of a Chinese Village, Cameron Highlands, Ma* 1968. 174 pp.
115. BURTON, IAN, KATES, ROBERT W., and SNEAD, RODMAN E. *The Human Ecology of Coastal Hazard in Megalopolis* 1968. 196 pp.
117. WONG, SHUE TUCK. *Perception of Choice and Factors Affecting Industrial Water Supply sions in Northeastern Illinois* 1968. 96 pp.
119. DIENES, LESLIE. *Locational Factors and Locational Developments in the Soviet Chemical In* 1969. 285 pp.
120. MIHELIC, DUSAN. *The Political Element in the Port Geography of Trieste* 1969. 104 pp.
121. BAUMANN, DUANE. *The Recreational Use of Domestic Water Supply Reservoir: Perceptio Choice* 1969. 125 pp.
122. LIND, AULIS O. *Coastal Landforms of Cat Island, Bahamas: A Study of Holocene Accret Topography and Sea-Level Change* 1969. 156 pp.
123. WHITNEY, JOSEPH. *China: Area, Administration and Nation Building* 1970. 198 pp.

124. EARICKSON, ROBERT. *The Spatial Behavior of Hospital Patients: A Behavioral Approach to Spatial Interaction in Metropolitan Chicago* 1970. 198 pp.

125. DAY, JOHN C. *Managing the Lower Rio Grande: An Experience in International River Development* 1970. 277 pp.

126. MAC IVER, IAN. *Urban Water Supply Alternatives: Perception and Choice in the Grand Basin Ontario* 1970. 178 pp.

127. GOHEEN, PETER G. *Victorian Toronto, 1850 to 1900: Pattern and Process of Growth* 1970. 278 pp.

128. GOOD, CHARLES M. *Rural Markets and Trade in East Africa* 1970. 252 pp.

129. MEYER, DAVID R. *Spatial Variation of Black Urban Households* 1970. 127 pp.

130. GLADFELTER, BRUCE. *Meseta and Campiña Landforms in Central Spain: A Geomorphology of the Alto Henares Basin.* 1971. 204 pp.

131. NEILS, ELAINE M. *Reservation to City: Indian Urbanization and Federal Relocation* 1971. 200 pp.

132. MOLINE, NORMAN T. *Mobility and the Small Town, 1900–1930* 1971. 169 pp.

133. SCHWIND, PAUL J. *Migration and Regional Development in the United States* 1971. 170 pp.

134. PYLE, GERALD F. *Heart Disease, Cancer and Stroke in Chicago: A Geographical Analysis with Facilities Plans for 1980.* 1971. 292 pp.

135. JOHNSON, JAMES F. *Renovated Waste Water: An Alternative Source of Municipal Water Supply in the U.S.* 1971. 155 pp.

136. BUTZER, KARL W. *Recent History of an Ethiopian Delta: The Omo River and the Level of Lake Rudolf.* 1971. 184 pp.

137. HARRIS, CHAUNCY D. *Annotated World List of Selected Current Geographical Serials in English, French, and German* 3rd edition 1971. 77 pp.

138. HARRIS, CHAUNCY D., and FELLMANN, JEROME D. *International List of Geographical Serials* 2nd edition 1971. 267 pp.

139. MC MANIS, DOUGLAS R. *European Impressions of the New England Coast, 1497–1620* 1972. 147 pp.

140. COHEN, YEHOSHUA S. *Diffusion of an Innovation in an Urban System: The Spread of Planned Regional Shopping Centers in the United States, 1949–1968* 1972. 136 pp.

141. MITCHELL, NORA. *The Indian Hill-Station: Kodaikanal* 1972. 199 pp.

142. PLATT, RUTHERFORD H. *The Open Space Decision Process: Spatial Allocation of Costs and Benefits* 1972. 189 pp.

143. GOLANT, STEPHEN M. *The Residential Location and Spatial Behavior of the Elderly: A Canadian Example* 1972. 226 pp.

144. PANNELL, CLIFTON W., *T'ai-chung, T'ai-wan: Structure and Function* 1972 (in press)

145. LANKFORD, PHILIP M. *Regional Incomes in the United States, 1929–1967: Level, Distribution, Stability, and Growth* 1972. 137 pp.

146. FREEMAN, DONALD B., *International Trade, Migration, and Capital Flows: A Quantitative Analysis of Spatial Economic Interaction.* 1973. 202 pp.

39, 41, 64

La Bibl